Righting the Educational Conveyor Belt

Second Edition

by

Michael Grinder

METAMORPHOUS

PRESS

Portland, Oregon

Published by

Metamorphous Press
P.O. Box 10616
Portland, OR 97210

Copyright © 1991 by Michael Grinder
Edited by Lori Stephens
Illustrations by Paul Hanson
Printed in the United States of America

Grinder, Michael.
Righting the educational conveyor belt / by Michael Grinder.--
2nd ed.
p.   cm.
Includes bibliographical references (p.) and index.
ISBN 1-55552-036-7 : $17.95
1. Teaching. 2. Neurolinguistic programming. 3. Learning.
I. Title
LB1025.2.G73   1991
371.3--dc20   90-19491

This is dedicated to

Gail

the balance in my life

Acknowledgements

We gratefully appreciate the following people
for their input and assistance:

Karen Asai
Suzanne Bailey
David Balding
Joe Beatty
Paula Bramble
Rosemary Brinkley
Lee Burkholder
John Christensen
Connie Connor
O.J. Cotes
Laura Eaton
Jay Erdmann
Marilyn Ewing
Jill Gomery
Polly Hobbs
Kelly & Adam's D.I.M. Service
Margo Long
Leslie McLaughlin
Dulcy Owen
Ron Rock
Sharon Sawicki
Lori Stephens
Glory Yankauskas
And Paul Hansen who was the doctor
of this "labor of love" from the
inception to the delivery room.

Table of Contents

Foreword

When I was a child in primary school, I remember being puzzled by the differences in attitude and performance in my schoolmates. How was it possible, I mused, that Joanie and Mike had struggled the year before to achieve minimum standards, yet found themselves leading the class with little or no apparent effort this year? How did that work? What was the difference that made this difference occur?

Roger Fisher, the head of the Harvard Negotiations Project, tells the following amusing and instructional story:

In the latter phases of World War II, a crack bomber crew was pulled out of active combat and given the task of testing a new bomber. On the particular day in question, their task was to test the restart engine inflight capabilities of this new aircraft. Having achieved the specified flight level of 32,000 feet, the pilot and co-pilot, closely observed by the flight engineer, shut down and then restarted each of the four engines one by one with no problems. They then shut down and restarted the engines two by two, and subsequently, three by three. Pleased with the success of these procedures, the pilot, exchanging a nod with his co-pilot, shut down all four engines. In the eerie silence that ensued, at just about the same time, both the pilot and co-pilot remembered that the officer who had done the briefing for the day's tests had said that to start an engine on this aircraft, one had to use either an engine that was already running or an external ground source. The co-pilot turned to the pilot and said, "Boy, are you in trouble!"

Estimates of how much trouble we're in in this task of educating ourselves here in the United States vary enormously, but I say that whatever the numbers, as long as there are *any* children, teenagers or adults who genuinely want to learn who are frustrated and fail to learn, then we are in trouble. Education is nothing more or less than our investment in and commitment to the future.

The teacher - student loop (the primary engine in education) is extremely complex. The interweaving of learning, relationship and socialization which constitutes the context in which teaching occurs makes the task of education a formidable one. The single most influential variable is the relationship between the student and the teacher. If the relationship is strong and constitutes a stable context for the student to learn, that student will learn, and more importantly, will learn to learn. Michael Grinder has, to my way of thinking, accomplished something quite extraordinary in this book. He has succeeded in taking some elementary patterns (i.e., representational patterns) modelled in the NLP technology and refined them significantly by tailoring them to the specific context of education. This is a fine and original piece of work. The thing, however, which I find extraordinary is the interweaving of relationship with specific techniques. The reader is offered explicit, precise descriptions of how to observe (both actively and passively) and classify the preferred learning styles of the student and how to adapt his/her (the teacher's) behaviors to meet the student halfway. The net result is not only a significant increase in the performance of the student (with its attendant payoffs for that particular student, the teacher and the other members of the class) but by successfully meeting the student halfway, the teacher enhances the relationship with the student. Thus, the careful study and incorporation of the patterns Grinder presents here does double duty; the use of the patterns are justified technically in that the student's performance is positively affected at a higher, logical level, and, simultaneously, they positively influence the single most powerful leverage point in education - the teacher/student relationship. I therefore urge anyone who recognizes that he teaches to master the patterns presented in this work.

On a more personal note, I did not need the quality in this book to inform me about the excellence with which my brother, Michael Grinder, conducts himself as a teacher. It is a special delight to assist in a very minor way in making this book available so that such information is presented to the rest of the reading public.

Well done, brother Michael. I salute the difference these patterns can make in the education of my children and yours and to all those wishing to learn.

Some thirty plus years ago, one of my finest teachers, Gregory Bateson, was engaged in an experiment concerning the sorting of the logical levels of learning and communication. Essentially, a dolphin - trainer loop was set up in such a way that the dolphin was to be rewarded if, and only if, the dolphin produced some piece of behavior for which it had never been rewarded. Within any particular session, the dolphin got a fish for repeating some specific behavior, but on the next (and subsequent) training session(s) no reward for previously rewarded behavior was given. Thus, for example, in the "nth" training session, the dolphin was awarded a fish when it did something it hadn't done in any previous training sessions. Bateson, however, caught the trainer throwing the dolphin an unearned fish. When he objected to her behavior, the trainer turned to Bateson and, to her credit and wisdom, pointed out that if the level of frustration in the dolphin as it strove to solve the "logical level leap puzzle" exceeded its tolerance for frustration, then the relationship between the trainer and the dolphin would be ruptured. She said, "And without a relationship between me and the dolphin, neither we nor the dolphin will learn anything."

In closing, I offer what I take to be one of the finest compliments a teacher can receive - in reading this book, I learned things I hadn't known about before.

John Grinder
Bonny Doone
Fall, 1988

Introduction

"Professional stretching prevents career arthritis."
- Gail Grinder

It seems as though every discovery in teacher communication comes about because of two ingredients; first, the person is PERCEPTIVE, and secondly, the person has a TECHNIQUE which is appropriate for the situation. If someone stumbles upon a technique that is effective, the reason that he discovers the technique is because he had the perception to do so.
An observer would only see the new technique, not the "spark" of perception in the discoverer. Without the perception, the teacher implementing the technique is like a newly hired disc jockey with lots of records available. The question is, "Does the d.j. know enough about his audience to properly choose which records to play?"

A technique employed without a grasp of the underlying perception is almost certainly destined to have the short life of yet another educational fad. This helps to explain the phenomenon which reoccurs every five to ten years; the same technique reappears under a new label.

Neuro Linguistic Programming may appear, on the surface, to be just another labeling of old ideas. But in the decade it has been around, it has emerged as truly a model of both PERCEPTIONS and TECHNIQUES.

The co-founders, John Grinder and Richard Bandler, studied people who were exquisite in their field and found that when they did exactly what the "experts" did, they amassed the same level of results. They varied their behavior enough to determine which mannerisms were present because of tradition and which were critical; in essence, they pioneered the now famous axiom: "Find the difference that makes a difference."*

For these modelers, the litmus test was teaching others the "difference" to determine if the validity of their observations held. This model of modeling was originally done in the counseling profession. Many titles were possible; one advantage of labeling it Neuro Linguistic Programming is that there is an instant reference to the body/mind relationship. "Neuro" means all experiences coming in through the five senses (nerves), and "linguistic" refers to the fact that what the brain experiences, it codes into language (words). Succinctly, NLP is the study of "words and nerves."

---

* Gregory Bateson, *Steps to an Ecology of Mind* (New York: Harper & Row, 1972), p. 453.

As NLP crossed into the education world, the tendency was to use the one-on-one therapeutic template.* Understandably those teachers with 28 or more students were frustrated by the NLP practitioners' inability to reformat the technology toward a "group process" setting. What was needed was an educational application that was more respectful of the culture of education.

As a former teacher with 17 years of experience on three levels of education, I have spent the last five years offering courses during the school year. Enrolled teachers are visited a minimum of three times in their classroom during my three credit, nine week class. Observation and feedback (and if appropriate, demonstration teaching) are done on the spot. By being in 100 different classrooms a month, I am able to observe patterns and techniques that are successful in a group setting. The patterns presented in this book are a result of this continuing *applied* research.

Since a training room is a much better medium to teach NLP's forte' of "perceptual skill development" than a book is, my attempt has been to partially bridge the gap between reading and real life experience through a format of explanation, vignette and worksheets. The reader who does only the first two will be, at best, intrigued.

It seems that during the first five years of a teacher's career, his progress is continuous. Sometime around the fifth year, a very precarious situation occurs. The teacher is quite adequate but professional growth slows. He understands the content, and classroom management is usually sufficient. The teacher is capable of finishing his career at about this level of competency.

After the first five years, a teacher's continued growth comes from training in process and perception as opposed to in-servicing about content. This allows the teacher to use his complete repertoire of techniques with great marksmanship as a result of exquisite eyesight.

One of the by-products of the five molding years is that the educator is acculturated into a lifestyle of bureaucracy. By then, one experiences a sense that there is a system that exists and is larger than the sum of all its parts. This results in an all-pervasive atmosphere where adults operate as if they are not empowered. It is in this mood that every fourth student is dropping off the educational conveyor belt.

The school's propensity to the left hemispheric way of thinking creates a centrifugal force which throws the right brain student off.

---

* Contact Grinder, DeLozier and Associates, 200 7th Ave, Suite 100, Santa Cruz, CA 95062, for a calendar of training.

Teachers need to be growing themselves to truly exemplify what learning is. The enclosed worksheets are a way of daily empowering instructors to realize that through their personal contact with the student, the educator can keep him or her on the conveyor belt. Hence, the cover of this book.

Agreement

Twice a year we all agree to change our time pieces either back or forward one hour. Reality doesn't change with the adjustment of clocks. Twenty-four hours later, there is just about the same amount of illumination as the previous day. What does change is our LABEL of reality. I live in the country, and on the morning of the last Sunday in October, the neighbor's cows moo and bang on the pasture gate, knowing their feeding time is past due. They don't have clocks; only the farmers do.

This book is about LABELS of REALITY. As long as the reader knows that labels are operational definitions of reality and not REALITY, we can communicate through "useful lies."

For example, the terms "visual student," "auditory student," and "kinesthetic student" are used throughout this book as if students could be categorized into these pigeonholes, and as if a specific teaching methodology could be prescribed for each type. However, this author has never found a student who is a single modality. LABELS of reality are like bicycle training wheels; they guide us as we develop a new skill, but once our balance is gained, they are a hindrance. The sophistication of the reader will provide guidance in interpreting the labels. If we "over generalize" labels, we run the "Fahrenheit Risk." When Fahrenheit perfected the transparent tube containing mercury, he asked an available patient to hold the instrument under his tongue. After the prescribed time, he withdrew the tube and placed a mark on the outside indicating the person's body temperature. To make it easier for all, he simplified reality by writing "100". Little did he know that his patient's body temperature was 1.4 degrees higher than the average person.

The "useful lies" which follow are a direct result of John Grinder and Richard Bandler's pioneering in Neuro Linguistic Programming. Because of the genius of both, and the generosity of the former, I offer an expansion of their work to education. The highest compliment will be if they don't recognize parts of it.

Note to reader: To facilitate the smoothness of reading, "he" and "she" are used throughout this book to connote a singular pronoun, not a gender distinction.

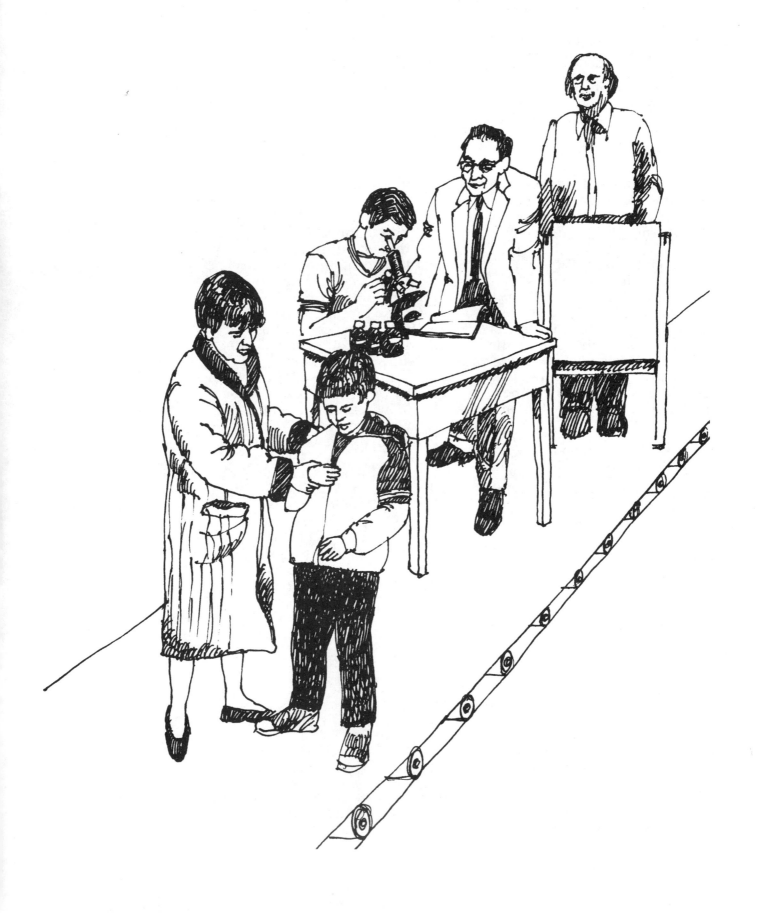

Chapter 1

The Culture of Education

"Doing what you like is freedom.
Liking what you do is happiness."
Thoreau

The school, like any other major corporation, has its own unique culture and within that, several subcultures, each with their own patterns of process and nonverbal communication.

Examples abound that indicate our profession's cultural beliefs and perceptions. The committee which was tasked to select the first *civilian* to ride the space shuttle agreed that the person had to represent a profession which the public perceived as "giving and being in service to society." Christa McAuliffe represented all teachers. A group of educators were surveyed after the space shuttle tragedy, and when asked if they would be willing to go on the expedition, knowing the possibilities, the response was a resounding YES.

There may be things that educators don't like about being public servants such as the pay scale (someone once said that our salary is like a rowboat with a leak and a good bucket; we stay afloat, but we do a lot of bailing). Nevertheless, we are proud, and we are privileged to influence. I know my kids spend more waking hours with their teachers than with me.

The first time I went to a cocktail party at the invitation of my income tax accountant, I realized two things: first, that I was the only non-CPA there, and second, how each profession *affects* its members. On almost every topic broached, the typical response was, "Do you find membership there a good investment for your dollar?" If CPAs are somewhat cloned, I, as a teacher, am also *affected* by my profession.

Because the developmental grade levels of children are markedly different from each other, each educational level produces its own unique cultural patterns of *effective* teaching styles. The levels tend to be grouped in the following categories: primary, third-fourth grade, early adolescent, high school* and Special Education. The subcultures are complete with their own perceptions and reactions.

Once I was moving transparencies to the front of an elementary faculty meeting room for a presentation. I inadvertently dropped several items, and immediately four teachers rose to assist me. I intentionally had the same accident in front of a high school staff

---

* Secondary teachers seem to be as much or more affected by their content area than their grade level. For example, a ninth grade math teacher will be more similar to a twelfth grade math teacher than he is to a ninth grade literature teacher.

(being highly kinesthetic, I drop things even when I don't mean to). As I gathered up my materials alone, I overheard one teacher whisper to another, "Looks like we have a clumsy presenter."

Just as nutritionists say "we are what we eat," teachers "are what they teach." The more we understand the developmental learning style of the grade level we teach, the more insight we have into how we are *affected*.

As you read through *Righting The Educational Conveyor Belt*, you will naturally identify with some sections stronger than others. Pay special attention to the sections to which other readers are more drawn than you, because each subculture (grade level) has developed and utilized patterns that are successful with the average pupil. Therefore, when looking for ways to reach students who don't fit the statistical norm, our answers are often found in the patterns common to another subculture. For example, the kinesthetic patterns learned in second grade may need to be taught or reemphasized to some fourth graders; likewise, the sixth grade teacher may have the solutions for the socially precocious fourth grader. This concept of switching to another subculture's way of perceiving and reacting is especially important in two areas: when working one-on-one (RETEACHING), so that you can act with the sensitivity and flexibility of a primary teacher, and when you finish the day, turn off the classroom lights, and (like the secondary teacher) have the ability to say, "Let's leave it here; I taught them and now I *deserve* a full home life."

Primary Students

When children are about five, they enter kindergarten and begin their journey on the educational conveyor belt. They enter kindergarten/first grade as primarily kinesthetic creatures.

Teachers at this level know that their students understand reality by touching, smelling, tasting, pushing, shoving, banging and taking apart their world. It is common practice on the primary level to "walk through" procedures and expectations. The following not-too-exaggerated example illustrates this point.

Sometime after Labor Day, the weather chills and it is time to teach the students where to put their coats. After the morning greeting, the teacher takes the students back out in the hall. With their coats on, they re-enter the room. She lines them up in the appropriate location to hang up their coats and makes a statement such as, "Ready? Take off your coats and hang them up." Once she spots those students who don't have their ears "functioning," she has several choices. One is to take the coat off the child. The adequate primary teacher who takes the student's coat off as she says the command runs the risk of setting up a precedent - when future directives are given, this child learns to expect the teacher to do the directive for him. A more appropriate choice is to consider the exercise a dry run, congratulate herself on detecting which students she needs to assist, and ask all the students to put their coats back on. The next time, she can station herself next to the student(s) she wants to assist as she gives the instructions to remove their coats.

A third alternative follows the axiom, "the meaning of the message is the response you get." The superior primary teacher places her hand on top of the student's hand as the student takes off his coat. These outstanding primary teachers are often behind their peers in the amount of content presented during the first month of school because of the amount of time spent kinesthetically teaching their students group procedures. However, by Thanksgiving, these teachers have surpassed their colleagues.

Intermediate Students

Between third and fourth grade, the format of the conveyor belt changes from kinesthetic to auditory. The students who are not able to make the switch are taken off the conveyor belt and put in a corridor. Each school district has its own label to describe its corridor: Special Education, Resource Room, Title 1.

Elementary Teachers

When educators of primary students were in college teachers' courses, they were motivated by the thought of working with 22-30 bright shiny faces. Their love for individual children was their source of inspiration. Their on-the-job training compelled them to naturally focus on learning - how each child perceives and internalizes information. They share this orientation with Special Education teachers.*

---

* A wonderful book for elementary and Special Education teachers is Linda Lloyd's *Classroom Magic*, available through Metamorphous Press, P.O. Box 10616, Portland, OR 97210. Both Metamorphous Press and Laura Grinder Resource Center carry a full line of NLP books and audio & video tapes (Laura Grinder Resource Center, 1803 Mission St., Ste. 406, Santa Cruz, CA 95060).

Workshops and seminars on "learning styles" are attended in greatest numbers by primary and Special Education teachers. Their preparation is the most kinesthetic of any level. They show caring by touching and being touchable. Someone once said that the successful primary teacher's clothing wears out in front first.

Junior High/Middle School Students

Sometime before high school, the format of the conveyor belt changes again and becomes primarily visual. The concepts presented are more abstract, symbolic and graphic. Students who are unable to make the transition to the visual format are taken off the conveyor belt and put into the corridor, which is composed of students who are predominantly kinesthetic and auditory.

Junior High/Middle School Teachers

This is the forgotten sub-culture of education. It is very rare to find a student teacher who *wants* to teach the 12-15 year old student. One local state college actually created a curriculum designed

specifically for this level of education. It only operated for one year because the creators couldn't find enough people to participate. One would have to humorously question the sanity of someone who wants to teach the "hormonal club of America," in which chemicals are being released so frequently and at such rapid speed that a student can feel as if he is living in a foreign body. Parents often refer to their adolescent offspring as U.F.O.'s (Unidentified, Formerly Ours).

Where do all the teachers who do instruct the emotional yoyos of the conveyor belt come from? They come from the other two sub-cultures. Those with a background in elementary teaching bring with them their love, their focus, and their sensitivities, all of which are reflections of their culture's teaching style.

The others are teachers who are waiting to get positions on the high school level. For them, May is the time of year to listen to the scuttlebutt regarding possible openings at the "big school." Like a plane waiting for permission to land at an airport, they circle and circle and run out of gas quicker than any other teachers except those in Special Education.

The successful teacher on this level knows his preparation is more emotional than anything else. Neuro Linguistic Programming offers assistance in much needed areas of establishing rapport, stress management, and preventive discipline. The teachers show their caring by talking to students and, even more so, by listening.

High School Teachers

High school teachers, by contrast, were motivated while in educational practicum courses by their love of content and their desire to impart knowledge and wisdom which comes with such information. Their focus, consequently, is on teaching and group dynamics. However, when one focuses on teaching without first understanding what learning is, one tends to duplicate his professor's style of teaching. Research indicates that 80% of high school instruction involves two teaching styles; lecturing and seat monitoring. Contrast this with the primary level classroom in which a teacher rotates through a minimum of four different teaching styles every 45 minutes.*

A high school teacher's preparation is the most academic of all levels. What draws these teachers to NLP are those techniques which increase content retention by students, which help the teacher to determine appropriate courses for the students (remedial, "par" or advanced courses), and which increase their understanding of how teaching styles affect student receptivity. In turn, they show their caring by helping students see their abilities and showing them options for the future.

The Conveyor Belt and the Corridor

Earlier it was noted that students who don't progress as expected on the conveyor belt are sent into the corridor to special programs and classes. What is the relationship between "conveyor belt teachers" and "corridor teachers" at your school?

Corridors

While no one ever intentionally sat down and consciously constructed the following scenario, it seems to be universally true. Any student who is precociously ahead of the predominant mode is perceived as "gifted" (i.e., a VISUAL student in the primary grades who reads two grade levels ahead). Likewise, any student entering a new grade level (especially third or sixth) who fails to adapt/adopt to the new mode (auditory and visual, respectively) of processing information is perceived as "below average." If money is available, the latter student is ushered off the conveyor belt and into the educational CORRIDOR. Some schools and school districts are more successful than others because they have the following VISION of the relationship between the conveyor belt and the corridor; they utilize the corridor as a place where the student's deficient mode is developed. In other words, the corridor is PROCESS oriented, whereas the conveyor belt is more oriented to CONTENT.

Comparison of the Scales of Learning

Conveyor Belt has heavy emphasis on **content**

Corridor has heavy emphasis on **process**

---

* It is no small coincidence that foreign languages are the only subjects associated with accelerated learning. It is predominantly the secondary level course which is taught much like the primary approach - multisensory. For more information and training in accelerated foreign language acquisition/suggestopedia, contact Charles Schmid of the Lind Institute, P.O. Box 14487, San Francisco, CA 94114.

"Less than successful" schools and school districts do not share the above VISION. Their conveyor belt teachers dictate the content to the corridor teachers, and therefore the corridor students' deficiencies are not addressed. For example, Mr. C. Belt tells Mrs. Cora Door, "Johnny will be coming down to see you fifth period every day. I'll send his math and spelling books with him." This forces Mrs. Cora Door to spend her time on CONTENT which is new to the students. The student actually needs assistance on PROCESS.*

The Scales of Learning are broken

The relationship between CONTENT and PROCESS is called the "Scales of Learning." When content is emphasized, the teacher has to use multisensory techniques so that students can choose which aspects of the presentation to pay attention to. Will they mostly watch, mostly listen, or mostly move and touch? Each student can select their familiar process. In order to avoid exceeding the student's frustration level, it is best to present a new process, such as visualization, with familiar content. If the conveyor belt class is working on multiplication tables and Johnny is having difficulty memorizing them auditorally, it is appropriate to spend time having Johnny first work with any familiar song/rhythmic saying. This will create the appropriate mental state. Once Johnny is repeating his song/rhythmic saying with his voice and moving his body in a metronome fashion, the teacher can mimic Johnny's movement and voice, thereby pacing and anchoring Johnny's auditory state. The teacher can move immediately into "2 x 2 is 4," mimicking the

rhythm of the nursery rhyme/song.

The success of this activity hinges on maintaining the auditory state while switching to content which is easier and more familiar than content being presented on the conveyor belt (i.e., "2 x 2 is 4" as opposed to "7 x 8 is 56").

One student, Sally, has her multiplication tables memorized auditorally but is unable to see them in her mind's eye. In this case, the corridor teacher would have Sally visualize familiar items such as her bedroom, living room furniture arrangement, and anything that has to do with visual properties: color, size, shape, distance, etc. When she was able to see these images in her mind's eye, her body would probably freeze and her eyes would move high in the socket. The teacher would then mimic Sally's physiology to anchor the state. Once the teacher was satisfied that Sally could maintain that state, the teacher could have the student "see" 3 x 3 in her mind's eye (more information offered in Chapter 6).

Since the purpose of the corridor is to offer an alternative to conveyor belt teaching, it is important for the corridor teacher to know the teaching style of the conveyor belt instructors and offer alternatives. If the conveyor belt teacher instructs primarily in one mode (such as auditory), it is helpful for the corridor teacher to see how the corridor student from that class responds to a multisensory approach (which is more often used by successful conveyor belt teachers). The corridor teacher might

---

* Recognizing that students are placed in the corridor for a variety of reasons, this section addresses only those who are there for learning style deficiencies.

consider teaching in a mode other than the primary mode used by the conveyor belt teacher. The sequence of the modes used by the conveyor belt teacher may not match the thinking of the corridor student. In such a case, it is the task of the corridor teacher to match the student's sequencing.

Conveyor belt teachers can adopt the current textbook publication program and work successfully with the majority of students. In contrast, the corridor teacher needs a separate program for each child, using a wide range of visual, auditory and kinesthetic styles, and needs to know how to match each to the appropriate student. The corridor teacher's ability to detect the learning styles of the students will be the basis of her success. The conveyor belt teacher can get away with a more limited perception and a fewer number of techniques.

Elizabeth, trained in NLP, is a corridor teacher who works with third grade learning disabled students. She took a cardboard box and made the top look like the top of a head and the front of the box look like a face. She made three flaps on the top, each labeled Visual, Auditory, and Kinesthetic. On the front, she did the same - three flaps, each labeled as the top had been. Within two months, every student knew what his visual, auditory and kinesthetic capacities were. When the students were to learn a new concept, Elizabeth called a student to the box and asked the student to describe the easiest way he received information. The top of the box represented the input channel. The teacher then asked, "In what form will your homeroom teacher require you to demonstrate that you know this?" The front of the box symbolized the output channel.

The students had a blueprint of HOW they would learn and retrieve (process); they were then ready for the WHAT (content).

Conveyor - Corridor Comparison Chart	
Conveyor	**Corridor**
Focus on group/ class as a whole	Focus on individual student
Emphasis on multisensory teaching	Consider initially teaching each student in his own mode
Oriented on new content	Oriented on new process
Focus on group teaching	Focus on learning
Success based on TECHNIQUE	Success based on PERCEPTION and matching technique to student's style

Relationship Between Conveyor and Corridor

The following questionnaire will assist you in recognizing the relationship between the Conveyor and the Corridor at your school.

Grade level: _____

Subject (for secondary teachers): _____

Are you a conveyor belt or corridor teacher?
(Suggestion: teachers of remedial classes are more corridor than conveyor belt.)

Percent of time spent (= 100%) in: Content : _____

                                        Process: _____

What is the relationship at your school between the conveyor belt and the corridor? Who dictates what content will be taught in the corridor?

_____

_____

_____

How does this relationship affect you?

_____

_____

Using the knowledge and insights presented so far (and if you had a magic wand), how would you alter the conveyor belt - corridor relationship at your school?

_____

_____

_____

Cultures of Education Summary Chart

	Elementary Teachers	Middle School/ Junior High Teachers	High School Teachers
Motivation	Kids	(background reflected)	Content
Focus	Learning	(background reflected)	Teaching
Preparation	Kinesthetic	Emotional	Intellectual
Students are:	Kinesthetic	Auditory	Visual
Show caring by	Touching, being touchable	Talking & listening	Helping students see abilities & options
NLP assists*	Learning styles	Rapport	Content retention
	Multisensory teaching	Group dynamics	Teaching visualization
		Stress management	Matching modes: course/teacher/ students
		Discipline with comfort	

---

* The areas listed above are of benefit to all. Research published by the National Education Association indicates that 82% of all teaching communication is nonverbal (Patrick Miller, *Nonverbal Communication*, Washington D.C., NEA Publications, 1981, p. 7. Reprinted with permission). Therefore, consistent nonverbal messages are the *single most important area in which NLP can assist.*

Chapter 2

Modalities

"At birth, the ape and human brains are 350 grams.
At adulthood, the ape's is 450 grams
and the human's is 1500 grams."

History of Learning Styles

The concept of Learning Styles has had a long history, extending back to the 1960's. Rita Dunn has done the most to awaken the education community to the differences among students. Those that follow her guidelines are encouraged to individualize *learning*, which the elementary teachers with their self-contained classrooms (30 students) find palatable.*

Bernice McCarthy's *4MAT* would have us focus on *teaching* and rotate through eight different stages of a lesson so that each type of learner gets an opportunity to operate in his comfort zone.**

Secondary instructors, with their attention to content, are attracted to a more generic view of learning styles that all levels of teachers will find easy to implement with practical benefits.

As Aristotle gave the ultimate compliment to his mentors, Socrates and Plato, by extrapolating beyond what each had taught, so, too, it is time to move on.

As a whole, teachers will not buy Dunn's ideas of creating individual learning packets, nor will they radically change their teaching style, as McCarthy would advocate. We need to find ways to work "smarter, not harder." This book is committed to finding those ways.

A New Look at Learning Styles

In a typical classroom of 30 students, there is an average of 22 students who have enough visual, auditory and kinesthetic *capacities* that the urge to pigeonhole them into VAK categories is senseless and impractical. On the other end, there are 2 - 3 students who are not learning from reasons other than their processing/learning style (i.e., psychological, home situations, etc.). The students in between these two groups are the "translators" of the educational conveyor belt.

---

* Dr. Rita Dunn, St. John's University, Grand Central Parkway, Jamaica, NY 11439.

** Dr. Bernice McCarthy, *4MAT* (Barrington, Ill.: Excel, Inc., 1981).

Typical Classroom

30 Students {
- 22 have VAK
- 4 - 6 translators
- 2 - 3 other factors interfering

These are the **V**isual **O**nly, the **A**uditory **O**nly and the **K**inesthetic **O**nly. (It's not just a coincidence that in sports, the initials "K O" stand for "knock out." These kids are "knocked out" of the educational system. In every study I have seen regarding "kids at risk," kinesthetics make up a vast majority of the 26% drop out rate.) They often do not quite qualify for Special Education. They are able to do functionally well some of the time and struggle most of the time. They have one preferred mode and very little capacity in the other two. Any information that enters through their sensory system has to be "translated" into their primary/only mode of storage. That is why when the instruction/content is in their primary mode, they do fine and, at times, even shine.

Example:

A **KO** student doing the lab section of a science unit is often quite adequate because he is able to physically grasp the concepts and yet is lost when reading about the same experiment in the textbook.

Likewise, the **VO** student can be quite overloaded by the tactileness of the lab experiment but the stillness experienced while reading the textbook allows the student to picture what the experiment was. The **AO** student attending the small group reading table at the back of the room does fine when that section of the lesson deals with the phonetic approach (such as Distar).

Glitches:

The above examples of **VO**, **AO** and **KO** dealt with a lesson which was taught primarily in one of the modes for an extended period of time. The more typical situation would be a five to ten minute time period during which all three modes would be utilized several times by the teacher. The teacher would switch from presenting in the translator's primary mode to other than that student's primary mode, and the student has to translate the information back into his primary mode. This requires the student to temporarily leave reality (be unable to hear or see the current information the teacher is presenting) in order to do this translation. Once the translation is complete, the student returns to external reality and continues to switch from taking in external information and closing off external reality in order to translate. The result is that the student has a series of gaps/glitches where he knows certain information and misses other bits of information. These gaps/glitches are especially apparent during review and on tests.

Observing Teaching/Learning Styles

When we teach using the students' sense of SEEING, HEARING, MOVEMENT and TOUCH, the class, as a whole, receives information in one or several channels. This multisensory approach also reinforces the use of their less developed senses.

This paper is designed to have one teacher observe another teacher (one who has volunteered). As observer, you will be tabulating how often students are engaged in SEEING, HEARING, MOVING and TOUCH. When the students are just utilizing one sense, put an "X"

in the outside circle part; if the students are using two senses, put an "X" in the inside triangle; if the students are involved with all three senses, put an "X" in the little inner circle.

On a separate piece of paper, talk about your reactions. Some helpful questions: What was the preferred sense? Least preferred sense? What was the main combination used? Did the predicates used match the activities? What kind of student would have an easy time? Hard time? What aspects were the same and different from my style of teaching?

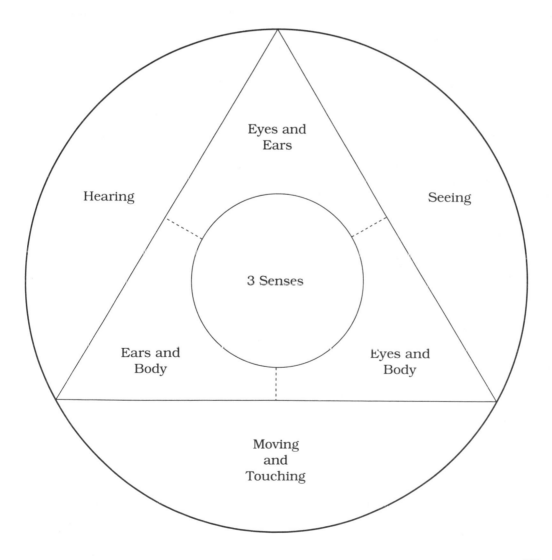

WORKSHEET

Modality Task Analysis of a Lesson

The following form is to assist you in identifying the glitches that occur in a lesson for translators.

1. Title or description of a lesson.

_____

2. Brief description of sequential order of content presented.

a. _____ (_____)

b. _____ (_____)

c. _____ (_____)

d. _____ (_____)

e. _____ (_____)

f. _____ (_____)

g. _____ (_____)

3. In the parentheses to the right of #2, using the initials V, A or K, list the mode that is required in order to follow the format.

4. As you present the lesson, notice where certain students (translators) temporarily leave attentiveness while they translate.

An example of the above is a secondary English teacher who is teaching figures of speech. When she comes to the onomatopoeia, the "AO" is in her area of strength, and the "VO" is temporarily lost; likewise, the primary teacher who uses a color code on the board to teach the 5 times table.

$$
\begin{array}{ccccc}
\textit{3} & \textit{4} & \textit{5} & \textit{6} & \textit{7} \\
\underline{\times 5} & \underline{\times 5} & \underline{\times 5} & \underline{\times 5} & \underline{\times 5} \\
15 & 20 & 25 & 30 & 35
\end{array}
$$

When the number that is multiplied by 5 is odd, the teacher has triangled it and put it in blue chalk (represented by italics) and has done the same with the 5 in the answer. The **VO** is helped by the color coding (italicized), the **KO** is assisted by both the color and the triangle, and the **AO** is asking, "Why did you do that?"

Indicators

There are external indicators which indicate which parts of the brain a student is operating from, whether it is auditory, visual or kinesthetic.

The charts which follow call attention to neurological and behavioral traits the student is likely to exhibit and respond to. The behaviors are a composite of characteristics gathered from NLP and Walter B. Barbe, Ph.D. and Raymond H. Swassing, Ed.D.*

	Neurological Indicators					
	Eyes	**Movement**	**Voice & Processing Speed**	**Process Location**	**Predicates**	
Visual		Still	Fastest	Movement/ changes around eyes, i.e., blinks, squints, eyebrows raise	focus see look watch clear	picture foggy reveal notice appears
Auditory			Metro-nome	Movement/ changes around ears/ mouth and sounds, i.e., "ah," "hmm"	listen sounds like said hear	talk speak rhyme
Kinesthetic		Lots of movement	Slowest	Changes and movement from the neck down	grasp feel "hold it," "I don't get it," action words	handle grab

---

* An excellent, inexpensive filmstrip cassette appropriate for educators, students and parents is "Teaching to Modality Strengths: A Common Sense Approach to Learning" (used by permission of Zaner-Bloser, Inc., Columbus, Ohio. Copyright 1979).

Behavioral Indicators

Visual	Auditory	Kinesthetic
Organized	Talks to self	Responds to physical rewards
Neat and orderly	Easily distracted	Touches people and stands close
Observant	Moves lips/says words when reading	Physically oriented
Quieter	Can repeat back	Moves a lot
Appearance oriented	Math and writing more difficult	Larger physical reaction
More deliberate	Spoken language easy	Early large muscle development
Good speller	Speaks in rhythmic pattern	Learns by doing
Memorizes by picture	Likes music	Memorizes by walking, seeing
Less distracted by noise	Can mimic tone, pitch and timbre	Points when reading
Has trouble remembering verbal instructions	Learns by listening	Gestures a lot
Would rather read than be read to	Memorizes by steps, procedure, sequence	Responds physically

Voice

Chin is up, voice high	"Marks off" w/ tone, tempo, shifts	Chin is down, voice louder

Learning

Needs overall view and purpose and a vision for details; cautious until mentally clear	Dialogues both internally and externally; tries alternatives verbally first	Learns through manipulating and actually doing

Recall

Remembers what was seen	Remembers what was discussed	Remembers an over-all impression of what was experienced

Behavioral Indicators, con't.

Visual	Auditory	Kinesthetic
Conversation		
Has to have the whole picture; very detailed	Most talkative of three modes; loves discussions, may monopolize; has a tendency for tangents and telling whole sequential event	Laconic, tactile, uses gestures and movements, uses action words
Spelling		
Most accurate of three modes; actually sees words and can spell them. Confused when spelling words never seen before	Uses phonetic approach, spells with a rhythmic movement	Counts out letters with body movements and checks with internal feelings
Reading		
Strong, successful area, has speed	Attacks unknown words well, enjoys reading aloud and listening; often slow because of subvocalizing	Likes plot oriented books, reflects action of story with body movement
Writing		
Having it look OK important, learning neatness easy	Tends to talk better than writes and likes to talk as he writes	Thick, pressured handwriting not as good as others
Imagination		
Vivid imagery, can see possibilities, details appear; is best mode for long term planning	Sounds and voices heard	Tends to act the image out; wants to walk through it. Strong intuitive, weak on details

Identifying One Modality Learners

The purpose of the following worksheet is to identify three students who are primarily one modality learners. Use the characteristics presented previously to identify these students. By filling out the form below, you will practice your observation skills.

1. Initials of a primarily visual student _____

Description of the behavior which indicates this:

_____

_____

_____

_____

_____

_____

2. Initials of a predominantly auditory learner _____

Description of the behavior which indicates this:

_____

_____

_____

_____

_____

_____

3. Initials of a mainly kinesthetic learner _____

Description of the behavior which indicates this:

_____

_____

_____

_____

_____

_____

The worksheet below was submitted by a teacher who participated in my "Learning Styles" course.

These are her descriptions of the single modality learners she taught.

Identifying One Modality Learners: Examples

---

1. Initials of a primarily visual student <u>MD</u>

Description of the behavior which indicates this:

A. ALWAYS looks at overhead as I explain a concept so she can SEE what I'm saying.

B. When I read from the text book, MD always reads the material for herself rather than relying on my reading.

C. Her English notebook is the most organized I've seen. It's all typed (she typed all of her handwritten notes from class). Each section is also indexed and subdivided with tabs.

D. She has a highlighter on her desk at all times. If I hand out a worksheet or a study guide, she reads through it for herself (again not relying on me) and highlights what is important to her.

E. MD consistently only misses one or two of the very difficult "extra credit" words on very difficult spelling/vocabulary tests.

2. Initials of a predominantly auditory learner <u>JS</u>

Description of the behavior which indicates this:

A. Whenever JS takes a test, he "talks" under his breath and mutters his way through it, much to the distraction of his quieter visual neighbors!

B. JS is a mimicker. He is able to repeat word for word what someone tells him (even when he appears not to be listening), AND he can usually repeat it in a near or exact imitation of the person's voice!

C. JS is able to mimic his various coaches' voices so well that he once dismissed practice early and everyone believed it was the coach who had spoken.

D. He has difficulty with math because he claims he cannot figure out where the numbers keep going. When he does his math homework, he talks to himself in his math teacher's voice!

E. JS often has to be sat in a corner of the room or at a table outside the room if he has any serious work to get done because he is so easily distracted even by a whisper in the far side of the classroom. During in-class essays, he has taken to putting himself away from the class so that he can get his essay done in the time allotted.

F. He is very creative in his writing, but his grammar, spelling and punctuation are lacking; however, he can TELL me the same essay and it SOUNDS better than how some of the other students' essays LOOK on paper!

Identifying One Modality Learners: Examples, con't.

3. Initials of a mainly kinesthetic learner <u>JLS</u>

Description of the behavior which indicates this:

A. JLS is the kid who gets up to sharpen an INK pen, just to move. (He actually did that one day and seemed genuinely surprised to realize that he did indeed have a pen rather than a pencil!)

B. When I am moving around the room helping students, JLS doesn't raise his hand and wait for me to get to him; he reaches out and GRABS me, by the wrist, the shirt, the skirt, whatever he can.

C. Whenever I am reading directions, he never looks at me. He touches the words on the worksheet or in the book, and he goes CRAZY if I have directions on the overhead. He has actually gone up to the overhead after I have given the directions and "read" the directions with his hands!

D. This kid could not learn grammar until I made HIM into different parts of speech and parts of the sentence and let him and his classmates BE the sentence and FEEL what it is like to be a verb placed either before the subject or after it, etc. Incidentally, JLS liked to be ACTION verbs or conjunctions. He really got into "connecting" two other people (parts of speech) together!

E. He is constantly reaching behind him, over his head, under his desk, etc., to touch the kid in back of him. Fortunately the neighbor is also kinesthetic, and they have at least two such tussles a class period; it seems to help each of them more than it bothers any of the rest of us!

Improvised Swassing and Barbe Diagnostic Activity

There are many educational situations where the previous model of identifying a student's "learning style" is insufficient. The legions of students who are under the umbrella label of "disability" fit this category. For these students, we need to separate the "input" from "storage" from "output" modes.

The Input-Output Diagram is an improvised activity originally established by Drs. Swassing and Barbe.*

The purpose of this instrument is to see if there is a difference in how easily a person can *store* and *retrieve* information. There are nine possible combinations of getting the information a certain way (input) and demonstrating that you remember it (output). We want to notice if the student has a combination(s) that is substantially stronger/weaker than the other combinations. No comparison between students is intended.

While most diagnostic instruments are biased towards the visual, this exercise circumvents such a weakness; in fact, its main weakness is that there is no provision for "visual output." In actuality, we are only able to do six possible comparisons; we skip the visual output (see the doubled asterisked "Visual Outputs").

Input (through which sense the information comes into the person)	Output (which sense is used to demonstrate the person has the information)
(V _____	V) **
V _____	A
V _____	K
(A _____	V) **
A _____	A
A _____	K
(K _____	V) **
K _____	A
K _____	K

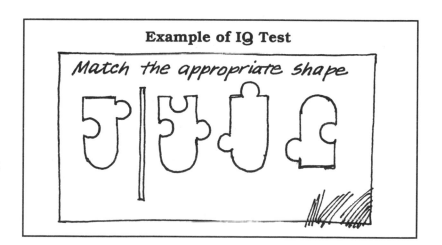

Example of IQ Test

Match the appropriate shape

---

* Contact Zaner-Bloser, Inc., 612 North Dark Street, Columbus, Ohio 43215 for information on their testing kit (used by permission of Zaner-Bloser, Inc., Columbus, Ohio. Copyright 1979).

** To do a visual output, we would need to show three possible output patterns and ask the person to select the correct one which, of course, is what commercial IQ tests do. Dale Seymour has excellent "visual thinking" kits. Write to Dale Seymour Publications, P.O. Box 10888, Palo Alto, CA 94303.

Directions

1. With a partner, gather three categories of eight items, each of which can be easily distinguished visually and kinesthetically (for example, one category could be coins; another, credit cards; and a third, paperclips).

2. Divide each category in half and allot four items to each partner. Partners are at a table, facing each other.

3. Set up a pretense for a test. For example, say, "Hi, I'm doing an exercise from a book and . . ." or "I want to test some ways to remember things."

4. Place any four items behind a divider (such as a large book). Ask the person to look at the items when you reveal them, and, after you cover them again, lay out his items to match your layout. V (in) K (out)

When the person has completed his layout, remove the divider for comparison. It is advantageous not to offer verbal feedback at this time.

NOTE: As the person is "inputting" the sequence of items you have laid out, he will give V, A and K clues of the process. If the person does well, use any of three variables to make the same exercise tougher. For example:

a. Shorten the time she is able to see the layout

b. Increase the number of items

c. Increase the complexity of the layout

Watch for the clues that indicate which representational system is being used when the person goes into stress (when the task becomes tough). If the person goes into stress before you have the clues, make the task easier.

5. Repeat Step 4, this time asking the person to tell you the sequence. V (in) A (out)

6. Again following the format of Step 4, tell the person the layout sequence and ask him to repeat it. A (in) A (out)

7. Then tell the person the sequence and ask him to lay it out. A (in) K (out)

8. Next have the person feel the layout without seeing it and describe it to you. K (in) A (out)

9. Finally, have the person feel the layout without seeing it and lay out one to match. K (in) K (out)

Remember, the purpose is to compare this person's input/output combinations in order to detect if one or more of the sequences is significantly stronger or weaker than the rest!

The Transition from Input to Output

The improvised Swassing and Barbe activity allows you to work one-on-one with a student. What about the class as a whole? When do they have to learn (input) in one mode and demonstrate (output) that they have it in another?

The learning process consists of a student receiving (input) and storing the information. The retrieving process is when the information is pulled from storage and demonstrated.

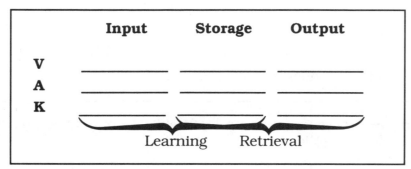

While we are still learning how to detect what is occurring in storage, we can certainly track the input and output. The majority of students can receive information via one channel (i.e., Auditory = hearing the teacher speaking) and demonstrate having received the information in another (i.e., Visual and Kinesthetic = writing it down). This happens during spelling tests; the teacher says the word (auditory) and the students write it down (visual and kinesthetic).

This week, record three examples of when the modes of input/output are different and comment on which students have difficulty.

1 a. What you did (their input channel):

_____

b. How they demonstrated they had the information (output channel):

_____

c. Comments on which students had what kind of difficulty:

_____

2 a. What you did:

_____

b. How they demonstrated they had the information:

_____

c. Comments:

_____

3 a. What you did:

_____

b. How they demonstrated they had the information:

_____

c. Comments:

_____

WORKSHEET

Successful vs. Unsuccessful Students

Sometimes a student finds it easy to learn specific *content* or do a procedure. Other students may find the same activity difficult. The difference between the two groups of students sometimes occurs because of the way they are *processing*. The two ways of processing are by single mode or by a combination of successive modes.

Directions

1. Skill/subject/topic selected:

_____

2. Initials of a student who does #1 with ease and success:

_____

3. Interview and learn the successful student's strategy of how he does the above (describe the neurological indicators):

_____

_____

_____

_____

4. Initials of a student who does #1 unsuccessfully or with difficulty:

_____

5. Interview and learn the unsuccessful student's strategy of how he does the above.

_____

_____

_____

_____

6. What is the difference between the two students, and how might you check to see if this pattern is true for a more representative group of students?

_____

_____

_____

_____

Teaching Styles

Because of our affiliation to grade level and, for secondary teachers, content area, we tend to hold certain beliefs. The more we are aware of our teaching styles and the underlying beliefs that support these styles, the better we understand the compatibility, or level of effective communication, between ourselves and certain students.

Appearance

We all would like to teach multisensory, and when we are doing so, we aren't aware of our individual preferred teaching style. However, there are times when we lapse back to our preferred teaching style. By knowing what that style is, and when we're using it, we can notice which students are having a difficult time. This section is intended to help you notice the small innuendoes which indicate a teacher's style. The following is a generic chart of descriptions which indicate a teacher's preference.

There is no mention of the auditory teacher's appearance, because, as a group, they are fewest in number and therefore, the author has not had many occasions to study them. Secondly, those studied seem to show a potpourri of visual and kinesthetic traits.

Teaching Styles Appearance

Area	Visual	Kinesthetic
Room Appearance	Neat, color coordinated	Lots of materials; several work stations
Work Space	Organized; arranged by size, color; stacks things in vertical filing cabinet	Functionally organized in stacks piled everywhere
Bulletin Boards	Visually pleasing; rotated periodically, color coordinated	Loves to display students' work; projects hanging everywhere; leaves things on board long after activity is completed (you know that it's Easter because the teacher takes down the Valentine's Day board)
Teacher Attire	Neat; tidy; color/ fabric coordinated; appearance is priority	Comfortable; emphasis on how it feels as opposed to how it looks

Teaching Styles: Instructional Presentation

Visual	Kinesthetic	Auditory
Talks fast	Talks slower	Speaks rhythmically
Uses visual aids (overhead, board)	Uses manipulatives (hands-on and handouts)	Likes class discussion
Likes to cover a lot of content	Has student involved projects (plays, simulations)	Teacher or student reads text aloud
Considers forms important (grammar, spelling, heading)	Considers concepts important (tends to de-emphasize spelling and grammar)	Tends to acknowledge student's comments by paraphrasing
Believes in visual feedback to evaluate individual (tests)	Believes in what students can do (create, demonstrate, etc.) to evaluate	Disciplines by talking to the student usually with memorized sermonettes which begin with "How many times? . . ."
Is due date oriented	Has students do boardwork, working in units and teams	Is easily disoriented from focus of lesson (war stories)
	Uses lots of demonstrations	Rarely uses visual aids, has a running commentary of words and noises (i.e., "Okay," "Uh huh")

Identifying Teachers With a Preferred Modality

The purpose of this worksheet is to identify three teachers who exhibit a preferred modality. Use the characteristics presented on the last two charts to identify these teachers. By filling out the form below, you will practice observation skills.

1. Initials of a primarily visual teacher:_____

Description of appearance and instructional presentation:

_____

_____

_____

_____

2. Initials of a predominantly auditory teacher:_____

Description of appearance and instructional presentation:

_____

_____

_____

_____

3. Initials of a mainly kinesthetic teacher:_____

Description of appearance and instructional presentation:

_____

_____

_____

_____

Visual-Kinesthetic Teacher vs. Kinesthetic-Visual Teacher

When asking teachers to identify their two preferred modes, the majority select the visual and the kinesthetic. Since this is the most common combination, it's pertinent to address the difference between when the visual leads the kinesthetic as opposed to the reverse.

Only the visual left mode has capacity for long term planning. A common joke among teachers versed in learning styles is not to get stuck on a district committee chaired by an auditory. The lack of the visual means absence of long term planning and the auditory means tangents composed primarily of war stories.

An asset of the visual (left brain) is the ability to pre-think about how to be systematic both in terms of management and content presentation. Another asset is the tendency to think in terms of the entire group and make sure that "the class" is on task before assisting individual students. Taken to the extreme, they're rigid and too schedule oriented.

The strengths of the kinesthetic are flexibility and being able to incorporate what's happening into the lesson being presented. The kinesthetic teacher tends to emphasize rapport (as opposed to the visual's "authority"). Students in a kinesthetic teacher's classroom often act as if they have permission to have a "private audience" with the teacher.

Oftentimes a teacher who is a visual-kinesthetic at school might be kinesthetic-visual when doing housework. For example, he does Saturday chores by picking up one item to put it in its proper place in another room, and on the way, putting two other items underneath each arm. The person is susceptible to being sidetracked from one minor, uncompleted project to another. By noon, the person has a sense that he has worked hard, accomplished little, and chased his tail all morning. This helter-skelter format also happens in the classroom, and certain content areas are especially susceptible to it: shop, arts, or other content areas which necessitate individual assistance. These courses often have the greatest collection of right brain teachers on secondary campuses. These are the times when it seems that five students are saying all at once, "Teacher! Teacher!" and are in desperate need of help. The teacher feels pulled in many directions at once. An old saying frequently seen on posters is, "When you are up to your elbows in alligators, it is hard to remember that you entered the swamp to drain it."

The following format is designed to help the teacher switch from a kinesthetic-visual to visual-kinesthetic day.

1. As you finish with one student, stand up and *breathe* twice. Use nonverbals to prevent the next onslaught of requests for help (such as a hand gesture for "stop").

2. *Look* around the room (go visual) and determine if you need to change directions for the entire group before assisting other individuals (see section on "When Routines Are Broken," p. 169).

3. *Decide* what to do next.

One teacher was able to remember the above method by thinking of her husband's underwear, **BVD** (**B**reathe, **V**isual and **D**ecide).

The following advanced technique was developed by a shop teacher. He noticed that he was helping students in the following order: He would help student A, then student B, then move on to student C and on to D. He would notice A was inappropriate and would return to A, then noticed B, then noticed C and D. His version of the BVD was to help A, then B, then look back at A again. His explanation was that because of his content area (shop), he has to make sure they are successfully engaged before focusing his attention on a third new student.

RETEACHING

The last section explained individual teaching styles. There are two main areas this work focuses on where styles come into play: TEACHING (direct instruction; large group) and RETEACHING.

TEACHING

When we are TEACHING, we want to present information in a multisensory fashion. The VAK approach will reach the vast majority of students. The VAK allows the student to receive the information in his choice of INPUT channel. Initially, multisensory TEACHING also helps students reinforce their retention because the "more channels the information is in, the more vivid the memory." TEACHING indirectly strengthens the students' secondary channel(s). The section on "What to Do With Important and Difficult Concepts," p. 184, will address the TEACHING part.

RETEACHING

When we finish the TEACHING, and we leave the front of the room/chalkboard/overhead, etc., to help students individually, we are then going to RETEACH. Our applied research shows that over 65% of RETEACHING time is spent with the same 4-6 students. These are the "translators," the pupils who are not multisensory enough to learn from some of our TEACHING presentation. They need to have information presented in just one or two INPUT channels.

WORKSHEET

A nifty idea from Carol Cummings' books is to put a check, at the end of every class period, next to the name of each student you've helped during the RETEACH phase.* Each check represents when you've walked to their desk to assist. Within four periods, you will have identified your translators. These are the only students whose learning styles you need to be aware of so you can adjust to them.

RETEACHING in Theory

For the purposes of this worksheet, we are presuming we have finished TEACHING (and we did it in a multisensory way). Now we are about to RETEACH. We are dealing with three students; the first is a **V**isual **O**nly learner, the second, an **A**uditory **O**nly learner and the third, a **K**inesthetic **O**nly learner. Have colleagues role play **VO, AO, KO** students (use charts on pgs. 19-21). Do a chunk of information with which you are familiar and RETEACH for two minutes.

1. Practice presenting this information to a **V**isual **O**nly student using words describing color, shape, size, location, etc., and pacing at a speed that is typical of their style. Be sure to hold your body still and stand in front of the student. Remember they learn by seeing. They want to watch you demonstrate the pattern over and over. Color coordinate the various points or aspects of the concepts being taught. Outline your plan here.

_____

_____

_____

2. Practice presenting this same information to an **A**uditory **O**nly student using different voices (volume, pausing, pitch, timbre, etc.) and predicates. Use a metronome body (especially the head) and pace at a speed that is typical of their style. Remember, if you can put the content in a sing song rhyme, they can remember it. Outline a plan to present material to an **A**uditory **O**nly student.

_____

_____

_____

3. Practice presenting this same information to a **K**inesthetic **O**nly student using locations, predicates, movement (gestures), touch, weight, texture, volume and pacing at a speed that is typical of their style. Remember they learn by doing through Muscle Memory; they're the "M & M" kids of school. Walk them through it over and over again. The greater the exaggeration, the easier the distinction is for their memory. Let them role play the different parts. Outline a plan to present material to a kinesthetic student.

_____

_____

* Dr. Carol Cummings, *Managing To Teach* (Edmonds, WA: Teaching, Inc., 1983).

RETEACHING in practice: Recording what you actually did in the classroom

Having done the above "RETEACHING", which was a theoretical practice which could be done with colleagues, complete the following form during this week. The former was done with peers simulating students with just a single modality. It is more likely that, in actual classroom settings, the student you reteach has more than one channel open. The following examples illustrate this point.

Example 1 Student's Initials: <u>CN</u>   Type of learner: <u>K</u>

After instruction on board, my kinesthetic "didn't get it." I put four books on the floor and had him walk from first, second, third and home base while I slowly talked through the analysis of the poem. He got to wear the baseball hat and also managed to fulfill his need to be the "class clown." When he did settle down to write his poem, he didn't need any extra help. He had "gotten it"!

Example 2 Student's Initials: <u>JS</u>   Type of learner: <u>AK</u>

Activity: I delivered a stimulating fifteen minute lecture on J. Steinbeck, the man and the philosopher. Students copied notes from overhead. Important pieces of information were squiggled. After lecture, students were to brainstorm possible quiz questions by reviewing squiggles.

1. A student was not engaged in activity; I approached from the right side and placed my hand on his shoulder.

2. I asked (A) him to point (K) to one piece of squiggled information on his notes.

3. I asked (A) him to climb (K) into my brain and see if he could see a question I might ask on the quiz. I asked (A) him to repeat (A) and write (K) it.

Example 3 Student's Initials: <u>RJ</u>   Type of learner: <u>VA</u>

Reviewing information on the last test, I went to that student and showed her the outline of the concept. While pointing to the parts (sort of a flow chart) (V), I rhythmically explained (A) it again and often asked her to repeat (A) back to me.

1. Student's Initials: _____   Type of learner: _____

Description of how you accommodated the student's INPUT channel:

_____

_____

_____

_____

_____

RETEACHING in practice: Recording what you actually did in the classroom,

2. Student's Initials: _____   Type of learner: _____

Description of how you accommodated the student's INPUT channel:

_____

_____

_____

_____

3. Student's Initials: _____   Type of learner: _____

Description of how you accommodated the student's INPUT channel:

_____

_____

_____

_____

There are at least two obvious benefits from RETEACHING. The first is as you help the "translator," you gather ingredients that will increase the sparkle the next time you "teach" the same concept. The dramatic flair which is necessary when RETEACHING the kinesthetic student often becomes the anchor used in your class presentation (See "Anchoring Concepts that are Important and Difficult," p. 189).

Secondly, the RETEACH is an indirect task analysis of the modalities needed by the students to understand the concept originally TAUGHT (see "Modality Task Analysis of a Lesson," p. 18). For example, when reteaching the "ing" suffix to the student, it becomes obvious that if "run" becomes "running," why doesn't "walk" become "walkking"? The coding of the pattern cannot be done by the visual alone. Likewise, the literature class that is covering poetry must use auditory abilities in order to hear the rhyming pace in poems.

Summary

Out of the average class of thirty students, twenty-two have enough visual, auditory and kinesthetic capacities to do well in almost any teacher's classroom. At the other end of the spectrum, there are approximately one to three students who have a difficult time with learning because of factors other than learning styles (home situations, psychological, etc.).

The four to six students in between these two groups are the "translators," those who are predominantly one modality learners. This results in at least five consequences:

1) When the information presented by the instructor isn't in his style, the student has to translate into his mode. For example, if a teacher shows an overhead or board presentation and the student is auditory, the student can be observed moving his lips while he *says* what he *sees*. While the predominantly one mode learners are translating, they are missing the next chunk of information that the teacher is presenting.

2) They also increase or decrease their attentiveness based on whether the current presentation style matches or mismatches their style.

3) The above results in the "translator" students knowing certain bits of information but lacking information that was presented in conjunction with the bit known. This causes the teacher to be confused when correcting a test/daily work and think, "How can the kid know 'X' but not 'Y'?"

4) It is estimated that we spend 60 - 80% of our "RETEACH" time on the same four to six students. They are the only ones whose "processing style" needs to be determined. We are already spending the time with them; we want to do it effectively.

5) We often are so multisensory that we find parts of our style listed under the visual, auditory and kinesthetic teaching styles columns. It is important to know which traits we have, especially those to which we revert when under pressure. We want to increase our flexibility and be compatible with each translator.

During this week, take short notes on how the five consequences apply to your "translators."

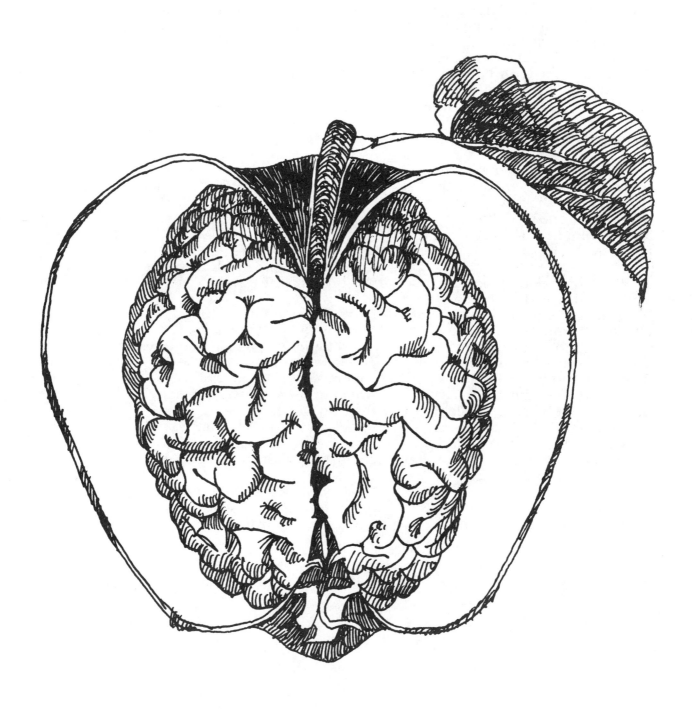

Chapter 3

Hemispherology: Another Model

*"The intuitive mind is a sacred gift, the rational mind a faithful servant.
It is paradoxical that in the context of modern life we have begun
to worship the servant and defile the divine."*
- Albert Einstein

The previously discussed model of VAK classifications has its assets and liabilities in helping teachers identify students' learning styles. The more models one has, the more sophisticated and precise one can be in detecting an individual's processing style.

A story illustrates this point. My neighbor's boy was borrowing tools from my automotive garage workbench to work on his bicycle. I noticed that some of the corners of the bolts were losing their shape and realized he was using the metric socket set. The tools worked well on most of the nuts, but when I introduced him to the standard socket set, he had a second model which was more precise for his particular bike and which, as a result, increased his effectiveness.

There is always a gap between model and reality. The greater number of models one has to choose from, the more appropriately he can match a model with a style he is trying to identify. My personal experience has been that the NLP neurological indicators and the Swassing and Barbe behavioral indicators correlate extremely well, with two exceptions:

Exception 1: A student "X" could be identified as a "visual" on the NLP neurological eyechart and a "kinesthetic" on the Swassing and Barbe behavioral chart. To resolve this apparent incongruity, I sought out a third learning style model. This section on hemispherology expands on this concept and resolves the incongruity.

Exception 2: The auditory person who is right brain (random in thought) presents a mystery. (If you have a plausible explanation, please write.)

Several years ago, a woman with epileptic seizures had tried all the standard chemicals to assist her condition. Necessity being the mother of invention, the medical community did an historical first; they severed the connection between the right and left side of her brain. The phenomenon of having two brains in one body allowed for testing of the functions of each lobe for the first time. The medical team designed a head apparatus that went from the middle of her forehead down the slope of her nose in order to simultaneously show her right eye one item (such as a pen) and her left eye another (such as a cup). When asked to *say* what she saw, she consistently described what her right eye had seen. Knowing that the right side of the body is connected to the left side of the brain merely confirmed what had been speculated for some time: the left hemisphere is the location of articulation.

What was intriguing was that when they presented her with a number of objects and asked her to *pick up* the object seen, she picked up the cup (what the left eye saw). This led to the understanding that kinesthetic

skills (movement and touch) are located on the right side of the brain. Since then, the list of skills and attributes associated with the hemispheres has been greatly expanded.*

The following is one of many explanations available on the commercial market.

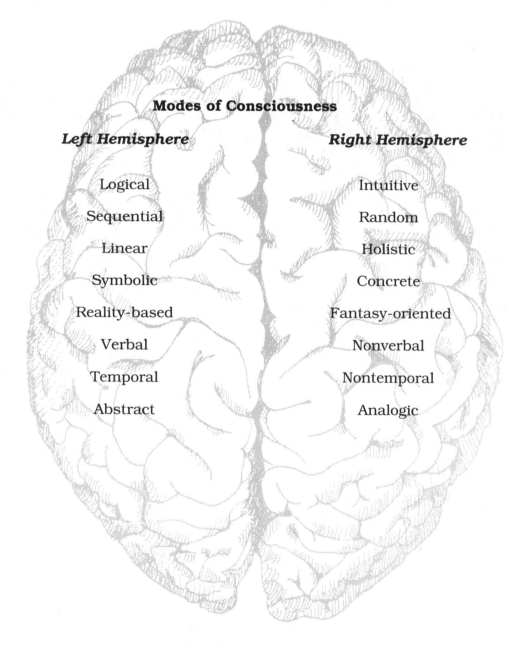

Modes of Consciousness

Left Hemisphere	*Right Hemisphere*
Logical	Intuitive
Sequential	Random
Linear	Holistic
Symbolic	Concrete
Reality-based	Fantasy-oriented
Verbal	Nonverbal
Temporal	Nontemporal
Abstract	Analogic

* Barbara Meister Vitale, *Unicorns Are Real* (Rolling Hills Estates, CA: Jalmar Press, 1982). Reprinted with permission.

Skills Associated With Hemispheric Specialization

Left Hemisphere	*Right Hemisphere*
Handwriting	Haptic awareness
Symbols	Spatial relationships
Language	Shapes and patterns
Reading	Mathematical computation
Phonetics	Color sensitivity
Locating details & facts	Singing and music
Talking and reciting	Art expression
Following directions	Creativity
Listening	Visualization
Auditory association	Feelings & emotions

---

* Barbara Meister Vitale, *Unicorns Are Real* (Rolling Hills Estates, CA: Jalmar Press, 1982). Reprinted with permission.

The correlation between the hemispherology model and NLP is shown in the following chart:

Left	Right
Auditory	Kinesthetic
Visual left	Visual right

While most hemispherology models place the visual on one side, this author vulnerably suggests an alternative: it is on both sides. The left brain visually "sees" symbols (letters, words, etc.) while the right "sees" specific concrete objects.

This resolves the previously mentioned conflict of student "X". The right brain visual student is in jeopardy of being a nonreader because his visual capacity is only of concrete, specific objects. The left brain, visual person sees letters and words (the abstraction of concrete reality). There is substantial research to indicate that mainstream education is a journey in which students are acculturated to prefer left brain skills. It is equally true that the majority of students in the corridor (Special Education, etc.) have right brain preference.

Anyone trained in detecting neurological indicators will be able to spot students with visual capacity. The question is whether we are identifying visual right or visual left preferences.

The visual left student is the one who fits in the 3.0 + grade point average category whereas the visual right is a 2.0 and below. Since the neurological eye indicators for the visual right and left are identical, one has to add behavioral indicators to know if you're looking at a visual right or a visual left student. If a student shows visual neurological eye indicators and kinesthetic behavioral indicators, his preference is right brain. If a student shows neurological visual eye indicators and visual behavioral indicators, you're looking at a visual left.

V. neurological eye Ind.
+ V. behavioral Ind.
= Left brain

V. neurological eye Ind.
+ K. behavioral Ind.
= Right brain

The following scenarios illustrate the difference between the two hemispheres.

Fifth Grade

Two students, Janet and Fred, have been identified by their teacher as pupils she needs to help RETEACH. As we enter the room, Fred immediately notices us and continues to watch us (distractibility is high right brain visual, kinesthetic). Janet has also noticed us but immediately returns to watching the teacher in the front of the room (doing what is expected/reality oriented is visual left). We have been there for five minutes and Fred has been constantly in motion; touching and tinkering with everything (self-entertainment is right brain).

Janet, on the other hand, has shown tremendous concentration following the teacher (visual left), but her forehead becomes furrowed when the teacher finishes the direction instruction segment of the lesson and, in a staccato voice, mentions the next three things to be done during independent work time. The visual left student needs clear, specific written directions. (See the section on "Exit Directions.")

The teacher is moving about the room monitoring/assisting. As she approaches Fred, she asks him if he knows what he's supposed to be doing. He says, "No." She reaches over and touches his shoulder as she repeats the instructions. The right brain responds to personal relationships much more than authority, and the contact at the shoulder greatly assists.

A section of their worksheet involves each student making up their own examples of the concept taught. Fred loves this section. (Visual rights love self-selecting assignments that involve creativity.) This is exactly the section for which Janet asks the teacher for assistance (the visual left, by comparison, is excellent at parroting back factual information and is somewhat uncomfortable with open ended, unstructured activity).

Reading

While it is certainly true that the latest research shows that reading involves both sides of the brain, the left to decode printed symbols called language and the right to find meaning from the decoding, visual right- and visual left-oriented students read very differently. The visual left appreciates and utilizes word attack skills. The phonetic/Distar approach is ideal for this student, because he learns from part to whole. The

Left Brain	Right Brain
Part, part	Whole

visual right, on the other hand, learns from whole to part.

The right brain method of reading uses context clues. The majority of commercial products on the market, and the method teachers are routinely trained to use, is the left brain approach. Therefore, it is not surprising that remedial readers prefer a right brain approach. The following is a third grade vignette:

The teacher is in the back of the room at the kidney-shaped reading table using a commercially prepared flip chart. The top of the page has three new vocabulary words followed by those words being used in sentences and underlined. For Miss Betty Bright, teaching the advanced reading group or the high average readers, the left brain approach is quite appropriate. She uses word attack on the first word with the students and has the students say the word again for reinforcement (part). After completing the same procedure for the other two words, she proceeds to the sentences which contain the new vocabulary words (whole).

The teacher in the next room, Mrs. Patty Par, is instructing the average reading group. She is using a mixture of right and left. As she does the word attack technique for the three vocabulary words at the top of the page, she is aware that the kinesthetic students pay little or no attention to this left brain portion of the lesson. When she

---

For further information on how to assist the different kinds of learners, see the section on "Reteaching," p. 33.

comes to the context sentences, she allows the more kinesthetic students to say, "Blank," when they come to the underlined new vocabulary words. Upon completion of the sentences (whole to part), the right brain student rereads the sentence and guesses which of the three new vocabulary words fits the context.

In the third adjacent classroom, Mr. Sam Snail is working with the remedial group. He skips the left brain word attack and has prepared three enlarged cards that have both a picture of the word and the word written in a raised form (Tulip Productions makes a "puffy pen" which will produce the raised and textured surface*). Sam is utilizing two insights with these cards:

1) The way teachers teach in first and second grade is the way the kinesthetic (remedial, slow) learners continue to learn. The picture is on the card (picture is right brain visual) along with the word (the word is left visual). It is in third grade that teachers tend to move away from pictures when teaching vocabulary.

2) The second insight is the use of exaggeration to reach the kinesthetic learner. One of the words is "harvest." Teacher Sam dons a red handkerchief around his neck as he places a straw hat on his head. Bellowing with a southern drawl, he has several students run to the window as he yells out, "Bring in the hay!" Another group runs to the back closet to bring in ears of corn. A third group retrieves canned jars from his desk. In controlled excitement,

they all gather around him as he looks at the ceiling and says, "This barn will protect our gathering." As he exchanges "high five's" with each student, he says it's been a good "harvest" and has the student repeat the word as the "give me five" is reciprocated.

In this example, one of the main differences between teaching whole (visual right) to part (visual left) is that the experience (whole/visual right) is provided before the label (visual left/vocabulary word = part). Vocabulary is best taught with multisensory involvement and with kinesthetic muscle memory.

Sam knows from past experience that the kinesthetic learners have to learn from their own sphere of experience. Each year he requests a higher portion of field trip money for his students than his colleagues do. He knows the students in Betty Bright's class can learn vicariously about life through reading, but his students have to experience reality before reading about it. Statistically, his pupils (and especially those in Special Education) are experientially deprived. Each year he seeks permission from the administration for money to rent movies which he shows the class *before* they read the corresponding book.

His colleague, Betty, often will not even show the students pictures when she's reading a library book aloud to them, because her students are capable of using a very active imagination. Sam has to provide the pictures so that reality is present. Sam also knows from experience that he only uses vocabulary verbs that are action oriented and abstract nouns. He

---

* Available through Tulip Productions, A Division of Polymerics, Inc., Waltham, MA 02254.

knows that his students find the verb "to be" very confusing because they can't see, taste, or touch it. Abstract nouns such as truth and beauty are avoided and homonyms such as "there/their." His mentor textbook is Sylvia Ashton Warner's *Teacher.**

Sam gives the three vocabulary cards to separate students and has each student act out their interpretation of the word's meaning. Mr. Snail wisely asks for variations of the interpretation from other students. He realizes this is important because the right brain is self-selecting and must have its own separate interpretation of the meaning.

ESL

English as a Second Language (ESL) students can be assessed as to their visual capacity on both the right and left side. For the visual left students, we can be extremely optimistic as to their quick acquisition of the language and a full participation as a member of the educational conveyor belt. The ESL classes in most schools are a corridor setting, and the success of these classes depends upon the flexibility of the teacher (see the section entitled "The Conveyor Belt and the Corridor," p. 9).

ERIC

One time, while coaching in an elementary school, I noted that the teachers were fascinated by the inservice I presented on "Hemispherology and Learning Styles." During my subsequent visit, I was directed to watch an enigmatic fifth grader, Eric. As I entered the class, I saw that his desk was pulled away from his peers and placed in the front of the room. He

showed capacity in all three modes, and I whispered to the accompanying principal, "How does Eric read?"

Previous visits to classrooms from second grade to college have taught me that if a person shows visual right behavior (preference) and is an above average reader (left brain capacity), you have the raw ingredients of a genius.

TAG

Expectations of such an individual's patterns and behavior can be much different from expectations put on an average pupil. For instance, a standard request made of students is to keep their eyes on the instructor during lecture. Since a good percentage of Talented And Gifted (TAG) students are multisensory, it is an insult for them to have to use their visual skills in order to hear (auditory). It is often better to occupy/distract one of their senses in order to get them to attend to their teacher with another sense. This is commonly done when a teacher asks a TAG student, during review for a test, to record papers in a grade book or some similar activity. This forces the student to attend to both recording and listening at the same time. What overloads the mind of the average student is often an appropriate challenge for the TAG student's brain.

This technique, of course, is anathema to most teachers and the standard left brain B+ and above student, but it was exactly what Eric was doing - distracting himself. He mumbled to himself while trying to use the clip part of his pen as the spring for a rocket launcher of spitwads. His eyes were never on the teacher, and he

---

* Sylvia Ashton Warner, *Teacher* (New York: Simon and Schuster, 1963).

was not doing his worksheet. When called upon, he sometimes knew the answer (to the astonishment of the teacher) and at other times, didn't even know he had been called upon. The principal informed me that his reading was above average. The suggested diagnosis was that he had a well developed left brain capacity and right brain preference.

In the debriefing later that day, it was revealed that Eric tested below his peers *during* all units and exceeded them at the end of the unit. This pattern held true for the quarterly grade level test compared with the *end* of the year grade level test. Eric was so smart that he retained all the individual parts the teacher presented (left brain approach) but didn't consciously pay attention to them because they lacked meaning until the end of the unit/year when the *whole* (right brain) came together and had meaning. At that point, he recalled all the *parts* that were taught along the way and fit them into the overall picture. That is a genius.

Math

Like reading, math is one of the better content areas to clearly show the difference between presenting material for the right and left brain and how students learn on their right or left sides. When a class is given a choice of possible answers, the right brain student, who is prone to guessing and jumping to conclusion, has a gambler's chance. Relying on intuition, he often picks the correct answer. Since most math teachers have been schooled to left brain teaching, they tend to ask for proof/justification of answers. Proof can only be done by the left brain, and examples of this abound on all educational levels. The second grade student checks his subtraction by adding the two lesser numbers to arrive at the larger number. A fifth grade student might check her long division by multiplying the divisor by the quotient to check to see if she comes up with the dividend. High school students may check a quotation answer by substituting the variable value back into the original statement to see if both sides of the equal sign balance.

What's amazing is that the "better" left brain students actually want to check their work, where the right brain students find checking a nuisance and often have to be forced to do it.

Another strong example from mathematics is the difference between algebra and geometry. Because of the spatial nature of geometry, some of the "weaker" students (right brain visual) will often actually shine when compared to their left brain peers. The former process, algebra, requires the logical, sequential thinking which is the forte of the left brain.

Story problems are a special bugaboo for math teachers because they require both right and left side abilities to interact.

IQ Tests

It may be of special note to mention here that a portion of IQ tests show a strong right brain visual capacity section, in which the test taker is given a configuration in the left margin and presented three choices to the right, only one of which matches the one on the left (see "Example of IQ Test", p. 25). The non-verbal nature of the test allows a diagnosis of mental capacity that we call IQ. This is mentioned because, in the author's opinion, the typical school setting is so left brain visual oriented that the correlation between IQ capacity shown on right brain visually oriented IQ tests and performance in school can be very slight. This discrepancy explains why some students have high IQ's and yet are perceived as underachieving, and why they are sometimes virtually nonreaders, much to the confusion of their teachers.

A speaker once said that teachers are worried about the kids who don't do well in the learning environment. The speaker's response to that concern was, "Schools have done such a poor job of patterning school after reality that those kids who are at risk do better, in fact, in reality than they do in school. Our biggest problem of right brain genius is trying to get those students out of the educational system with their self-esteem still intact."

VIETOR'S FUNNY BUSINESS

"Revenge is sweet. I got D's in history, C's in algebra, F's in philosophy, but I just sold the company for $39 million."

Copyright 1988, USA TODAY. Reprinted with permission.

Identifying Visual Right From Visual Left

The following is a worksheet to practice identifying the visual right from the visual left students. You will be using the neurological and behavioral indicator charts listed on pages 19-21. Go into a classroom where you don't know the students. With the teacher's permission, place yourself in such a way that you are to the side and toward the front of the room so you can see the students' eyes. Act in such a way that the students behave in as normal a manner as possible.

1. List here the grade level and, if above sixth grade, the content being taught.

_____

2. Identify a visual left. Find the student whose neurological eye signs (pupils high in eye socket) and behavioral indicators are visual, and list the observable neurological and behavioral indicators noticed in a five minute span.

_____

_____

_____

3. Identify the visual right. Find the student who has very similar neurological eye indicators to the visual left and yet whose behavior is that of a kinesthetic. List the observable behavioral indicators seen in a five minute span.

_____

_____

_____

4. How has this activity assisted in understanding some of your past and current students?

_____

_____

_____

Internal vs. External Focus

The descriptions of the behaviors associated with visual, auditory and kinesthetic right brain/left brain are lengthy. Sometimes what we need is a simpler way of identifying these different learning styles. One simple way of understanding the auditory person is to remember that that "there are no rhetorical questions." Auditory people respond to everything.

A trademark of the kinesthetic learner is that he is committed to entertainment. This commitment is to entertain or be entertained, whether it is positive or negative, and if the teacher doesn't provide it, the student will.

What is the main difference then, between the visual left brain and the visual right brain? The visual left is able to see letters, words, sentences and passages. The visual right sees concrete objects in their minds. To a great extent, the visual left brain has internal focus capacity and the visual right has external focus tendencies. The latter stimulation comes from their environment and from outside themselves; hence the high degree of distractibility associated with the right brain kids. That is why the kinesthetics who are right brain are considered the "kids at risk." In watching a student in a classroom, when his body goes still, he is indicating a capacity for internal concentration and focus. The longer the length of the stare or the fixed position and the higher the frequency, the greater the capacity. Use the worksheet below to practice analyzing this ability.

1. List three students' initials whose visual capacity you would like to identify. Make sure one of them is a student you know to have a difficult time with school, especially in the area of reading, another student you know who has an easy time with reading, and the last being a student in between.

Student A _____ Student B _____ Student C _____

2. Watch each student for a five to ten minute period and, using the second hand of your watch or common sense, notice how long he is able to keep his body still during this time. The suggestion is that there is a tremendous correlation between the stillness of the student who has the easy time and the constant movement and lack of stillness on the student who has a difficult time.

3. On a separate piece of paper, list your reactions and insights from the above task. Pay particular attention to the idea that there is a tremendous correlation between internal focus and the ability to read.

4. With permission, enter a classroom in which you do not know the students (choose a grade level that is not the same but is within two grade levels of the students you teach). Pick out two or three students who immediately make you curious about their internal visual capacity. Watch them for a three minute period, using your stopwatch, and count the length of time that they're able to hold their eyes fixed on something which is internal. Internal includes both reading a book (which is making pictures in their mind) and daydreaming in a stare. List your findings and some conclusions you may draw on a separate page. Then check with the teacher for verification of their reading levels.

Hemispherology Summary Chart

Left Brain Student	Right Brain Student
Sees symbols (letters, words)	Sees concrete objects and is in jeopardy of being a nonreader
3.0+ grade point average	-2.0 grade point average
Uses visual NLP eye indicators & visual behavioral indicators	Uses visual NLP eye indicators & kinesthetic behavioral indicators
Needs clear, specific, written directions	Distractibility and self-entertainment are high
Parrots back factual information	Responds to personal rather than authoritarian relationship
Uncomfortable with openended, unstructured freelancing	Loves self selected assignments that involve creativity
Wants to check work	Guesses and uses intuition; checkwork is a nuisance
Wants information in written form	Wants information in a demonstration, graph, or chart
Focuses internally	Focuses externally

* See "SPECIALTY," p. 62

Hemispherology Summary Chart, con't.
Reading

Left Brain Student

Uses word attack skills
(Phonetic, Distar)

Analyzes from part to whole

Experiences life by reading
about it

Reads book, then views movie

Right Brain Student

Analyzes from whole to part

Experiences reality before
reading about it

Likes to view movie
before reading book

Needs to have pictures
provided so reality is present

Chapter 4

Communicating With Respect

"Until you let me be an 'I' the way you are,
you can never come inside my silence
and know me."

Children of A Lesser God (movie)

As humans, we comprehend well when given information in a compare-contrast format. That is why while the former chapters are an excellent map of learning styles, they are susceptible to being used in an inflexible manner. The previous presentations on **V**isual, **A**uditory, **K**inesthetic and **L**eft/**R**ight brain, and all that follow, are like tools on a workbench. Their functional usefulness is dependent on the craftsman.

This chapter is a plea to go beyond the tendency toward pigeonholing and statistical averages. The 1970s are a case in point. During this period, we saw an increase in awareness of nonverbals as evidenced by the many books on "body language." There are still major corporations which test nonverbal sensitivity by using a commercial product which shows quick video footage of a face. The viewer is then given three descriptions and asked to select the one that best describes the face. The same detection is done with voices.

As we move towards the new century, "high tech" has to be balanced by "high touch."* People want to be more than a "statistical average"; they want to be measured individually. Teachers who preface comments with "I always" or "I never" are part of the statistical average. The more sophisticated and successful teacher finds each person/group unique in itself.

One of the hallmarks of NLP is to personalize our sensitivity to each student. Therefore, this chapter opens with five cautions on how to be respectful when using indicators and devotes the second half of the chapter to "Kids at Risk."

---

* John Naisbitt, *Megatrends* (New York: Warner Books, 1984).

Using Indicators

1. Calibration

When interpreting behavior exhibited by another, calibration is an essential process. The better you can identify a person's normal, base behavior, the easier it is to detect an increase or decrease from that base.

The first form of calibration is "cultural calibration." Behavior stemming from cultural upbringing isn't necessarily indicative of a person's modality preferences or tendencies. For example, a person who is kinesthetic talks slower than the person who is visual, according to statistics; however, if a kinesthetic cab driver from New York is compared with a visual Ph.D professor from Texas, the driver skews the chart unless culture is considered. Likewise, someone raised in a traditional Italian culture who is visual will actually stand closer to other people than a kinesthetic who has been raised in a German culture. Culture precedes the individual.

A second rule of thumb of cultural cultivation is that cultural traits tend to be part of base behavior and have a propensity to be consistently present.

2. Information

Information can be placed on a continuum with "readily available" at one end and "not readily available" at the other. In order to use the neurological indicators as a basis for detecting one's modalities, the following information needs to be included.

Information Readily Available

Information that is readily available does not force the person to search for the information and therefore, the neurological indicators are absent. Since most people think in terms of content, if we ask "what questions," very little searching is done because of the familiarity. Hence, the eyes remain the same, as in the picture below.

Information Not Readily Available

Information that has to be sought allows the observer to watch the process of searching. The neurological indicators are seen during the search (see "Strategy Elicitation", p. 58). By asking someone about the process (a most unfamiliar emphasis) he used to arrive at the content, we increase the likelihood of the person's searching for information. "How questions" activate this process. The illustrations below indicate the change.

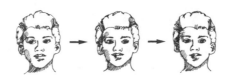

Separating Cultural From Individual Indicators

People exhibit behaviors that are a combination of both cultural habits and individual preferences. Without separating the two elements, we misread a person's modality tendencies. For example, a person may talk fast because he comes from the East Coast or another talks slowly because he comes from the South. In these instances, speed of voice is a cultural indicator and not an identifier of individual modality tendencies. For the purpose of this worksheet, culture is being used in the loose sense to mean any behavioral traits that one exhibits because he is or formerly was a member of a group that collectively acts that way. In this sense, a family can be a cultural unit.

1. Identify two people who come from the same cultural group.

\# 1 _____   \# 2 _____

2. Describe the common behavior they share from their culture:

_____

_____

_____

3. Respectfully watch the two people and notice how each of them exhibits the same behavior mentioned in #2 in a slightly different way from the other. For example, if they are culturally Italian and commonly stand close to others, the one who stands closer is more kinesthetic than the other. This worksheet will help to prevent you from pigeonholing people as being certain modalities. It will encourage you to look at people on a more comparative basis with other people. The phrase, "more kinesthetic than" is much more useful and respectful than "is kinesthetic." (This is especially true in personal relationships such as couples.) In the space below, describe the people in #1 above as "more" or "less," using your observations from #2.

_____

_____

_____

_____

_____

_____

_____

_____

3. Special Notes on the Auditory

The Swassing and Barbe research indicates that only 22% of elementary students prefer to have information initially received via the auditory channel. Among the adult, "educated" population, those who show the auditory as a preferred modality are less than 15%. One can only surmise that although the "lecture teaching approach" increases from the secondary level on, it doesn't seem to increase the percentage of people who select the auditory as their primary channel.

Several interesting side notes are corollaries of this statistic.

A. While the main modality ingredient needed in order for a classroom teacher to get his administrative credential is the visual (because of the necessity of reading the textbooks), the main channel used as an administrator is the auditory.

It is estimated that managers spend 65% or more of their time listening and talking, and yet they got to their positions through the visual channel. The switch from visual to auditory is one of the major factors which determine whether one has the compatible make-up to be a successful administrator. Another major ingredient is the ability to be disassociated (see p. 129).

B. The student population of the inner city is primarily auditory and kinesthetic. The expression along with the accompanying hand slap, "give me five!" symbolizes the auditory and kinesthetic culture. It is no small wonder that the transition from being a visually oriented college student to a teacher in an inner city is a major cultural shock.

C. In the visual educational world, the auditory person is an emotional minority. At social gatherings, it is common for people to open their wallets and show pictures of their family. Since the visual is not my preferred modality, I may be more acutely aware than others of visually oriented people. When my friend at a cocktail party flips open his wallet and shows his grandchildren and the family dog, I have the urge to jovially pull out a tape recorder and say, "Would you like to listen to my daughter?" or "Here's our dog, Drummer, barking at the UPS delivery truck."

D. The "a" in adolescent stands for auditory. As a cultural group, they are in an auditory development phase. They are very sound oriented, as evidenced by their Sony Walkman tape players and "ghetto blasters." It is important to note that often the junior high/middle school population is married to their output, auditory channel and at the same time, their input channel is terribly weak. In other words, they can't remember what they heard the teacher say but want to talk about it anyway. It is because of this auditory propensity that the age old axiom, "whenever possible, discipline the adolescent away from his peers," holds true.

One of the truest tests of a person's auditory orientation is whether they fit the proverb, "There are no rhetorical questions." Statements such as, "Jamie, don't you have anything to do?" or "Hank, do I have to tell you again?" or "Jennifer, would you pass out the books?" are statements which can be interpreted as questions. Questions elicit the auditory channel in the listener.

This is especially true for the adolescent.

I once visited a ninth grade classroom in which the teacher was teaching scientific notation and circulating about the room helping individuals. Everyone was on task except one kinesthetic student who had appropriately been given a separate activity. The light bulbs had just come on, and they were in the "aha!" stage of insight. The teacher said in passing, "Isn't this fun!" Half the class said in unison, "No!" while continuing to do their work. I swear they never consciously knew they said it.

Junior high/middle school teachers could increase the longevity of their energy and their careers by more fully understanding the auditory nature of the adolescent. The easiest addition to your repertoire of effective classroom management is to switch to nonverbal cues as soon as you have the students' attention. The instructor who says "Fred!" to get Fred to look at him and then uses nonverbal gestures to indicate appropriate behavior will avoid the common blunder of a power struggle and confrontation.

Once, at a training session in Anchorage, I offered what the kinesthetic's equivalent of the auditory's tape recorder might be by saying, "Would you like to feel some locks of my son's hair when he was born?" or "Here's some fur from our favorite cat." The participants laughed differently than other audiences had. Sensing that I was missing something, they explained that it is common in Alaskan culture for family pets to be brought to community social gatherings. Their culture is so kinesthetic that instead of bringing pictures of their pets, they bring the pets.

Most teaching staffs of twenty or more include one person who is auditory. This is the faculty member with whom people are afraid to get caught. Remember, there are no rhetorical questions for this individual. Being polite and asking an auditory person how his weekend was could cost you ten minutes at the teachers' boxes, and if it happened to be a three day weekend, he may talk for fifteen minutes!

4. The Adolescent as an Auditory

You have to be flexible with teenagers if you want to utilize their structure. Working with them is like flying on a plane to Hawaii; 95% of the time the pilot is off course, but he still gets you there.*

One very successful junior high school teacher explained that he does well because he perceives himself as an emotional Monty Hall from the television show, *Let's Make A Deal.* "Come on down! Let's make a deal!" is his line. In his role as "Monty," he has taught adolescents long enough to know what they need and when they need it. During the days when it's likely they will want to "talk about it" and whine, "Why do we have to do this?", he covers the homework on the board with a pull down chart/map. When the "why?" question occurs, the homework is revealed and Monty steps to the side and shows that he is more than willing to listen and chat. The class knows that the home

---

* Used with permission from Phil and Norma Baretta, Southern California Center for NLP, 929 Barhugh, San Pedro, CA 90731. Contact them for a list of their fine NLP seminars.

work is assigned, and they must decide collectively whether to let him give further instruction about the homework or take up class time with adolescent griping.

Monty has an intuitive sense about when the class needs to have a releasing and relieving session. In such cases, the homework is not revealed and therefore not used as a nonverbal signal of "You better let me finish my lecture." He has a separate place for this type of facilitative listening (see section on "Decontaminating the Classroom," p. 182). Monty also uses presuppositions very well. He only gives the students a range of choices, each being acceptable to him. For example, at the start of a period when the students are restless and in an inappropriate mental state to do well on that morning's test, he would ask the class, "Do you want to start the test now or have 10 good minutes to review before we begin?" This is a much different approach than simply announcing, "You have 10 minutes before the test starts. You better review."

The teacher who maintains a completely democratic format that can be activated on the whims of the class is not teaching "reality."

Monty also realizes that "assertive discipline" is a wonderful program for 80 - 97% of the students. It is neat, systematic and sequential; in short, it has all of the ingredients that the visual left brain world loves. Typically, however, it is not the left brain students who need discipline systems.

A remark by Carol Cummings changed Monty's way of perceiving what discipline is. She defines

"consequences" as something the student wants and may not get unless he acts in a certain way, or something the students don't want and will get if they act in a certain way.* 5 - 15% of the student population will not consider the various levels of assertive discipline to be of "consequence" to themselves. They're not motivated by rewards if they do fine or threatened by punishment if they don't. Monty realizes that this population is lacking successful relationships with adults. Because of Monty's success, the counselors place a higher percentage of the 5 - 15% population in his classes. Mr. Hall knows that he has to make person-to-person contact with these students.

5. Strategy Elicitation

The following is a formal process known as "strategy elicitation." There are two occasions where this process can be used in a profitable manner. One is when you are trying to figure out HOW successful students process as compared to unsuccessful students. This gives the teacher a successful strategy which he can consider teaching to others.

The second category is when you are working with colleagues, parents, and superiors and you need to know in what sequence to present information.

A. Establish rapport by respectfully mirroring. Some rules of thumb for respectfully mirroring are:

1) You can mirror up to 100% of the other person's voice, tone, pitch, speed and volume as long as you both have the same cultural background.

---

* Dr. Carol Cummings, *Teaching Makes A Difference* (Edmonds, WA: Teaching Inc., 1980).

2) Mirror up to 75% of the person's facial expressions.

3) Mirror up to 50% of the person's body slant and body posturing.

4) When it is your turn to talk, mirror up to 100% of the other person's gestures.

The purpose of establishing rapport is that the more rapport you have, the more resourceful the other person can become. The more resourceful they are, the greater access to all modes and the greater the animation of the indicators. You will then have an easier time detecting the indicators (see "Verbal and Nonverbal Rapport," p. 65), and they can use more parts of their brain.

B. Start with an introductory sentence which, in a generalized way, mentions the purpose of the interaction (such as, "Mr. Principal, thank you for arranging to see me during prep time to discuss an idea of how to . . ." or "Mrs. Parent, thank you for coming in to discuss your child's progress . . ." or "As members of this department, it is that time of year when we need to meet and discuss . . ."). A person's strategy (sequence of modes) is based on the context. The sequence of thought used to decide which flavor of ice cream to order might be very different from the sequence used in purchasing a car! The purpose of this step is to have them access memories of previous examples of the same topic/context.

C. Next, you want to find the best representation of how to go about presenting the information. Ask the person to recall a setting similar to the present one that they found to be successful. If they do not have a previous suc-cessful representation, your back-up question is to ask them to imagine a successful one. Once the person has a "best representation," ask him to share with you what made it successful.

D. When someone is accessing information that is not readily available, the pause before he speaks will contain one or more neurological indicators. The order in which the indicators appear indicates the actual sequence in which the person wants to review the information. For example, if the principal looks up and then makes a sound with his mouth (like "tch"), the sequence is visual/auditory. Likewise, a parent who moves while silently thinking and then freezes his body just before speaking is indicating a kinesthetic/ visual sequence. The pauses before a person speaks during a five minute conversation may equal a total of five seconds.

E. Verification Statement: Having made your guess at the person's sequence, make a statement which uses predicates from the same modality indicators. Use them in the same sequential order presented. With a principal, use the words, "If I understand correctly, the best way for us to deal with the idea is to give you a picture (V) and then discuss (A) it." With a parent, use the wording, "Let me give (K) you a picture." (V)

The purpose of making the verification statement is to see if your identification of the process shown during the pause is accurate. Accuracy is determined by the congruency of the person's response during and immediately following your verification statement. For example, an increase in head nodding and relaxation of breathing would indicate congruent agreement. Holding the breath or furrowing the forehead would indicate a lack of accuracy.

There is a major difference between the visual right and the visual left in terms of the form in which he prefers to receive information. The visual left wants to see it in written form with linear, sequential descriptions of the whole picture. The visual right desires a demonstration or example of the overall idea. The visual right will tend to prefer graphs and charts more than the visual left.

When the pause indicates a visual mode, it is best to offer a menu of two statements when making the verification statement; one with a visual left and one with a visual right. In the above example of the principal, the menu could appear in the following form, "I am thinking there are at least two ways to deal with the idea; one is for me to leave you a written proposal (visual left) and then we can discuss it (auditory), or secondly, I know someone else who is already implementing the idea. You can visit their classroom and see for yourself (kinesthetic and visual) and then we could discuss it (auditory)." The offering of choices allows you to calibrate which visual form is more to their liking. It is interesting to note in passing that, culturally, administrators are supposed to prefer the visual left written format. This ambiguity is illustrated by a right brain administrator, who, when the menu is given, will nonverbally indicate her personal preference to see a demonstration of the concept, and yet will verbally state she would prefer to have it in written format. The obvious maneuver is to do both. For example, the teacher could state, "Of course, you will be receiving this proposal in written form. Would you rather have it before or after you see a demonstration of the idea?"

If you get a congruent response, present it in the same sequence of your verification statement. If you don't get a congruent response, offer alternative verification statements until congruency is obtained.

Kids at Risk

```
I        I
N        N
O        O
```

Any examination of our educational woes has to include the "kids at risk." The report *A Nation at Risk,* which popularized the idea of kids who are "at risk", recommends **more**:

* More homework and better books
* Longer days and school year
* Rigorous standards and tests
* Emphasis: English, Math, Science, Social Studies and Computer Sciences.

However, John Goodlad's most thorough study of education finds that we spend almost 80% of instructional time on basic skills.* Clearly, the answer is not **more** work but **effective** and **different** work. "During the past fifteen years, teachers have been exhorted to take account of and provide for student individuality in learning rates and styles; however, this is not something often or readily done."*

The dropout rate of 26+% will only increase unless the system encourages, trains and supports greater sensitivity toward this population. "At risk" is an umbrella label that houses two kinds of groups; those who qualify because of *psychological* reasons and those who have *learning styles* which are incompatible with the predominantly visual, left brain mode of schooling.

Like Thomas Armstrong's *In Their Own Way* ,** this section believes that much of the ailments of all kids at risk can be greatly helped through preventive changes. The following sections of this book are highly recommended for rereading:

1. "Teaching Right Brain." The "at risk" students' days are mostly right brain days.

2. Nonverbal Communication: Decontaminating (p. 182) **C**oncepts Which are **I**mportant and **D**ifficult (p. 184)

3. RETEACHING: especially working one-on-one with the kinesthetic (p. 33).

4. The Importance of Visualization: this is what they lack and need the most (Chap. 6).

The kids who are at risk, because of their learning style incompatibility, are from beginning to end kino. Sometimes they are culturally kinesthetic (i.e., "inner city" kids are kinesthetic with external auditory), and sometimes they are individually.

---

* John Goodlad, *A Place Called School* (New York: McGraw-Hill, 1984), p. 105. Reprinted with permission. For an illuminating discussion see Thomas Armstrong's *In Their Own Way.*
** Thomas Armstrong, *In Their Own Way* (Los Angeles: J.P. Tarcher, Inc., 1987).

The right brain individual is a SPECIALTY item on the educational conveyor belt. What are the specific traits of the right brain student? And more importantly, what are the teacher traits needed to respect and build rapport with the right brain student?

SPECIALTY	
Student Traits	**Teacher's Necessary Traits**
Slow processing	Talk slow. "One thought driven home is better than three left on base." (see RETEACHING, p. 33)
Person to person; very self selecting	Rapport, rapport, rapport
Entertainment; committed to random behavior. Often short attention span	Watch how easily distracted they are. Help control external stimuli and assist in their planning
Concrete objects needed for their muscle memory	They need immediate reinforcement Provide tactile manipulatives
Intuitive, fantasy oriented	Teach holistically and seek outlets for their creativity
Associative mind	Connect things with their experiences and emotions (see A.C.I.D., p. 189)
Lousy left brain visualization ability	They absolutely need Visualization (Chap. 6)
Touch	Touch
Y "Why?"	Realize that the students make "left brain" statements, but are only satisfied when the teacher uses rapport and associates answers with the students' experiences

In real estate, they say there are three rules: location, location, location. The equivalent in communication is rapport, rapport, rapport. Rapport can be effectively defined as one person entering another's world. Left brain students can enter the teacher's world.

You can act as a calm ⟵————————— Left Brain
competent professional   Student

High school teachers are the most left brain of all levels of the conveyor belt and expect the students to join their world. This perception of reality, something like "blinders on a horse," is not limited to our profession. It seems the longer the person was on the conveyor belt, the more they believe the plaque (diploma) allows them to be inflexible. Think of lawyers and doctors. For a complete discussion of "plaque mentality," see Marilyn Ferguson's *Aquarian Conspiracy.** With right brain students, often we have to enter their world (this is known as the pace or "pacing").

Teacher ————————— (enter) ⟶ Right Brain
                                                  Student

Then the teacher can use the established contact to "lead" the student back into the highly structured, predictable, sequential and logical left brain atmosphere of school.

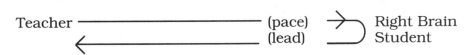

Teacher ————————————— (pace) ⟶ Right Brain
          ⟵————————————— (lead)   Student

How often do you have to "pace and lead" a right brain student? The answer lies in understanding that left brain people take their values from society; therefore, you can motivate them with facts, statistics and your own credibility. Right brain people are motivated by their own unique inner world. Through rapport, they share "what makes them tick," and then you can *package* motivation in terms which make sense to them. Compared to left brain individuals, right brain persons are more different from each other than they are the same. Therefore, how often you pace and lead must vary. You can lecture to a room full of left brain people, but often you have to work one-on-one with right brain persons.

The rest of this chaper is devoted to increasing your understanding of right brain students and your flexibility in regard to respect through rapport and sensitivity.

---

* Marilyn Ferguson, *Aquarian Conspiracy* (Los Angeles, CA.: J.P. Tarcher, 1980).

WORKSHEET

Verbal Rapport with "Hard to Reach" Students

1. Initials of a student who fits the 5 - 15% "hard to reach" population (usually right brain and more or less not affected by standard discipline systems): _____

2. Briefly describe the behaviors that qualify this student for this category.

_____

_____

_____

3. When acting in a capacity other than that of the authoritarian position of teacher (during transition time, at school events, passing in the halls), find the student's two or three highest positive topics of interest. List them here:

A. _____

B. _____

C. _____

4. When presenting in a TEACHING or a RETEACHING situation, spice the conversation with items from the student's high interest areas to hold his attention. List two examples of how you did this.

A. _____

_____

B. _____

_____

5. Describe the increase in the student's attentiveness.

_____

_____

_____

Note: The timing of when to do this exercise is described in the section on "Positive Reinforcement," p. 67.

Verbal and Nonverbal Rapport

The previous worksheet showed how you can verbally utilize the right brain students' high interest areas and thereby increase your rapport through verbal pacing. Since the nonverbal level is more powerful than verbal, this worksheet illustrates both verbal and nonverbal pacing.

Pacing is respectful when the student is unaware that you are mirroring the student's physiology. Mockery is when the individual is aware and disapproving. The guidelines for being respectful are (Strategy Elicitation, p. 58):

1. Mirror the voice up to 100%

2. Mirror the facial expressions up to 75%

3. Mirror the body movements up to 50%

4. Mirror the gestures (when you speak) up to 75-100%.

When you have been pacing and you want to see if you have enough rapport, test the rapport by leading. Switch from following the verbals and nonverbals of the pupil and do your own to see if the student will follow your lead. Remember each student is unique and your ability to notice how much mirroring is respectful is essential.

Pick a hard-to-reach student and do the following:

1. Find something of high interest to him. List it here.

_____

2. Use the "how" questions to identify his mode or sequence when talking about the area of high interest. For example, if the person responds with: "When I see the outside of the arcade, my heart races," the sequence is: V = (see) and K = (races). (For assistance, refer to "Strategy Elicitation," especially D and E, page 59.)

_____

_____

_____

Verbal and Nonverbal Rapport, con't.

3. Instead of continuing to interview, chitchat and share by using the same mode or sequence the student used. List two or three sentences you used (you match by using the predicates listed under "Neurological Indicators").

_____

_____

_____

_____

4. Make sure you're gradually and *respectfully* mirroring the other person's body. Describe what aspects of their nonverbals you initially mirrored and how you increased the mirroring.

_____

_____

_____

5. Describe the increase in animation and rapport you developed with the other person.

_____

_____

_____

_____

_____

_____

_____

_____

Positive Reinforcement

A survey of educators indicates that when teachers are more "people oriented" than "idea oriented," their energy level is higher and their self image greater when they give students "positive strokes." Conversely, their energy level and self image decrease when they discipline. It is obvious that methods which increase the teacher's use of "positive reinforcement" and decrease "negative reinforcement" are most welcome.

Often the difference between a stroke and a reprimand is the *length of time* between strokes. *Example:* the teacher is at the transparency projector calling students up to demonstrate ability on the overhead screen. The teacher has judiciously placed Sam (a highly kinesthetic student) in the front row to keep him *on task*. The teacher does a variety of techniques to interrupt his inappropriate behavior and put him back on task. The teacher is using a disciplinary response. For about 30-40 seconds Sam stays on task. The teacher is intervening every 60-90 seconds. If the teacher gives positive strokes every 25 seconds, the length of time the student will stay on task often increases and the teacher feels better using positive actions.

Here is another way of looking at switching from "negative interaction" (disciplining) to "positive interaction" (stroking). Each time the teacher does disciplinary intervention, she follows with visual, auditory or kinesthetic praise within 20-25 seconds. This assures the teacher that the student knows what behavior the teacher wants and that the student can get attention in a positive way.*

This concept is especially true for right brain students because of their SPECIALTY traits of:

1. Person to person interaction
2. Short attention span
3. Distractibility
4. Need for immediate reinforcement

The following exercises will help you practice this concept.

1. Describe a student's repeated inappropriate behavior.
2a. Do your normal process of disciplinary intervention.
2b. How often are you doing it?
2c. How long does the student stay on task?
3. Do #2b and then praise the student for appropriate behavior while student is still on task.
4. Briefly describe the results. Does the length of time "on task" increase?

* See Carol Cummings' *Teaching Makes a Difference* (1983) and *Managing to Teach* (Edmonds, WA: Teaching Inc., 1980).

Social Manners

The educated live in a visual world; that's what college is. Whether we, as teachers, are visual individually or not, collectively, we're members of a visual culture. Think of it this way - how many of us have pictures of people which we carry around in our wallets or show in professional settings (such as your desktop)? Compare that with the number of people who carry around auditory tapes of the voices of the people they love, and compare that even further with carrying around tufts of hair or clothing or emotional touchstones from these people. Sound ridiculous? It just shows that we live in a visual world.

The students who have a difficult time in school are usually not visual. These nonvisuals need special help. The most vivid example is Special Education and those who are in remedial classes. With these "blind" students, we often expect them to act with certain social politeness without understanding that without a visual representation of a social manner, they are confused. The two examples that follow illustrate this point well.

Example 1

Two adults are talking or a teacher is talking with a student and another student walks between the two people. The teacher pulls the student back and tells the student to walk around. If the student is a Special Education

student, he often will comply without understanding why he should do so, especially if the amount of room behind each of the people is less than the amount of space between the two people. Educated people visually superimpose a visual and oral corridor between two people's bodies and assume that to walk between them would be to interrupt. We presume that other people, such as students, also understand this. Because of their "blindness," they do not see this invisible corridor. We have to teach them through visual representations. The following technique would work: the teacher speaks into a can that has a string attached to another can that the listener is holding to his ear. To the Special Ed/remedial student, this visual representation helps the student "see" why social manners are so important.

Example 2

Another example is the student who gets too close to our physical body and "invades our space." For teachers who are highly visual, this infringement on their personal space can shake up the pictures in their mind and fog their internal screen. A visual representation to assist would be to place a Hula Hoop$_{(R)}$ around the teacher, held out from the body with suspenders attached to the hoop. When the student approaches the teacher and gets to the outer perimeter of the Hula Hoop$_{(R)}$, he has a visual representation that he must not go any further.

Teaching Social Manners Through Visual Representation

1. Think of one or two students who are oblivious to social manners and list their initials here.

_____

2. List one or two social manners they do not recognize.

_____

_____

3. Construct and explain a visual representation of the social manner (because they are "blind", be blatant).

_____

_____

_____

_____

4. Try this representation for a week.

5. List your results here.

_____

_____

_____

_____

_____

_____

_____

WORKSHEET

Using Gestures to Symbolize Concepts

We learn from research that 82% of all teacher's messages are nonverbal. We also know that the younger the child or the more kinesthetic he is, the more he learns from muscle memory. Combining these two facts allows us to consider associating both the teacher's gestures and the students' duplication of those gestures with a concept. For example: a teacher is teaching a class how to count by two's, and as she throws her hand across her body in a downward motion, she says "one" very quietly and then, using the same hand, swings it in a downward motion to the same side and says, much louder, "two." If she continues to do the odd numbers in a whisper on the left and the even numbers louder on the right, she is teaching the students how to count by two's by using gestures to symbolize. Likewise, when she teaches three's, she makes a triangle in the air in front of the student and, speaking loudly just when they come to every third point (3, 6, 9), she allows the students to understand the concept symbolically with muscle memory. With four's, she makes a box and says every fourth number quite loud.

1. Make a list of the concepts in a lesson you will be teaching. Next to each of the items list a nonverbal gesture that could symbolize it.

_____

_____

_____

_____

_____

_____

3. From the fifth grade on, you may have to end up doing the muscle memory for the students by demonstrating. Below the fifth grade, actually have them do it with you.

4. List your results.

_____

_____

_____

_____

Note: see "Auditory Storage with Kinesthetic Movement," p. 88.

Kinesthetic Predicates Used Last

When students hear a teacher use a kinesthetic predicate (as opposed to a visual or auditory predicate), their bodies are activated. When the body is activated, hearing decreases as the body increases in movement. When a teacher says, "Take out your book and turn to page three." Hearing the words, "take out . . ." will activate the students to start to pull their books out of their desks. They won't be able to hear the page number and the teacher ends up repeating it. There are a couple of ways of getting around this.

1. Whenever possible, say the kinesthetic predicate last. "On page forty-three, you will find your assignment in the book you're now taking out."

2. If you have to say a kinesthetic predicate early, then use a nonverbal such as your hand forward in a "traffic cop" stop position as you say, "In just a minute you're going to be taking out your book and looking at page forty-three."

This week use this new technique three times and describe results.

1st time; describe what you did:

_____

Results:

_____

_____

_____

2nd time; describe what you did:

_____

Results:

_____

_____

_____

3rd time; describe what you did:

_____

Results:

_____

_____

_____

Single Modality Messages

An expert in communication was once asked what the main difference is between teachers who communicate well and those who are less proficient. Being an expert, he, of course, rephrased the question and answered, "One belief gets in our way; we think our words have the same meaning for others as they have for us." His suggestion was that we visit other countries and learn nonverbal communication. The purpose of this assignment is to apply this idea to discipline.

The right brain students get in much more trouble than the left brain students. It is estimated that 70% of the penal population is right brain dominant. Most of the school disciplinary *system* works wonders for over 80% of the student body. This must mean that the system is geared for the left brain. The system is usually logical, sequentially geared, long term oriented, verbally delivered, and easy to justify.

There is a range of behavior that fits under the general term of "inappropriateness." The realm of handling "grave infractions" is beyond the scope of this paper, but for the "run of the mill," daily, off-task behaviors, the following skill building worksheet is offered.

For each of the next six days, practice interrupting inappropriate student behaviors with nonverbals. Record a very brief description of what you did to discipline (i.e., "Looked with a frown on my forehead, my hands on my hips") and the student's reaction ("Student's mouth dropped open; a minute later was on task").

Why would we want to increase nonverbal messages?

1) Because the right brain actually is more sensitive and responds quicker to them than the left brain;
2) To avoid the students' auditory channel (see "Adolescent as Auditory," p. 57);
3) Lastly, because our tongue wears out faster than any other part of our body, and this approach saves a tongue.

For two days, use at least three visual signals per day, signals the student sees without your touching him or making any sounds. You can attempt to use the signals both in discipline and during instruction.

Day 1

_____

_____

_____

Day 2

_____

_____

_____

WORKSHEET

Single Modality Messages, con't.

For two days, use at least three kinesthetic signals per day (signals the student feels without seeing or hearing you). Again, attempt to use these while disciplining, although it is okay to use them while instructing as well.

Day 3

_____

_____

_____

_____

Day 4

_____

_____

_____

For two days, use at least three auditory signals per day. These are the hardest to do; they are nonverbal messages conveyed through speed, pitch, timbre, pause, length of sentence - anything that is heard that is independent of the words used. A suggestion is to use sounds for the first day and only on the second day attempt using words.

Day 5

_____

_____

_____

Day 6

_____

_____

_____

_____

Also see "Pace of Lesson," p. 203.

"Getting Rid of Houdini"

When we present information and then show it rearranged, the kinesthetic student is confused because she doesn't get to see the information move from one arrangement to the next. Information appears, disappears and reappears. By removing the disappearing column, the kinesthetic learner in the classroom has an easier time.

English: An example is when we have students identify the subject and predicate of a sentence by listing them off to the right in columns for each category.

Appear	Disappear	Reappear
		Subject Predicate
The boy ran.		Boy ran

If the student were allowed to identify the subject and the predicate in the actual sentence she would have an easier time. It also allows her to learn location cues that normally the subject comes before the predicate.

Contractions: We show the student two words, "can" and "not" (appear); they are removed (disappear) and then replaced by "can't" (reappear). By having the "can not" on one card and folding the card so that the second "n" and the "o" are tucked in, Houdini is removed from the classroom. As a wonderful serendipity, a paperclip holds the fold and acts as a natural anchor for the apostrophe because its function is metaphorically explained.

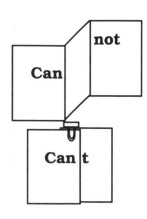

Test: When we ask students to use a test booklet or to write their answers on another piece of paper, whether it be IBM computer cards or just an answer sheet, it is a gigantic use of the "disappear."

Kinesthetic students actually score lower on that form of a test than a test where they can write their answers on the same paper/booklet.

Reading: When we have students read aloud and, at some point, the teacher stops, makes a parenthetical comment, and then continues, the student who is highly kinesthetic with poor visual capacity becomes frustrated trying to track where to refocus his eyes in the book.

Math: An example is when we teach the conversion of a fraction to a decimal, we show:

Appear	Disappear	Reappear
$\dfrac{5}{6}$		$6\overline{)5}$

It's the disappearing column that confuses the at-risk student. When we use a chalkboard or an overhead, if the numbers are not visably represented as tangible objects that can be moved, the students are confused by the disappearing column. For overhead usage, have moveable numbers; for boardwork, have numbers on pieces of paper so the pieces of paper can be moved, or use magnetic numbers for the chalkboard.

In addition to the fraction example, story problems cause a lot of confusion because they involve both the right and left hemispheres. If students were allowed to write the processes on the story problems by putting common math symbols over the corresponding written words, they would have an easier time translating the problem. An example would be a coded poster which indicates that "is" is the equivalent of the "=" sign and "of" is the same as "x".

Math Ability Through Hemispherology
"Two-Fisted Math"

The section on "Getting Rid of Houdini" explained how teachers tend to present information in one format and then make the information reappear in a different arrangement. This is confusing to kinesthetic students; they need to see the information actually move.

A corollary to the above is when we process items in a sequence which are mentally done simultaneously. The kinesthetic students miss the connection; they have to do the processes concurrently.

1. Example:

$$\text{Reducing:} \quad \frac{1}{8} \quad x \quad \frac{3}{5} \quad x \quad \frac{4}{9}$$

If we cross out the 8 (leaving a 2) and then the 4 (leaving a 1), the vast majority of students understand the connection between both (they are both being divided by 4), but the kinesthetic/remedial students need to understand the connection by simultaneously crossing out both the 8 (with the left hand) and the 4 (with the right hand).

2. Example:

$$\text{Fractions:} \quad 8 \quad \div \quad \frac{4}{5}$$

Instructions: have the left hand "x" out the division sign while the right hand writes the reciprocal.

$$8 \quad x \quad \frac{5}{4}$$

3. Example:

Algebra: $Y \quad 10 = 23$

Instructions: left hand writes "+ 10" on the left side of the equal sign while right hand writes "+ 10" on the right side. $Y - 10 + 10 = 23 + 10$.

4. Outline how you plan to incorporate "two-fisted" math in your area:

_____

_____

5. Describe the results, focusing on which students tend to really benefit from it.

_____

_____

WORKSHEET

Math Ability Through Hemispherology
Color Coding

The majority of students learn because of their ability to adjust to the instructor's style. Other students, especially those at risk, need additional help. One very helpful learning tool for right brain students is color coded information.

Examples:

1. Addition:

$$\begin{array}{r} 4 \\ 3 \\ +5 \\ \hline 12 \end{array}$$

ones in a given color (i.e., blue; represented here by *italics*)

tens in a separate color (i.e., green; represented here by **bold**)

2. Multiplication

$$\begin{array}{r} (4) \\ (2) \\ 48 \\ \times \mathbf{5}3 \\ \hline 144 \\ \mathbf{240}0 \,* \\ \hline 2544 \end{array}$$

Ones digits are in a given color (i.e., blue; here in *italics 3*) as well as all numbers affected [*(2), 144*]

Tens digits are in a separate color (i.e., green; here in **bold 5**) as well as all numbers affected [**(4), 240**]

3. Algebra:
color code items

	A	+4		=	10	
	A	+4	-4	=	10	-4
		A		=	6	

(This is the same concept as the one on the previous page)

4. Outline how you plan to incorporate color coding into your lessons.

_____

_____

_____

5. Describe the results, focusing on which students tend to benefit from it.

_____

_____

_____

_____

Suggestion: buy half a dozen pens that have four colors in the same pen tube. See "Anchors; Transferring from Teacher to Student," p. 192.

* Some teachers like to color code the last 0 of 2400 to indicate it is connected to the "ones operation"; therefore it is italicized.

Special Education

One remedial teacher with a limited supply of books couldn't afford to have the students write in the books, and yet she knew she needed to help the students "get rid of Houdini." Her solution?

She paperclipped a clear transparency to the workbook page and the student used a felt tip marker. When the student was done, the teacher put it on top of her own teacher test booklet to do the correction.

Getting Rid of Houdini

1. Identify at least one area in which you use Houdini in the classroom.

2. Describe your plan on how to get rid of Houdini.

3. For this week, notice which students benefit from this extra assistance. Describe them here.

Diagnosing Visual Capacity in General

We know that there is a great difference between those who have visual capacity and those who do not. The vast majority of students have the capacity - the difference is whether they have the visual capacity on the left brain side (being able to see words in their mind's eye) or the right (being able to see concrete objects). The former group does well in school; the latter doesn't.

The intention of this worksheet is to provide practice in detecting the two visual hemi-spheres. Interview three to five students with varying degrees of academic success. Have them each do the following: a) think of a topic of high interest, b) describe the topic, c) ask for spatial location of items (visual right), d) ask them to "see" some let-ters/words/sentences/passages about the topic (visual left). Report on each one. For example, a student likes motorcross bikes and you ask him to see his favorite bike in front of him. Once the vision is established, then have him point to where the logos are located and describe them.

Student 1 initials: _____   Academic success level _____

1A _____

1B _____

1C _____

1D _____

Student 2 initials: _____   Academic success level _____

2A _____

2B _____

2C _____

2D _____

Student 3 initials: _____   Academic success level _____

3A _____

3B _____

3C _____

3D _____

Diagnosing an "At Risk" Student for Visual Capacity

The first step, of course, is to assess the student's visual capacity. When someone is in stress, he tends to "close down" to only one sensory channel.

Someone once said that this "closing" process is like being in a rowboat that is starting to sink. We tend to jettison our least valuable assets (capacities in all modalities) and cling to those that are the most precious (preferred mode).

Likewise, when someone is relaxed or energetic, he opens up to all his senses. Since our objective is to detect visual capacity, and the student may not be primarily visual, we want him to stay relaxed. The following exercise helps determine in which senses a person has capacities.

1. Talk about something of high interest to him. The topic is:

_____

2. Respectfully mirror him to increase his accessing of different parts of his mind. Generally this will increase the external indicators. Describe how you respectfully mirrored him:

_____

_____

3. Usually the student will exhibit two modes of processing. The two detected are:

_____

_____

4. The student has probably shown you two modes. Which mode have you not seen (or seen the least)?

_____

Use the questions below that relate directly to the least shown mode.

    a. To check for visual capacity, ask about color, size, shape, distance, etc.
    b. To check for auditory capacity, ask about conversations, music, etc.
    c. To check for kinesthetic capacity, ask about movement, touch, temperature, weight, texture, etc.

WORKSHEET

Interviewing for Modality Capacity

1. Initials of person interviewed who is at risk: _____

2. Topic of high interest:

   _____

3. How you gradually mirrored the person:

   _____

   _____

   _____

4. Which mode was most evident?

   _____

5. Mode(s) in which you explored capacity:

   _____

6. Which mode(s) have you not seen or least seen?

   _____

Use the questions below that relate directly to the mode(s) in which you are still checking for capacity.

a. To check for visual capacity, ask about color, size, shape, distance, etc.
b. To check for auditory capacity, ask about conversations, music, etc.
c. To check for kinesthetic capacity, ask about movement, touch, temperature, weight, texture, etc.

Which is the mode you want to check for first?   _____

List the three questions that you used to check that mode:

_____

_____

What is the next mode for which you want to check?   _____

List the three questions that you used to check that mode:

_____

_____

_____

CAUTION: Notice if this student's visual mode follows another mode. If the student has visual capacity, it is okay to force the student to operate in the visual mode. However, be sure that the student's level of frustration is not exceeded. The "Scales of Learning" indicate that when "reviewing" it is safer to require visual behavior.

Moving A Student From the Visual Right to Visual Left

We know that the more someone is interested in something, the greater the access to his modes. This provides the teacher an opportunity to practice getting a less than academically successful student to see letters, words and sentences.

1. Initials of a less than academically successful student:

_____

2. Short description of how this student qualifies as "less than academically successful."

_____

_____

_____

3. Topic of high interest to student:

_____

4. Visual Right:

Describe how you established the picture of the concrete setting (i.e., spatial location, sizes, colors, etc.).

_____

_____

_____

_____

5. Visual Left:

Once the visual right is permanent, have the person focus on left brain visual specifics. For example, if the topic was skiing (#3), the visual description was color, width and shape of new skis (#4), the focus for the left visual (#5) is "Where is the brand name and what are the letters?"

_____

_____

_____

_____

Summary

A SPECIALTY item on the educational conveyor belt is the student who has a right brain preference and yet has great left brain capacity.

This chapter can be best summarized by relating the following true story. One summer, as I was driving from Western Washington to Eastern Washington, I picked up a hitchhiker. Once in the car, his nonverbal signals, especially his breathing pattern, indicated he was kinesthetic with a visual capacity. Consequently, I was slow to talk and paced him for some time. Having established enough rapport, I broached the subject of destination.

"Where are you going?"

"Where you headed?" was his reply. The lack of a standard answer further confirmed my initial impressions.

"Pasco," I said.

"I always wanted to go there," he responded.

As we dropped into a silence, I reflected with a quiet chuckle on a joke I had recently heard about the right brain individual who interviewed for a job.

It went like this:

Interviewer: "We need to ask you a few questions; this one is in regard to your general fund of knowledge. How many days of the week start with the letter 'T'?"

Applicant: (after some thought) "Two."

Interviewer: (after wondering at the length of time it took to respond) "By the way, which are they?"

Applicant: "Today and tomorrow."

Interviewer: "Let me switch to a mathematical problem; how many seconds in a year?"

Applicant: (with very little thought) "Twelve."

Interviewer: "I'm curious; how did you arrive at that?"

Applicant: "January 2, February 2, March 2 . . . "

Interviewer: "This is a spelling question. How many 'd's' in Rudolph The Red Nosed Reindeer?"

Applicant: (after bobbing his head for some time) "Ninety-seven."

Interviewer: "How did you get that?"

Applicant: "Da, da, da, da, da, da, da . . ."

For the next hour, I was respectful both verbally and nonverbally, and as the hitchhiker gradually grew to trust that I sincerely cared, he became increasingly more comfortable.

During the next hour, his "life's history was revealed like a good book; the farther he went into it, the more it began to make sense."* His father was valedictorian of Cornell University in the late 1920s and two of his children presently attended Cornell. The

---

* *Reader's Digest*, March 1988. Taken from Harold Kushner's *When All You've Ever Wanted Isn't Enough*, Summit Books.

hitchhiker had walked off a job five years ago, and when the last paycheck was spent and the car finally sold, he began living as a hobo. His clothes were all less than a week old as he went from shelters to door jambs to missions.

Reflecting on his fine level of articulation, I began to suspect that I was dealing with a brilliant mind. Respectfully I asked him what his IQ was. He paused for a long time as if assessing the safety of the atmosphere.

"How did you know?" he asked. I vulnerably shared what I do for a living. His long poignant silence was punctuated with his answer, "160+."

Slowly, because he was letting someone enter his private sanctuary for the first time, he painted me a cryptic picture. He said that he spent no less than five hours a day, five days a week, reading in the public libraries.

As we approached the three hour mark, we entered Pasco, and he pointed to a twenty-four hour truck stop. As we arrived, I asked what coffee cost now. He said with a knowing chuckle, "Fifty cents."

As he opened the door, I ventured in a voice patterned after his own, "Could I write family and say we have met and you're fine?"

Having no way of knowing what his unique artwork of synapsis would produce, I waited as he pondered. He asked for my business card, and said he would ruminate on it and might stop by sometime.

That night as I lay in bed, I reflected on all that I had learned. This gentleman had great capacity but had chosen to follow his own drummer. Because societal pressures were too great for him, he had created a disguise that allowed him to make sense of his life.

I dreamed of past students who might become hitchhikers and how I could help future ones.

"Little decisions are easy when you are multisensory--it's the 'biggies' that are rough . . . because I have to make sure my pictures, internal dialogue and feelings all agree."
Kelly Day Rogers

Chapter 5

Storage

*"As you store,
so shall you reap during retrieval."*

- Krista Grinder

	Input	Storage	Output
Visual	_____	_____	_____
Auditory	_____	_____	_____
Kinesthetic	_____	_____	_____
	Learning	Retrieval	

Since the 1960's, the educational conveyor belt has had a love-hate affair with "learning styles." Educators are attracted to the idea that they can learn how a student thinks. They are also confused by the question of whether to adapt a *system* to an individual or an *individual* to a system.

Neuro Linguistic Programming has made it easier for the educator to diagnose where the learner is from moment-to-moment rather than depending on the use of a static commercialized test. "Learning styles" focus on input and output channels of the learner. If the issue of adaptation is to be seriously addressed, the educational microscope must include the question of storage.

Characteristics of Auditory Storage

	Input	Storage	Output
Visual	_____	_____	_____
Auditory	_____	Sequential, Entire Chunk	_____
Kinesthetic	_____	_____	_____
	Learning	Retrieval	

The two characteristics of Auditory storage are "sequential order" and "entire chunk" (from beginning to end). A teacher once said, half jokingly, that she did an autopsy on an auditory student, and in examining the brain, realized his was a cassette recorder. When an auditory student hears a question, he selects the cassette which contains the answer; the cassette is inserted, and he runs through the whole bit of information until the answer is located. There is a tendency for the cassette to continue to play even after the answer is found.

All people are likely to have three items that they have stored auditorally. By paying attention to how your mind responds to these questions, you will vicariously experience how the auditory mentality operates all the time. As you hear these questions, pause and notice how your mind inserts the cassette, starts at the beginning and has a tendency to continue even after the information is re-accessed.

First Question: How many days are in the month of May? Pause now and answer. Did you find your inner voice and body starting a metronome as you sing-song the rhyme, "Thirty days has September, April, June and November. . ."

Second Question: What's the third line of the "Star Spangled Banner"? Some musicians *see* the third line of the "Star Spangled Banner," but most of us start at the beginning of the song, *hearing* the lines.

Third Question: The alphabet appears in every primary classroom, but because of the style in which it is taught, it is stored auditorally instead of visually. As you read the following letters, think of which letter follows them in the alphabet: J_, P_, T_, X_. Now compare the speed of recall with the following task: when you see the letter, think of the letter that comes just before it: _Z, _L, _R, _V. Did you access the former letter responses quicker than the latter? When information is stored auditorally, any item in the list can readily be obtained as long as the preceding item is mentioned first; however, when a person is asked to retrieve an item that precedes the designated item, he has to rewind his cassette and begin at his natural break. In the above samples of alphabet letters, when someone recalls the letter before "L", he normally begins at "H". We've all memorized the song "A, B, C, D, E, F, G (pause), H, I, J, K, L, M, N, O, P." Can you imagine your mind perpetually operating this way? The auditories do!

Where does auditory storage appear in the classroom? On the primary level, most information is stored auditorally because of the immaturity of the student's visual ability.

In one kindergarten classroom, the teacher opened the daily routine by looking at a bulletin board display which showed the month, date and day of the week.

"Today is Wednesday. What is tomorrow?" the teacher asked.

"Thursday," the students responded in quick unison.

However, when the teacher then asked, "What was yesterday?" there was silence. When the teacher then prompted them with, "Remember, class, 'Sunday, Monday . . .'", the class remembered.

The teacher was asked to try the same activity the next day, and when she said, "Remember, class . . ." she moved her head and her voice in a metronome fashion. The kindergarten instructor found that some kids got to the answer before she got to the day; some students have "fast forward" on their cassettes.

On the intermediate level, a principal opened every school assembly with the "Pledge of Allegiance." Each year an effort was made to get the student body to pause orally in conjunction with the commas and periods of the pledge. The only students who were able to do that were those who could visually see the pledge written out in their mind's eye. For the vast majority of students, the pledge is stored orally and a student's pause is based on the rhythmic length of their breath.

At the junior high/middle school level, when students have a fill-in section on a test, questions can appear in the following three forms:

Test

1. Blah, blah, blah_____.

2. Blah, blah ____blah, blah.

3. _____ blah, blah, blah.

The student who has the information stored auditorally has the easiest time with the first example and the most difficult time with the last. The axiom is, "Auditory storage is retrieved only by activating the initial/preceding bit of information."

Think of a time when you woke up to the second half of a song on the clock radio and the rest of the day the ending kept repeating itself in your mind, but you couldn't remember the first section.

Parents of junior-senior high secondary level children who want help with questions at the end of the chapter can either assist them in finding the answer, or, if we don't want to teach, do the following:

As we're continuing with whatever activity we're presently involved with, we can ask this series of questions.

"How many questions are there?"

"Fifteen," the child would reply.

"What question do you want help with?"

"Number five."

In our mind's eye, we convert their response into a fraction (for this example, we'll say 1/3.)

"How many pages are in the chapter?" we ask.

"Twenty-one."

Mentally we multiply the fraction by the number of pages and say that the answer will be on the seventh page of the chapter (give or take a page).

As adults, we often snap our fingers and hum when we're trying to recall a piece of information. It is as if our fingers are a band conductor's baton and we're readying the orchestra of our mind for a performance.

Guidelines for Auditory Storage

Since the two characteristics of auditory storage are "sequential" and "entire chunk" (beginning to end), in what situations is it beneficial for material to be stored auditorally?

1. When people are unable to visualize, i.e., in kindergarten and first grade.

2. When the input and output channels are both auditory, i.e., when situations involve music, lines of a play, songs, etc.

3. When the information has consecutive steps and all the steps are to be done (procedures or processes such as math, analyzing a sentence in English, etc.).

The following is a form to assist you in developing a procedure students will use in doing an academic skill. The example given is from the area of math, but the form can be applied to all subject areas.

Do the following worksheet on a separate sheet of paper.

Auditory Storage With Kinesthetic Movement

List Essential Steps	List Corresponding Body Motion	Actual Words Said Metronome Fashion
a. _____	_____	_____
b. _____	_____	_____
c. _____	_____	_____
d. _____	_____	_____

Title/description of the same procedure is used in the example that follows.

Auditory Storage With Kinesthetic Movement: Example

The quickest, most permanent way to remember consecutive steps is to have symbolic full-body motions that accompany a sing-song voice. Example: Long division, 4980 divided by 18.

Essential Steps	Symbolic Body Motion	Actual Words
a. Round off divisor to nearest 10's	Have hands move around an invisible basketball	Round off
b. Divide divisor into dividend	Place one arm horizontally in front of chest, other hand with fingers on top of and then under to form the division symbol	Divide dividend
c. Multiply quotient by divisor	Cross arms out from body to form multiplication symbol	Multiply
d. Subtract product from dividend	Slice air horizontally with right arm at chest level	Subtract
e. Bring down next number from dividend	Take hand raised high and dropped to waist level	Bring down
f. Repeat above steps until problem is finished	Place hand down and do half circle going up	Start over

---

Disadvantages of Auditory Storage

It's okay to learn information auditorally. If the entire chunk is going to be used in the same sequential order, then leave it <u>stored</u> auditorally. If the information is to be used in a different sequence, it may need to be stored visually.

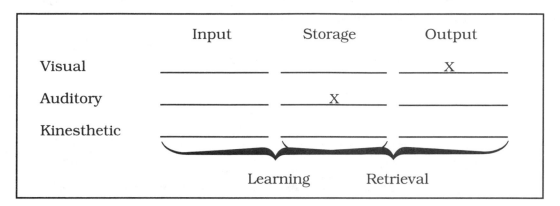

	Input	Storage	Output
Visual	_____	_____	X
Auditory	_____	X	_____
Kinesthetic	_____	_____	_____
		Learning	Retrieval

We tend to teach auditorally and test visually. If a student has information still stored auditorally when taking the test, he has to transfer during the test situation. This puts him at a severe disadvantage compared to students who have the information stored visually. For example, the student who has memorized a laundry list of information in a certain sequential order has to do the following:

1. See the question;

2. Insert the cassette;

3. Start it from the beginning; listen to the inner voice;

4. Get information and write it down;

5. If the next question the student looks at is at a different place on the cassette, the student has to continue listening to the whole cassette or start it over. This is obviously a time-consuming task and is likely to create stress in a student who sees the test period slipping away faster than he is able to answer the questions.

Information that is stored visually can be scanned as a whole chunk, focusing in on the pertinent information. The auditory retriever doesn't have the capacity to "fast forward" and still hear the information. It's as if the visual person can fly in a helicopter, hover, select a part of terrain it wants to focus in on, and zoom in for a closer, more detailed look. In contrast, the auditory person has to crawl along the ground, stay on the memorized road, and go laboriously from one point to the next.

There is a tendency for publishers to put "end of the chapter" questions in the same sequential order as the information appears in the chapter. This is the motif of "daily work." However, final test questions that come from the teacher's edition are usually in random order. We know what problems this can create for the auditory student; in essence, the system of assigning final grades is based on whether the student has the information stored visually or auditorally as opposed to whether the student has stored the information.

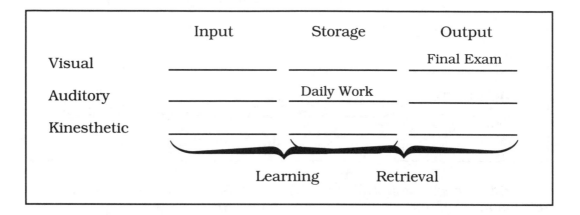

What are the characteristics of visual storage that allow the brain to do so well on tests?

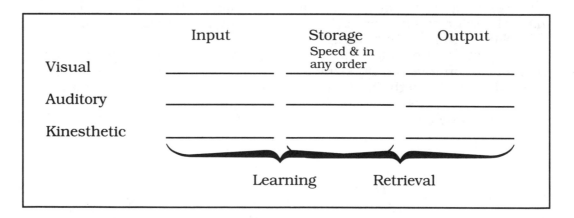

Summary

We have examined "input," "storage," and "output." My own crystal ball shows that the essential value of "learning styles" will only be realized when we focus on the least understood but most valuable aspect: STORAGE.

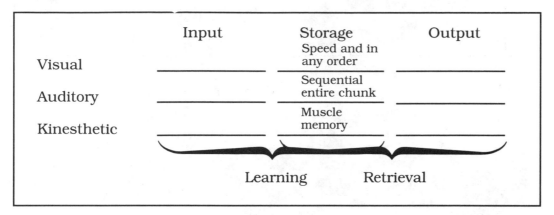

Chapter 6

Importance of Visualization

"The secret of education is respecting the pupil."
- Ralph Waldo Emerson

In the last chapter, the advantages of visual flexibility were highlighted. From the fourth grade on, the ability to see words in the mind's eye is the key to academic success. These skills can even be practiced in preschool. This chapter will cover the following areas:

1. How students see "in their mind's eye";

2. How to increase the visual capacity of students who aren't "seeing" and what teaching strategies assist;

3. The purpose of review, which is to move information stored in **A**uditory to the **V**isual in preparation for test;

4. Examples of visualization;

a) Reading
b) Spelling
c) Math

How do Students "See"?

The students who have the least difficulty with the conveyor belt format are students who can immediately convert information heard (input) into internal (storage) visual form. The most common way of doing this is through notetaking. The majority of notetakers are literally attempting to see what they hear. While the kinesthetic is involved in notetaking, it is a minor aspect.

When giving a presentation, sometimes I take a pen out of my shirt pocket and offer to swap it with one of the avid notetakers in the front row. I explain that the ball in the ballpoint is greased with a clear lubricant which enables the participant to get the same fluid muscle movement that their pen offers but it won't produce anything on the page. This offer distinguishes the kinesthetic notetaker from the visual notetaker. While conceding that notetaking is a combination of both visual and kinesthetic, my offer to swap pens distinguishes, in their own minds, their purpose in taking notes. Given a choice between writing what they hear without seeing it or receiving what they hear in typed form, most visuals will choose the latter.

There are four ways that students who innately visualize do so. These are listed from most commonly used to least used but most sophisticated.

1. The most common style is shown by the student who attends lectures, takes notes on what was heard, looks at the notes and forms a picture in his mind's eye (see chart below).

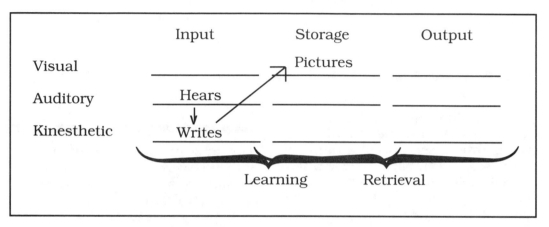

2. The second most popular style is shown by the student who reads the book, takes notes, looks at the notes and thereby forms a picture in the brain (see chart below).

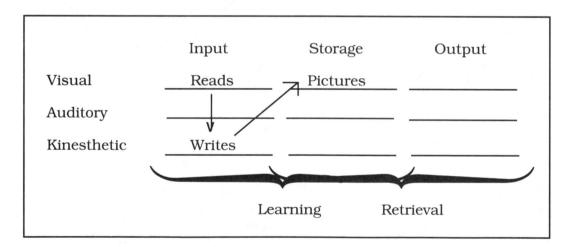

The differences between these first two styles of "seeing" are whether the instructor follows the book for composing the test or if he adds the lecture material to the test, and additionally, which initial input mode the students prefer, Auditory or Visual.

3. Notetaking is an example of visual storage through "external seeing" with kinesthetic assistance. Some students prefer the external visual without the kinesthetic assistance; they are the ones who prefer being given the typed form. It would be interesting to offer these people the option of getting the content of the presentation in typed form or the same content in their own handwriting. How would you choose to study? (See figure below.)

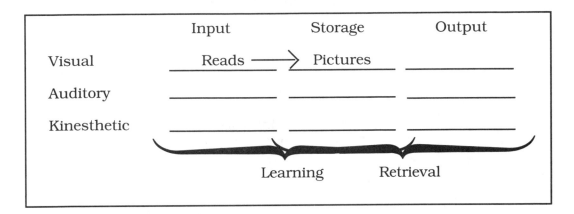

4. There are some students who can store visually without seeing information externally. These students are able to create a picture in their mind without the assistance of seeing it externally first. These students are the envy of their classmates. In college, they usually don't buy textbooks or take notes and still get high grades (see chart below).

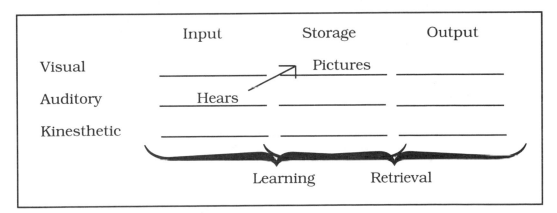

The four types of visual processing are:

1. Auditory external through notetaking to internal visual;
2. Visual external through notetaking to internal visual;
3. Visual external without kinesthetic to internal visual;
4. Auditory external to immediate internal visual.

Students employing any of the first three modes have an easier time in school than students who store information internally in auditory form. The student who auditorally hears and immediately stores in visual is often interpreted as "talented and gifted."

Increasing Visual Capacity

In Chapter 5, we examined how the system of grade assignment correlates with the student's preferred mode of storage--visual or auditory. It
was noted that problems can arise for auditory students when "end of
chapter" review questions are presented in sequential order and final test
questions in random order.

	Input	Storage	Output
Visual	_____	_____	Final Exam
Auditory	_____	Daily Work	_____
Kinesthetic	_____	_____	_____
	Learning	Retrieval	

It is imperative that the teacher know the visual left capacity of a student
to allow him to store information visually. It would be nice if we could
assess and test individual students in their preferred mode; however,
their overall success and ease of accomplishment on the school conveyor
belt will be in direct proportion to their visual left capacity. It is the
single most important variable from the fourth grade on and can be
practiced from preschool on. It is possible to help a student shift storage
from the auditory to the visual.

How do we increase the visual capacity of students who are still learning
to see in their minds?

First, we can use certain nonverbals (still body, flat soft voice, increase
slowness of pace and length of sentences--see p. 97).

Secondly, we have to have the patience of Job and great rapport skills.
The students who already "see" will tend to become bored--we have to
have rapport so that they are patient. And, we have to do two to four
weeks of visual right seeing before adventuring into the visual left.

There appears to be a correlation between being resourceful and being
able to access a wide range of modality capacities. Therefore, the more
fun the activity is, the more that students breathe. The result is that
they are more apt to be resourceful and able to use visual capacities.
Keep it lighthearted and model breathing. One optimistic note: the
younger the student, the more they believe what you believe of them
(see "Increasing Congruity," p. 205).

On the following pages are techniques which enable an educator to
assist students in learning to "see content in their minds." This is the
key to high school graduation and the ticket to "doing college."

Teacher's Behaviors to Assist Student Visualization

Research indicates that the instructor's nonverbal behavior greatly influences student learning. When we want students to "see" in their mind's eye, the teacher's behaviors that best assist the class are:

A) still body/arms

B) flat high voice

C) talking at a slow pace

D) increasing the length of the sentences.

As a project, we are going to examine if this is true.

1. On a typical day, do the above recommended behaviors when doing an activity that encourages students to see in their mind's eye. Report the class' reaction(s):

_____

_____

_____

_____

_____

2. Now, in a similar situation, do the exact opposite behaviors.

A) move body/arms

B) low voice with inflections

C) talk fast

D) change length of sentences. Report the class' reaction(s):

_____

_____

_____

_____

Introducing a Class to Visualization

The process of visualization is readily done by some students and not others. Therefore, your initial use of visualization in the class needs to be done with ease and an atmosphere of fun. Visualization is a process which is often easier for children who have never done it than adults who have a history of feeling incapable of doing it. The adult pattern of going into stress in regard to visualization is more embedded than for students. My guess is that kids know how to breathe better than adults. The following exercises are best done over a two to four week period before any visualizing of academic content is attempted.

The following is a generic format that will need to be adapted based on the particular grade level you are teaching.

Formula

Step 1: Teacher provides the students with a non-descriptive scene (a sentence with a simple subject and predicate, such as "The boy and the dog went outside.").

Step 2: Teacher asks students to fill in details of the scene with the following specific visual properties. The students add adjectives to "boy" and "dog" such as big, brown, furry, and adds adverbs to "went outside" such as quickly, eagerly, etc. You may want to encourage students to close their eyes for this activity.

Colors

_____

Distance

_____

Sizes

_____

Foreground/background

_____

Shapes

_____

Other

_____

Introducing a Class to Visualization, con't.

Step 3: Conclude the activity by having students share their particular visual properties. The debrief time is very important because by sharing, students provide models for each other. Remember to indicate both verbally and nonverbally that any and all answers are correct.

The next page contains visualization exercises which are listed in progressive order of difficulty. Use the ones that are appropriate for your grade level and your community's values. Use this chart to record your progress.

Day 1 Activity:

Day 2 Activity:

Day 3 Activity:

Day 4 Activity:

Day 5 Activity:

What changes have you noticed during this first week of daily visualization activities?

Day 6 Activity:

Day 7 Activity:

Day 8 Activity:

Day 9 Activity:

Day 10 Activity:

How have the students responded differently the second week from the first week?

Visualization Exercises

Below is a series of exercises to be done 10-15 minutes a day for two solid weeks. These are designed in a progressive order and, therefore, you have to realistically progress fast enough to keep their interest. For example, while a primary teacher could spend two months on the first three steps, the secondary instructor might only allot 2-3 days for the same steps. In all cases, the outcome is the same: increase awareness of and confidence in their Visual Right capacities by progressively improving their specificities.

1. To each student pass out an envelope with two examples of three familiar objects. Two paperclips, two rubber bands and two pennies could make up the envelopes. Show these real objects in juxtaposition on an overhead. Have the students, at their desks, duplicate the pattern. Tape a piece of heavy paper on the overhead so that it can be flipped up in a tachistoscopic fashion so that you can show the objects and then quickly conceal them (if you turn the lamp off and on the bulb burns out very quickly.) There are three variables you can alter to challenge them: (a) number of objects shown, (b) sophistication of the pattern of the objects (i.e., a display of four objects such as "penny, penny, clip, clip" is easier than the display of three objects of "penny, rubber band, and clip"), and (c) the length of time the objects are shown.

2. Same as #1 with this additional instruction: "We will count aloud from 100 backwards to 95 and during the counting you will be shown the objects." This occupies their internal auditory and thus increases their visual.

3. Do #1 above without passing out the envelopes. This starts the transition away from the kinesthetic toward the visual. Do the same for #2 above.

4. Have them recall familiar objects and pretend to touch and notice details. Using "bedroom" as an example, you might say, "Touch the four sides of your desk. Pretend they are the four walls of your bedroom and you are on the ceiling looking down on the room. Touch the wall your window is on, the door, your bed, closet," etc. Another example is, "There is a small cat on your desk. Which way is it facing? Stroke the back of the cat. Have the cat turn and stroke it again."

5. This step uses Nanci Bell's *Visualizing & Verbalizing* concepts of "category" versus "menu."* The first is the label/heading for a concept. The latter is the actual choices under that label. Give an example of a familiar object and offer the class kinesthetic (category) choices (menu). Example, "There is a dog on your desk. What is its size? (category) Is it big, medium or small?" (menu). The kinesthetic categories are size, texture, shape, temperature, etc. Likewise, the auditory categories are volume, pausing, speed or voice, etc. Example: "The dog is barking (category). Is it loud, soft, or in between?" (menu). The visual categories are colors, foreground-background, direction, number, size, and shape. Example: "What is the color (category) of the dog? Is it brown, white, black?" (menu).

The axiom is to teach several days/weeks on categories with menu choices before instructing a class to perform only on the categories level. Example, "There are some apples on your desk. Notice the number, sizes, shapes, and colors."

* Nancy Bell, *Visualizing & Verbalizing* (Academy of Reading Publications, 1120 Filbert St., Paso Robles, CA 93446 (805) 238-2008. Copyright 1986).

Advantages of Visual Right Before Visual Left

In other sections, the difference between <u>V</u>isual <u>R</u>ight (sees objects and seeks to understand the "whole") and <u>V</u>isual <u>L</u>eft (sees words and seeks parts) was presented. Elsewhere, the suggestion was made that since school is progressively *left brain visual* and "kids at risk" are *right brain visual,* they have to be taught how to SEE words. The way to do this is to increase their awareness of and confidence in their *visual right* capacity. This is accomplished by having them be more specific and detailed in their visualization of objects before introducing them to SEEING letters and words.

The purpose of this worksheet is to focus on the by-products of doing the <u>V</u>isual <u>R</u>ight before the <u>V</u>isual <u>L</u>eft.

I. Reading: When visualization is done prior to reading, the student has an overview of the theme/purpose/plot. He then can more correctly place the individual parts, as he reads, into the larger scheme. This results in more accurate and complete comprehension, plus longer term memory.

II. Writing: When visualization is done prior to writing, the final product is more detailed, specific, and longer. This includes having students draw before writing.

III. Math Story Problems: When the student does stick figure graphic representations above the English language sentence, he has an easier time.

The following allows you to implement the above:

1. Content area:

_____

2. Describe how the <u>V</u>isual <u>R</u>ight was done:

_____

_____

3. Describe how the <u>V</u>isual <u>L</u>eft was done:

_____

_____

4. Compare these results with the results from your former method(s):

_____

_____

_____

_____

A Philosophy

The teaching of visualization in a group setting is a peculiar operation. The students who already have the ability are the better students and might interpret the time spent teaching others how to do it as minutiae. The teacher has to have enough rapport to ask them for their patience and enough cleverness to challenge them. At the same time, those who don't possess the ability tend to have a belief that they "can't" see. If the educator in any way brings the class' attention to what they are doing, their emotions of "can't" are activated and the teacher has to swim upstream. To respectfully assist the latter, the instructor has to make sure the students DO it enough so that they have to shift their belief. The best way to circumvent their belief is to have them DO it BEHAVIORALLY without being aware of what it is they are doing. Hence, initially, the emphasis is on high kinesthetic activities. For two weeks, avoid the impulse to say "see in your mind"; the kinesthetic equivalent of "see" is the word "sense."

The second philosophical consideration is to make sure the activities are fun . . .keep in mind that when people are having fun they are breathing, and when that occurs, they have greater capacities . . . which is what we are trying to increase.

Finally, encourage a lot of student sharing of how they are doing the activity. The class will have more models than you could ever dream of, and because of the nature of the approach, students seem to try out their peers' templates; hence, they obtain a wider range of possibilities than if the teacher presented the same alternatives.

Visual Configuration of Printed Material

The following is a series of exercises to assist students in creating a picture of printed material in their mind's eye. The theory behind these exercises is that those students who have "internal left visual" (seeing words) capacity have an easier time in school. Since most students have "internal right visual" (see objects/configuration) capacity, if we increase the specificity of the right capacity, the student increases access to seeing left.

The exercises are arranged from least "visual ability" required to increasingly requiring more visual ability. Students who already have left visual ability will have a reaction to the initial exercises ranging from "Easy!" to "This is too easy, it's stupid to do!" The class composition and your relationship with the higher ability students will dictate the speed at which these exercises are done. The higher the ability group, the higher the percentage of students having left visual capacity. They will want to go through them quickly. We are not doing the exercises for these students; therefore, GO SLOW and yet maintain rapport/permission from the higher ability students. Make it FUN.

Each exercise can be done several times and over several days. An initial exposure isn't enough . . . PRACTICE, PRACTICE, PRACTICE. In the exercises that follow, clarification/instructions are in parentheses. Comments in brackets are for the educator's consideration.

Comparing Outputs

1. Students open to announced page; put finger in book and close.

2. Students instructed to slip finger to next page without looking (it is helpful to select pages with pictures, graphs, boldness, etc.).

3. Teacher says "open" (pause) "close" eyes and book. (The length between "open and close" needs to be varied.) (Place a marker/finger in the book so that it can be easily reopened.) [This is visual input].

4. Teacher says, "Outline on your desk with your finger the different components/parts/items seen." [This is kinesthetic output].

5. Repeat # 2 and # 3 with a new page and this time say, "Tell a neighbor the general layout of pages." [This is auditory output].

6. Discuss with class which was easier or what were the differences between # 4 [kinesthetic output] or # 5 [auditory output]. Watch which students sense a difference. They are indicating a preference. Remember during debriefs students can *model* from each other. Note that those students who naturally gravitate towards the "big outline" are more "global" (*visual right*) and those who are tending to look for specifics and sequential order are *visual left*.

7. Do # 2 - 4 with a new page and then announce, "Use pencil/pen and sketch the picture from your mind on paper" (have paper and pen/pencil already out).

8. Debrief comparing kinesthetic finger outlining (#4) with auditory (#5) and kinesthetic with visual (#7).

Second Looks

9. Do the above but after each output #4, 5, 7, have student "open" again and "add to/further clarify." Debrief. Watch again for opportunities for modeling during the *sharing* and individual student's tendency towards "global (visual right) - to - specific parts/sequential" (visual left)]. You can eventually have them look a third and fourth time, adding to/further clarifying each time.

10. Do the above but this time have them keep their eyes closed and turn their heads toward the open book. Give the "open and close" commands. This time students' bodies are still as they just mentally picture the page.

11. Debrief comparing outputs: kinesthetic (#4 and 7) vs. auditory (#5) vs. visual (#10). Hopefully those who needed the auditory and kinesthetic practice have had enough success to try visual output. Be sensitive to which students tend to be uncomfortable with this approach. Because you cannot go as slow as they need you to, you have to look for opportunities to work one-on-one.

12. Do #10 with # 9, "adding to/further clarifying."

13. To add to the above exercises, the teacher can run off blotted out components of a page, cut the components out, and place the cut parts in envelopes on the students' desks. After opening their eyes and looking at the page, they then close the book and take the components out of the envelope and recreate the page. The first two times you do this, use duplicates of the actual page size. On the third and subsequent practices, you can reduce the size of the duplicate pages. [This is what the

primary teacher does all of the time: prepare materials. Although it takes the teacher time, the kinesthetic students really appreciate the effort.] Have them do "second looks" to further clarify. Also, at the end, have them open the book to verify their representation. This is one of the most important classroom activities for the kinesthetic members.

14. Now select pages with pictures/graphs/charts. The purpose is to notice the size of the paragraphs. Select pages with definite different sized paragraphs (length, width, bold print, italicized, underlined, etc.) Do "open," "close" and outputs of a) kinesthetic, b) auditory and c) visual.

Tachistoscope/Scanning

15. A. A good warm-up exercise is having them stare at a point and wiggle index fingers in front of glazed eyes. They continue to stare and wiggle fingers as they spread their fingers towards their farthest peripheral view.

15. B. Students' eyes are closed, book is open, head towards book (as in #10), and this time direct the students to keep their eyes on the crease between both pages. Make sure the length of time between commands of "open" and "close" is short. (Use different outputs with each round; do "second looks" and debrief.) If an actual tachistoscope is available, use it with words.

15. C. Select an item that stands out differently from the rest of the items (i.e., date, year) and have the students race to find it. Make this one FUN (they are no longer focusing their eyes on the crease). Give the following instructions:

1. "Open to page ___"

2. "Put your finger in book, close book."

3. "Eyes on board." (Teacher reveals question.)

4. Students search and raise hands when they find it.

[15 C is the first exercise in this series in which the teacher is seeking visual left information.]

Location of Information

16. A. Pick a passage in which paragraphs contain different information which is easy for the students. [See "When to Have Class Visualization; Parts 1 and 2," p. 106.] The greater the difference in each paragraph, the better. In other words, pick passages in which the author describes only one concept per paragraph. Have the class read either aloud or silently. The students have a blotted out copy of the page in front of them. After reading have them close their books and ask a question to which the answer is only found in the first paragraph. Students point to appropriate paragraph on blotted page. Continue to ask questions until all 5 - 7 paragraphs have been covered in sequential order. Once you are certain that knowledge is retained and associated with the corresponding paragraphs on blotted out page, you can emphasize location. You are helping the class to approach and practice the fundamental ability commonly titled "photographic memory." Now ask the class the same questions but in random order. Have the students again point to the location of the answer on the blotted out copy. This level of visual sophistication can be practiced on a daily basis. When they are ready to increase the complexity of their skills, ask questions such as "Is

the information at the beginning, middle, or end of the paragraph?"

16. B. # 16A dealt with the ability to recall location of original information with *external representation* (i.e., book, blotted paragraphs, etc.). This level of exercises transforms seeing external information into the *internal representation* level. Have the class look at a single bit of information in a book, on an overhead, or from the board. Use the wording: "Either close your eyes or look somewhere else in the room and see it." Simultaneously use nonverbal teacher behaviors which assist visualization: still body, chin up, flat voice, slow speech. The students will most likely be in a frozen body with a stare/glazed look in their eyes. Then say, "Very slowly, nod your head to indicate you are seeing it." If some students are having difficulty, it could be because of the term *"see"*. The kinesthetic prefers the wording, "or have a *sense* of its location," so when you say "see," add the wording, "or have a sense of."

Have the class look at the next single bit of information and use this wording "Again, either close your eyes or look somewhere else in the room and see it." When you do this same process with the third bit of information, add the following wording, "Again go to *your favorite place* and see." Make sure you *debrief*. The students may share their strategies and possibly model each other. This word usage quickly makes "your favorite place" an anchored mental state which the students can use during *review*; after information has been learned and they are *storing* it for the test. Of course, when passing out the tests, remind them to use their "favorite place" for retrieving information during the test.

16. C. Do the same as 16B above only when you add the second and other subsequent bits of information, ask them to see all the bits together. Suggested wording could be, "Look at #2 on the board. Go to your favorite place and see this second item. (pause). While there, see the first item (pause). Slowly nod your head to indicate you are seeing them." 16C is a major jump for some students. Remember: keep them breathing and make it fun. Debrief by sharing strategies and providing models for each other.

16. D. This is like #16C but with a wider focus. When they see the second item, have them "focus between the first and second item and see both simultaneously." This is an internal visual tachistoscope. This may be the maximum skill level for the majority of students.

17. *Superimposing.* This exercise can be done after each exercise outlined in #16. If the class is hitting their limit during one of the #16 exercises, take a break. When you return, start with #17. Whatever level of #16 you stopped at, say the following: "See the item in your favorite place (pause) and gently nod your head (pause). Look at your desk and pretend to see a quiz/test question asking for that information (pause). Nod your head as you do (pause). Now superimpose the item from your favorite place to the paper and see the answer (pause). Nod your head (pause). Now trace over the answer." This is the skill used by the visual. This level is worth practicing. Some students will even report that they feel as though they are cheating when they take tests.

18. Do # 16A - C and #17 with new information.

The Purpose of Review

When to Have Class Visualization, Part 1

Since most students can "see" concrete objects (right brain) easier than letters/words/sentences/passages (left brain), it is important to know when to ask the class to "see" letters. "Seeing" is a process. There is a tendency for teachers to go heavy on content and light on emphasizing process.

As concepts become more familiar, the students can see visually left with greater ease. The following "Scales of Learning" explains this concept:

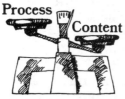

Initial Learning

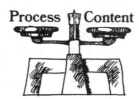

Review

1. Using the above ideas, outline how to plan to initially present an idea/unit in a multisensory fashion (make sure they can see/hear - talk/touch).

_____

_____

_____

_____

2. During review, emphasize the students' ability to "see."

_____

_____

_____

_____

_____

WORKSHEET

When to Have Class Visualization, Part 2

In Part 1 of this worksheet, we discussed the fact that *review* is when we want to emphasize the class "seeing" letters, words, sentences, and passages. This worksheet explores the *review* phase in more depth (see the chart below).

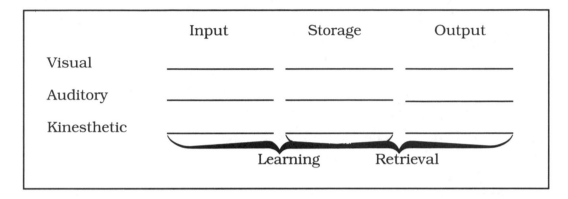

First Review:
The purpose of the first review is to *check* that learning has occurred. This is often done by giving the students choices of ways to prove they have learned something: showing (visual), saying (auditory) or demonstrating (kinesthetic). Describe how you will/did do this.

_____

_____

_____

_____

Second Review:
Since the final test changes the sequential order of the information, the second review involves having the class practice utilizing the information in a random order. The two characteristics of "visual storage" are "speed" and "in any order." Second review is often a variation of the final test. Describe how you will/did do this.

_____

_____

_____

_____

_____

WORKSHEET

Testing, Part 1

The American education system does a good job of getting the learning *in*. We are still learning how to get the learning *out*. In another worksheet, the difference between information stored visually vs. auditorally was explored. Basically, the auditory information is stored from beginning to end in a sequential order, whereas the two characteristics of "visual storage" are speed and retrieval in random order.

When the student does daily work, the answers to the questions at the end of the chapter are in the same order that the information was presented. Daily work presented in sequential order does not pose a challenge to the auditory brain. On final tests, the questions from the textbook are often not in the same order of sequence. As a result, the students with "cassettes" in their minds are at a disadvantage.

Comment on when you or the textbook you use presents information in a sequential order (the input):

_____

_____

_____

Describe *how* the students demonstrate they have received the information and whether they have to change the sequence during output.

_____

_____

_____

What insights about learning did this activity provide?

_____

_____

_____

_____

_____

Testing, Part 2, Visual vs. Auditory Student

In "Testing, Part 1", we explored the idea that auditory storage of information is effective for "daily work" but inappropriate for "testing."

This worksheet further examines the difference between the visual and auditory students. The following chart suggests the differences.

Type of Student	"Daily Work"	Test results compared to "Daily Work"
Visual	Not studying	Much higher
Auditory	Not studying	Same as daily work
Visual	Studies	Same as daily
Auditory	Studies	Lower than daily

Select a student for each of the four classifications above (interview other teachers to find a representative for each category). List the student's initials and comment on any differences between their daily work and their test results.

1. Initials of a visual who doesn't study _____
Comments:

_____

_____

2. Initials of an auditory who doesn't study _____
Comments:

_____

_____

3. Initials of a visual who does study _____
Comments:

_____

_____

4. Initials of an auditory who does study _____
Comments:

_____

_____

WORKSHEET

Testing, Part 3

In "Testing", Parts 1 and 2, we explored the idea that tests present information in a different sequence than how it was presented during "daily" work and that there is a difference between the test results of the visual compared to the auditory student. This worksheet further focuses on these differences. The purpose is to trace where the information which appears on a test comes from and determine if the type of source influences the results for the visual compared to the auditory student.

Steps

1. Identify students in your class who are highly visual and considerably less profi- cient in their auditory skills. List initials here (you may have 1 - 6 students out of 30).

_____ _____ _____ _____ _____ _____

2. Identify students in the same class who are highly auditory and considerably less proficient in the visual mode (you might have 2 - 4 students out of 30). List initials here.

_____ _____ _____ _____

3. Look at a test and identify the source of the questions (perhaps there is a greater correlation with major tests compared to weekly tests). The source of answers to most test questions is a combination of both visual (they appear in a textbook) and auditory (they were covered in the lecture). For our present purposes, we are only interested in sources that are just, or mainly, one mode. Which test questions come from just the book (pages were assigned and the information was not covered by the teacher's oral presentation)? Put a "V" (for visual) out in the margin next to these test items.

4. Next, identify those test items that come exclusively or almost exclusively from an auditory source (lecture, class discussion, etc.) by putting an "A" (for auditory) out in the margin next to the test number.

5. a) After correcting the test and recording the results in a grade book, go back and pull the tests of the visual students (#1 above).

   b) Make up a score of how these visual students collectively did on visual questions (#3 above).

   Record percentage here _____

   c) Make up a score of how these visual students collectively did on auditory questions (# 4 above).

   Record percentage here _____

   d) Is there a substantial difference between # 5b & 5c?

   Yes _____ No _____

Testing, Part 3, con't.

6. a) Pull the tests of the auditory students only (#2 above).

b) Make up a score of how these auditory students collectively did on visual questions (#3 above).

Record percentage here ———————

c) Make up a score of how these auditory students collectively did on auditory questions (#4 above).

Record percentage here ———————

d) Was there a substantial difference between #6 b and #6 c?

Yes _____ No _____

7. Is there an overall pattern that the source of information affects the proficiency of the learners (matched vs. mismatched)? Are # 5 b and # 6 c collectively higher than #5 c and # 6 b?

———————————————————————————————————

———————————————————————————————————

———————————————————————————————————

WORKSHEET

Outlining vs. Mindmapping

The traditional way of presenting is to organize our lectures around the *outline* format.

I. Outlining is formal
   A. Sequential and numbered
   B. Usually complete ideas or sentences
   C. Logical content and structure
      1. Concepts follow in order/priority
      2. At least two subconcepts per concept
II. Outlining has a beginning and ending

1. This structured, logical, orderly, sequential style is highly "left brain." The "right brain" equivalent is known by several labels: "mapping," "clustering," "webbing" etc.

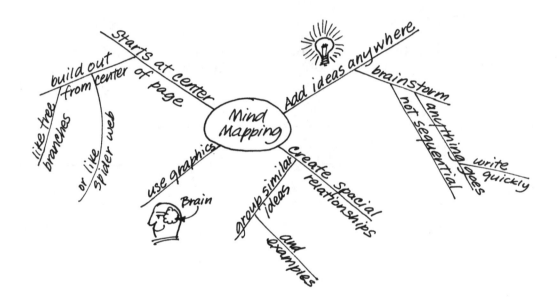

Organize a 10 - 20 minute presentation in which you pass out the left brain, skeleton outline. Have the class fill theirs in as you model on the board/overhead while lecturing.

2. Give another 10 - 20 minute presentation of equivalent difficulty in which you pass out a mind-map. Again have them fill in theirs while you model during the lecture.

3. Discuss individual students' reaction to both. Keep in mind the two-sided sword of "novelty and unfamiliar." Is there a pattern to which students like which style?

_____

_____

_____

Sorting Content Into Visual and Auditory Categories

The two characteristics of auditory storage are sequential and entire chunk. The two characteristics of visual storage are speed of processing and being able to retrieve/ rearrange the information in any order. The purpose of this worksheet is to have the teacher sort which material will be readily understood if taught visually. Keep in mind the characteristics of each modality, sort one or two items under each of the modalities, and briefly explain how that sorting was done. List the characteristics of the content which corresponds to the selected modality.

For example:

$$\begin{array}{r} 6 \\ \times 4 \\ \hline 24 \end{array}$$

This content is appropriate for auditory storage because of the rhythm of your voice (6 times 4 is 24).

$$\begin{array}{r} 8 \\ \times 7 \\ \hline 56 \end{array}$$

This content is appropriate for visual storage because there is no metronome and the numbers are visually consecutive (5, 6, 7, 8).

Content for auditory storage:

_____

_____

Explanation for selection:

_____

_____

Content for visual storage:

_____

_____

Explanation for selection:

_____

_____

Examples of Visualization

Visualization of Reading

Since one of the two characteristics of visual storage is speed, increasing the pace of material covered increases visualization. In order to work on a new process, the content needs to be familiar ("Scales of Learning," p. 106). Get material two grade levels below the reading capacity of the class. Let them read at their own speed and calibrate how long it takes the average student to cover one page. Then set up a system so they turn the page when a signal is given (clapping hands, clicking, etc.). Have the system be slightly faster than their independent level. Have the students read a short section, then have them stop and describe how they are picturing the scenes.

Read Pause Picture

Preface: There are some students who are multisensory and can adapt to any mode of presentation. Likewise, there are some students who have difficulty even when given a choice of modes. The following section especially addresses those students who fall in between the two extremes.

Education goes through pendulum swings of emphasizing, and often overemphasizing, an approach which will match nicely with a certain segment of the population's learning style. At other times, the pendulum reverses direction because there are populations of students who are not getting the current approach. Then it swings too far over to the other side again, and some of the students who were successful under the former approach now have difficulty (see chart on p. 209).

We know that reading involves both sides of the brain; the left side specializes in coding and decoding, the right side in comprehension or overall meaning. Using this as an operational definition allows teachers involved with reading to determine which side of the student's brain is deficient when diagnosing his reading ability and formulating a prescriptive plan of how to increase his reading. When a student is able to code and pronounce words disproportionately to his comprehension, his left brain is working in excess of his right brain. This symptom will be especially true when the youngster you are dealing with comes from a school system that emphasizes the phonetic approach (the left brain).

The following technique is designed especially to assist those students with the above symptoms.

1. Check first to ensure that the students have the ability to picture in their mind's eye. For example, have them look at their desks and pretend that their desks are really their bedrooms and that they are on the ceiling looking down at the four walls and everything inside the bedroom. Have them point to the wall where their bed is, the wall(s) with windows, point to the door, closet, etc. Do this exercise again with the layout of the whole house. This exercise ensures that they are making mental pictures of concrete, right brain objects.

2. Have them read a very short segment. For some students, it is a noun; for others, it's a phrase and for others, it's a sentence. The sentence is the easiest unit to use for this particular method.*

3. As they complete the chunk of information, have them stop, go into a stare or close their eyes, whichever is more comfortable, and picture in their mind what the sentence described. Make sure you're using nouns that are concrete objects and action verbs as opposed to the verb "to be." "To be" verbs and abstract nouns confuse the students and prevent them from using right brain picturing abilities (see "Reading," pgs. 43-44).

4. Have the students describe the color, size, shape, foreground, and distance of the picture in their minds. If the reading book passage is accompanied by a picture, you may want to cover it up and either not show the picture, or, if you're going to show the picture, after they have finished their mental construction, use the following respectful wording: "Let's see if their picture is as good as the one you've created in your mind."

5. Having taught the skill mentioned in Exercises 1 - 4, our new goal is to find out how many items the students can include in one picture before they have to go to a second picture. Sometimes their skills are based on the passage, their picturing abilities, or the interaction of both. *As a second picture begins to form, the student needs to stop reading, pause, and cement the first picture before going on to the second picture.* The brain has five to nine slots of information it can entertain simultaneously. When it gets beyond its capacity, it has a tendency to lose information which was placed previously in order to create a spot for new information. Students who find it easy to create pictures and entertain large amounts of information have a facility to take information spread on several slides and regroup them onto one, thereby creating new spots for new information. A dramatic example of this is when students are taught multiplication tables. They learn a certain number of tables, but when moving on to the next number, they begin losing the ability to remember some of the previous factors. What the teacher needs to do is to cement the first picture just as the second picture is starting to be formed. The sensitivity and external directing of the student as he learns to do this is the key to comprehension. It is suggested that you work with one student in particular and record your sense of how this student pictures, how you knew when he was starting to form the second picture, how you cemented the first picture, and how you taught him to do this skill on his own.

6. Comprehension questions are taught by having the student recall the individual pictures he had; the first picture, the second picture and the third picture, and that, basically, is what comprehension is.

---

* Nanci Bell, *Visualizing & Verbalizing* (Paso Robles, CA: Academy of Reading Publications, 1986). Also contact June Jackson of Learning Pathway, 6000 E. Evans Bldg., Ste. 256, Denver CO 80222.

Selecting Books for the Visual, Auditory and Kinesthetic Reader

In a class of thirty, twenty-two students have enough visual, auditory and kinesthetic capacities that it is often unnecessary to take time to individualize and accommodate them. There are also two to three students whose learning problems are other than learning styles deficiency. Between those two groups are four to six "translators"; those people who use one modality and need the instructors to adjust to them in order for them to comprehend and learn. For these particular students, it is helpful to understand what ingredients in a book make it attractive or repulsive.

Of the three ingredients in any kind of literature (plot, setting and characterization), only the visual person has an appreciation of and an attraction to setting. Books by James Michener are supreme examples of a writer who spent a great deal of time setting the picture in the reader's mind of what is about to occur. The nonvisual readers are oblivious and are repulsed by the opening setting of some classic books. If you know of a book with a good plot or dialogue, and you know the student will enjoy it, you can tell her to skip those "setting" pages in the beginning and in subsequent chapters. In fact, if it is a paperback, you may want to mark those sections out so that the nonvisual reader knows which ones to skip.

Auditory people love dialogue because they can hear the different voices of the people talking back and forth. Kinesthetic people are action-oriented plot lovers. They could not care less about the setting and the internal composition of the person. They just want the external action. Books by Louis L'Amour would be examples of plot-oriented reading.

To analyze a book, open the pages and flip forward or backwards and look at the indentation on the left side of the page. Indentations indicate change in paragraphs. The more frequent the changes, the more likely you will find dialogue. The longer the paragraph, the more visual it will be with lengthy descriptions.

A kinesthetic person also wants fewer words on a page. I once saw an extremely effective remedial reading teacher who knew her students were kinesthetic buy two sets of paperbacks and cut the pages in half so that the students would be turning the page more often. Remember that the kinesthetic person likes and needs movement. Some suggested books for these students include *The Outsiders* and *Durango Street.*.

One insightful librarian realized that the nonvisual (especially the kinesthetic) reader goes into stress when in a library because it is associated with "failure" and "lack of movement" (the proverbial "shh."). She marked the paperback tops in a color code, blue for kinesthetic, green for auditory. She left the visual books blank because visual people like things neat and orderly.

1. Initials of a highly auditory student in your room/grade level: _____

Selecting Books for the Visual, Auditory and Kinesthetic Reader, con't.

2. Ask her what books/stories she has enjoyed and list titles here with the reasons she enjoyed the book.

Title	Reasons
_____	_____
_____	_____
_____	_____

3. Correlating her reasons with the suggested guidelines from the previous page, pick a book/story and offer it to the student. List the student's reactions to the book here.

_____

_____

_____

4. Initials of a highly kinesthetic student: _____

5. Interview him about books/stories he has enjoyed. If none, switch to movies.

Title	Reasons
_____	_____
_____	_____
_____	_____

6. Correlating his reasons with the suggested guidelines from the previous page, pick a book/stories and offer (or read aloud) to the student. List reactions here.

_____

_____

_____

Visualization of Spelling

Example 1

Step 1 Write the words on the board and say to class, "As you see the letters, say them aloud forward." Use an auditory nonverbal cue (i.e., snap of fingers) to indicate the pace of saying each letter. Repeat.

Step 2 Have them look anywhere in the room but the board, see the letters, and recite aloud together (use the same auditory nonverbal cue). Repeat.

Step 3 Have students look back at board and say, "As you see all the letters, say all the letters backwards." (Use same auditory nonverbal cue.) Repeat.

Step 4 Say, "Look somewhere else in the room, see the letters and spell the word backwards."

Step 5 Say, "With eyes still in same place as before (in #4), say word and spell it forward."

Example 2

Step 1 Select a word with an odd number of letters (i.e., catch).

Step 2 Have the students wiggle their fingers in front of their eyes and gradually move off to peripheral vision.

Step 3 Say, "Look at the middle letter" (i.e., t of catch).

Step 4 "As you look at the middle letter, (t), at the same time, look at the letter to the right (i.e., see tc)."

Step 5 Say, "As you look at the middle letter (t) and see the letter to the right (c), at the same time, see the letter to the left (a)."

Step 6 Continue to do the process above, spanning to the right and then to the left until the whole word is completed.

Example 3

Step 1 Teacher writes a word on the board and underlines each letter (p r i d e).

Step 2 "Look at the board and memorize each letter and their relationship to the letter on each side."

Step 3 "Indicate that you have it memorized by nodding your head."

Step 4 Teacher erases the letters leaving dashes (_ _ _ _ _).

Step 5 Teacher points to dash; students recite aloud.

Step 6 Once teacher is satisfied the students have dashes memorized, the teacher changes the order to more random selection of dashes.

Example 4

Step 1 Same as #3 only this time two words are put on board, one on top of the other, as follows:
l o d g e
g r o u n d

Step 2 Once students have memorized them, the letters are erased. Dashes remain.

— — — — —
— — — — — —

Step 3 Once the teacher is satisfied the students have the dashes memorized with corresponding letters, teacher points to dashes from one word to the dashes in the other word and students recite aloud.

Odd Number Letter Words

1. Either in pairs or directing the whole class, write on the board or on a piece of paper, an odd number letter word with a line going through the middle letter.

Example:　　　　d　a　|t|　e　s

The student is asked to see the middle letter (t) and continue to focus while spanning his eyes to see the letter to the immediate right (e) and the letter to the immediate left (a). Continue seeing the letter in the middle and the letters immediately to each side and then span the eyes even farther to see the next letter to the far right (s) and the next letter to the far left (d). Continue to do so until all letters are seen at the same time.

This ability is the same as a tachistoscope machine. To reinforce and test the visual storage of the word, do the following:

1. Ask someone to look somewhere else in the room, see the middle letter and ask for the letter to the right, letter to the left of the middle and then span out from there. Once the letters of the word are able to be seen visually, the teacher can call for middle letter, immediate right, far right, immediate left, and far left (in the case of a five letter word).

2. Incorporate the above into your format. Do this daily for a short time period for several days in a row and record the results. Especially notice which kinds of students benefit most.

_____

_____

_____

_____

_____

_____

_____

_____

_____

_____

_____

_____

Using the Student's Neurological Location for Spelling*

1. Have students pair up as designated by Student X and Student Y.

2. Have them look at a spelling list or select a word on their own and write one word down on a piece of paper that is thick enough so that they're unable to see through from the back side, preferably right in the center of the page.

3. Student X gives his paper to Y, Y holds the paper and asks X to *see* and *spell* the word. X does so forward twice and then Y asks X to spell it backwards. Student does so and then spells it forward again.

4. Y asks X to look somewhere else in the room and see the word and as X sees it, to spell it. Student X does so.

5. Y directs X to keep eyes at that location and attempts to move the paper in the same location that X is looking. X nonverbally adjusts the distance and height of the card by using hand gestures.

6. Y again asks X to see and spell forward twice, backwards once and forward once again. Y, keeping body frozen, very slowly and gently turns the card over and X again spells forward, backward, and forward. If at any time X would like to see the card again, X will so direct with nonverbal gestures or Y may, at a pause, very slowly turn the card over. When X finishes, they swap and do the same exercise in reverse roles.

7. Incorporate the above into your format. Do this for a short time span for several days in a row and record the results. Especially notice which kinds of students benefit the most.

_____

_____

_____

_____

_____

_____

_____

_____

* Special credit to Dr. David Lundsgaard for the development of the above techniques.

Reducing the Number of Pictures to See Words

Ask students to select words of their choice and, in pairs, have one partner instruct the other to study a word and then look somewhere else in the room and see the word. As they see the word, notice how many pictures it takes in order to spell the word. The purpose of this worksheet is to reduce the number of pictures so that the word takes fewer number of frames in the student's mind to see the word. The goal, of course, is to expand the number of letters that can be seen in the picture. This is a tachistoscope visual/mental skill (see p. 104).

It is important to note that we separate words by syllabication, with each syllable being a separate picture. This latter method is very auditory and left brain visual. The right brain visual tends to separate a word in ways that standard teaching methods consider peculiar (i.e., Was hing ton).

1. Have the student look at the first picture. When they can clearly see it, have them nod their head and then say the last letter of that picture(s) (which is " . . . s" in the word Was hing ton).

2. When they can clearly see the second picture, have them nod their head and then say the first letter of that picture (using the word "Was hing ton", this would be the letter "h . . ."). Then ask them to make a new picture of the last letter from the first picture and the first letter from the second picture
(". . . sh . . .").

3. Have the students look at the picture again and tell you how many pictures they have for that word. Of course, our purpose is to have two pictures ("Washing" and the second picture, "ton").

4. Have them look at the last letter of the new first picture (". . . g") and the first letter of the second picture ("t . . .") and have them make a new picture with those two letters (". . . gt . . ."). Ask them again how many pictures they have for the word. The purpose is to decrease the number of pictures it takes to see the word. Some students will need to have two pictures because of the length of the word. Other students will need only one picture for it.

_____

_____

_____

_____

Visualization of Math

Example 1

When students learn math (such as addition), the information is used in the next level (subtraction). The cumulative nature of math is difficult for the student who has information stored auditorally. The students who have 3 + 1 = 4 stored auditorally are unable to use the information to solve the problem 4 - 1 = ? because subtraction changes the sequential order of addition. The question is how to store information that was learned auditorally so it can be used in a different order for the next level of math.

Step 1
Change the linear order of 3 + 1 = 4 by putting it in a triangular form.

Step 2
The student puts a finger over one of the corners of the triangle.

Step 3
The student answers the question, "What is the missing number?" The student learns the cluster or family of the three numbers. The pyramid has broken the linear structure and the student is able to do subtraction.

Example 2

Repeat the above, using the triangle with multiplication in preparation for progressing to division.

Step 1
Change the linear order of 7 x 7 = 49 by putting it in a triangular form.

Step 2
The student puts a finger over one of the corners of the triangle.

Step 3
The student answers the question, "What is the missing number?" The student learns the cluster or family of the three numbers. The pyramid has broken the linear structure and the student is able to do division.

At all times, remember the "Scales of Learning" axiom, "A new process (visualizing) is best done with familiar content." In the above examples, 3 + 1 = 4 or 7 x 7 = 49, it is presumed that the class has already learned these, and we are concentrating on having them stored visually.
On a separate piece of paper, do the following:
    Step 1: Fill in a linear math concept
    Step 2: How would you graphically rearrange it to break the possible auditory storage of this concept?
    Step 3: What would be the wording for the student to use to ensure that the information is being stored visually?

Summary

By the fourth grade, written tests challenge students to reaccess information in a different order from the original sequence in which it was presented. Professionally, we are doing a good job of getting knowledge into the student. We are just starting to understand how retrieval is a different set of skills than initial learning. The secret lies in understanding how information is stored. This is the key to the ease of retrieval. To teach the process of seeing in the mind's eye, we have to have permission to slow down the amount of content covered ("Scales of Learning," p. 106). The vast majority of students can see objects in their mind (visual right). We need to increase their confidence in doing this before we ask them to see words (visual left). Our goal is to let all students have the facility that the better students have. The way the 3.0+ students take tests is to see the questions on the paper, recall a picture of the answer, superimpose the answer on the test sheet, and practice their handwriting by tracing the answer.

TEST

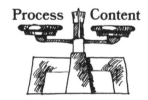

Second Review =
ready for test

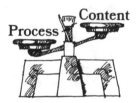

First Review =
ensures that learning
has occurred

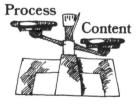

Initial Learning

Chapter 7

"Wellness" Model

"Experience doesn't guarantee wisdom.
The latter comes from Reviewing the Past and Rehearsing the Future."
- John Grinder

Overview

Career counselors are famous for saying there are three kinds of occupations or combinations thereof; working with your hands, working with ideas, and working with people. The last category, statistically, is more susceptible to stress than the former two.

Benefits of Wellness

Educators are in the "people business." Our wellness is like the battery of an automobile. We have twelve cells (months) and as we draw from them, we need to utilize them wisely and know how to recharge them.

The following definitions and by-products of wellness (being in a resourceful state) are briefly mentioned here and further expanded in this chapter.

1. The nature of stress: There's a difference between "gradual stress" and "surprise stress" (trauma). Our understanding of the relationship between the mind and the body gives us more choices on how to coordinate and increase the co-operation between both parts.

2. Associated/disassociated: When you are associated, you are inside your body and looking out. You are able to see, hear, and move and still know what you are feeling. When you are disassociated, you are outside your body and can see your body and environment; you can hear sounds and watch your physical self move, but your access to how your physical self feels is greatly reduced or totally eliminated. There's a direct correlation between one's wellness and the ability to go from associated to disassociated (and vice versa) at appropriate times in both our personal and professional lives.

3. Disciplining with comfort: An operational definition of discipline is *"doing what they need you to do in order for them to be okay."* The key to disciplining with comfort is the ability to disassociate (not know how you're feeling).

125

The nature of gradual stress:*

A. Tension: Stress experts say that the balanced life is one in which the body/mind alternates between periods of tension and relaxation/recovery and the mind interprets both phases as meaningful. Research shows that tension is the contracting of the body, which means a "grimace" and a "cry" might be the same amount of contraction. Statistically, there's as much contraction when one attends a wedding as a funeral; as much when one receives a $5000 pay increase as the same amount decreased; when one gets married or when one gets divorced. The amount of tension, or adjustment of the central nervous system to the events, is equal. Since tension is tension, how the mind interprets what the body experiences is of major importance.**

During the invasion of Italy in World War II, a U.S. medical doctor kept statistics on the soldiers he treated during one particular campaign.*** Only 30% of the men survived the initial phase. When the convalescing injured were offered morphine, 80% of them told the medical staff to save the pain killer for others. The doctor was so amazed at the soldiers altruistic refusal to take the painkillers that when he returned to private practice, he duplicated the study (the same statistics,

considering age, race, religion, and level of education). The most common equivalent in his private practice was auto and industrial accidents. Eighty percent of the civilians not only accepted the painkillers, they demanded more. The interpretation of the two groups is that the soldiers felt fortunate to survive and could look forward to life; the civilians, on the other hand, saw their accident as dramatically altering their life in a negative way. A simple way of understanding the relationship between the mind and the body is shown in the following chart:

```
┌─────────────────────────────────┐
│ Body-mind Relationship          │
│                                 │
│ M E A N I N G                   │
│                                 │
│ I                               │
│                                 │
│ N                               │
│                                 │
│ D                               │
│                                 │
│ B A R O M E T E R               │
│                                 │
│ O                               │
│                                 │
│ D                               │
│                                 │
│ Y                               │
└─────────────────────────────────┘
```

The body is a barometer to the mind, like an advance early warning system to the brain. One way to think about this is to imagine ourselves like a vast country such

---

* Since there is a relationship between "words and nerves" and the word that is used throughout this section is stress, I strongly recommend you breathe deeply and slowly every time you read "stress."

** Holmes, Thomas and Rahe, "The Social Readjustment Rating Scale," *Journal of Psychosomatic Research*, 11, (1967), 213-218.

*** Henry K. Beecher, *The Measurement of Subjective Response* (New York: Oxford University Press, 1959).

as the United States. In the out-reaches of our "Alaska," highly so-phisticated devices monitor for UFO's (unidentified foreign objects = stressors). Once they are regis-tered on the screen, the military at that station (brow of the fore-head) responsibly contact the central office (the mind). Tension is the contact. The mind has several choices as to how to inter-pret the tension. When tension is ignored (no acknowledgment to the "servicemen" in "Alaska"), the sys-tem is skewed. Out of obligation, the "military" must increase the tension, turning a slight tightening of the forehead into a furrow. If no response from Central Headquar-ters is received, the station con-tacts other outposts (neck, shoul-ders, etc.) and the tension in-creases until there is a response.

The above metaphor has been verified through medical research. For example, statistically, people who are prone to migraines have at least three early signals that, if ignored, will escalate to the mi-graine. This is why the body is called the barometer. It doesn't know how to rationalize; only how to gauge a person's well being. The earlier that the signs of ten-sion are detected, the easier they are to satisfy. According to stud-ies, the medical equivalent of this concept is that the earlier you take aspirin, the more effect it has.

Teachers, as a group, have se-lected their career to serve others. While this is a great motivational asset, it is simultaneously a liabil-ity. We tend to ignore the tension so that we can continue to give. This is where the seasonal aspect of our careers comes into play. Whether we say, "It's Wednesday, I can make it to Friday," or "We get a vacation in two weeks, I'll make it," we tend to ignore signs of tension. The enthusiasm and energy of elementary teachers is saintly in this aspect. In Septem-ber, they take on more commit-ment and adjustment and are tired in a far different way in November than secondary teach-ers who think more in terms of their "rights" and tend to pace themselves differently.

B. Gradual Stress: Teachers are seasonal workers; they just don't migrate. The commitment, energy and enthusiasm during the first week of school is not the same as the two weeks before Christ-mas. Our season is like a motion picture with the sprocket holes in the side.

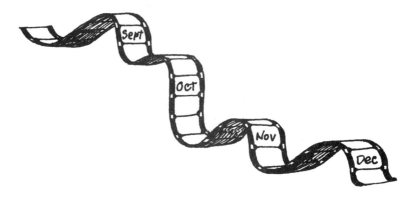

Our batteries need to be recharged on a regular basis. The person who knows one's self and knows one's needs and how to fulfill them has the choice to be systematic in replenishing one's energy. We all need revitalizing because we're in the people business, and those who teach Special Education, re-medial students/subjects and junior high need to be even health-ier than the rest of us.

Giving Yourself Love (Recharging)

1. List 3 - 5 activities that make you feel good about yourself.

a. _____

b. _____

c. _____

d. _____

e. _____

2. After having listed the above, interview yourself or ask someone to assist you. Find the essential ingredients that make these activities so fulfilling. It is suggested you do this in written form. Some variables to think about are:

· Are they done with people or alone?

· Time of day or week

· Location/environmental factors

· Internal/external focus

· Are they primarily visual, auditory or kinesthetic activities?

· Are there necessary prerequisites?

· Which of your senses tend to become renewed or refreshed by these activities?

· What contracts or agreements do you need to make with yourself or others in order to indulge?

3. One of the purposes of having done the above is to de-mystify the superstition that only certain activities replenish us. By reflecting on the common ingredients in the majority of "renewing" activities above, you can discover the "difference that makes the difference." Then you can substitute activities that contain some of these essential ingredients.

Associated/Disassociated

This section will cover the concepts of being associated and disassociated. Each state has assets that save energy when used properly.

Algebra is a mathematical model that incorporates and is much more sophisticated than the models of addition, subtraction, multiplication and division.
So, too, NLP has models within models.*

The Visual, Auditory and Kinesthetic model is the building block of understanding perception and processing styles. It is superseded by the concept of "sequence." A sequence is the modalities one uses when thinking (i.e., making a decision to go to a movie); likewise, the model of "mental states" supersedes sequence.

```
┌─────────────────────────┐
│  M E N T A L   S T A T E │
└─────────────────────────┘
  ┌─────────────────────┐
  │     Sequence        │
  └─────────────────────┘
  ┌─┐┌─┐┌─┐┌─┐┌─┐┌─┐
  │V││A││K││V││A││K│
  └─┘└─┘└─┘└─┘└─┘└─┘
```

A mental state is one of your identification cards from your emotional billfold. For example, my roles as a spouse, parent, and teacher are each a separate state, involving different decision-making strategies (sequences) and relying on different modes or combinations of modalities. Two major mental states which are of great importance to stress management are "Association and Disassociation."

Think of a pleasant past event (vacation, celebration, etc.). Can you see yourself (disassociated) or are you inside your body remembering the experience (associated)? Mentally go through a small scrapbook of events, especially ones which have different emotional connotations attached to them. We all have experiences that we can recollect in which we can see ourselves. There are others in which we find ourselves inside our body in the original setting. There's a third set of experiences in which we are able to switch back and forth from being associated/disassociated about the same memory.

The purpose in recalling these activities is to make it clear that we already have in our repertoire the mental states of being both associated and disassociated. Two pertinent questions to ask ourselves are "When would I want to use these states?" and "How do I do them on command?"

---

* Gregory Bateson, "Logical Categories of Learning and Communication" from *Steps to an Ecology of Mind* (New York: Harper & Row, 1972).

Methods For Becoming More Associated

Out of necessity, our professional world often demands that we be disassociated (we don't have to feel what is occurring when we make stressful types of decisions). The only way that I know that a person replenishes himself after a disassociated period is to become associated and have it be pleasant. Both need to be present for the recovery process to occur. The following exercises are for practicing that process and are not necessarily listed in any particular order. For those who have a bent towards hemispherology, the left brain tends to specialize in labeling, interpreting, filtering in/out, and making sense of reality; whereas the right brain tends to experience reality apart from the labels or articulation. Therefore, much of the following processes involves engaging the right brain without interference from the left brain.

1. Set some time aside on a daily basis (five minutes is appropriate) in which you close your eyes (this will decrease the external and internal visual, thereby giving an opportunity to increase the other senses, heightening the experience for those senses). Start by taking a couple of deep breaths in a very relaxed way. Allow all stimuli from smell and hearing to come in through those senses unfiltered and allow yourself to remain in the present with those sensations coming in (sitting outdoors is helpful). Describe how you are able to increasingly notice if your mind is making pictures and labeling/identifying or identifying what the stimulus is. Notice if you respectfully pay attention more to the external stimuli, and thereby decrease the left brain interpretive level. Describe the difference in your energy level as you perfect this method.

Day 1 _____

_____

Day 2 _____

_____

Day 3 _____

_____

Day 4 _____

_____

Day 5 _____

_____

Day 6 _____

_____

Methods For Becoming More Associated, con't.

2. Safety seems to be a very strong factor in becoming associated. For the following activity, select someone with whom you feel extremely comfortable (this may or may not be your spouse). Have the person prepare food without you being aware of the particular food. For a seven minute time period, with your eyes closed and without either of you saying any words, have the person nonverbally communicate with you while feeding you. You may make any sounds you want, without saying any words. Have them offer your palate a wide variety of tastes, textures, and temperatures with dutiful respect to you. The purpose is to try to focus on tastes and smells. As your brain tends to want to identify, know that this is the left side working - try to ignore it while you stay with the right side. Note your results here.

_____

_____

_____

_____

_____

3. This is similar to #2. This time, have your friend take you on a "blind walk," where your guide exposes you to sensations of temperature, texture, volume, size, and shape through the use of your kinesthetic and your auditory capacities. You may be intrigued to try occupying your left brain in order to heighten the experience of the right brain. For example, you might try counting backwards from 199 (left brain) while the rest of this is going on. Comment on your increased ability to notice sensations.

_____

_____

_____

_____

_____

"Why Would I Want to Disassociate?"

Teachers choose their career because of a desire to be involved with future generations, growth, learning and the acquisition of skills and attitudes. On days when we are doing these things, we feel successful. At the end of the day, we often feel spent. As one veteran teacher told me, "It's a *good tired*." On days when we have to discipline beyond the norm, our energy is scattered, erratic, and low. If we have several days in a row like this, we contemplate whether we're "getting too old" and/or should have considered a different profession. As a whole, teachers are not motivated by being a martinet. Those are days of "*bad tired*." Truly, then, if we could find a way to do the necessary discipline and yet have emotional amnesia during and after the discipline, our memories would be obscured and only our memory of the teaching/imparting would remain clear. Being disassociated while disciplining allows this. In addition, disassociation allows us to be outside of ourselves so that we can logically, instead of emotionally, determine the type and amount of appropriate action.

Many teachers discipline from an associated mental state, and when they do, they utilize an internal scale of justice. They don't allow themselves to react harshly to inappropriateness until the class/individual has clearly tilted the scales and violated the teacher's rights. The associated teacher is therefore susceptible to relieving the pent-up frustration more than doing effective discipline. *Effective discipline is when we act the way they need us to act instead of how we feel.* Another by-product of releasing frustration while the teacher is associated is that he feels guilty afterwards. This compounds the situation because of the incongruity which is portrayed to the class.

"How do I Disassociate on Command?"

Process of Disassociation

Read through the following processes. You can memorize them, have someone read them to you as you are doing the exercises, or listen to a tape as you do it (use the nonverbals outlined on p. 97, "Teacher's Behaviors that Assist"). For each ellipsis which appears, pause one second.

Round 1 = Sit comfortably and take two deep breaths. Gradually close your eyes or go into a stare . . . If you were going to be somewhere else in this room, would you choose someplace off to the right . . or the left . . in front of . . behind where you are now? . . Would that place be higher . . or lower . . or the same as where your physical body is? . . As you have a sense of that location or the direction of the location or pretend you do, very gently nod your head . . . . From the new location, look at or have a sense of where your physical body is.

Reassociating: When you have established a way of memorizing the direction and picked a location from your physical body, and when you have arrived there,

---

Note: Some kinesthetics prefer the word "sense" rather than "see/look" when doing disassociation and visualization.

gently nod your head . . . gradually come back and slowly reenter your body. As you feel the part of your body that is touching your chair, slowly open your eyes and, if you feel like it, stretch your body like a cat coming out of a nap.

The previous exercise is one everyone can do. To increase the speed and functionality of it, do the following:

Round 2 = After the line that reads, "from the new location, look over at or have a sense of where your physical body is," continue with the following: nod your head as you have a sense of the physical distance (number of feet) between your new location and the physical self you are looking at . . . For example, you could say to yourself, "He is sitting at the far end of the couch, ten feet away from the windowsill." Nod your head as you have a sense of an object that is at this new location or logically could be (such as a door, corner of ceiling, windowsill, chair, etc). Think to yourself, "I am over at the window and there is an end table with a round lamp on it between my vantage point and where he/she is," or nod your head as you specifically think of the object you are at, such as, "I am at the bay window seat in the top left corner of the middle pane." Having done this, continue with the rest of the exercise. Reassociate as outlined in Round 1.

The above round identified the distance and clarified the distance/object. These maneuvers stabilize the disassociation so that one can get to that location quickly and remain there.

Round 3 = This time, after being at the disassociated location, instruct

yourself to do the following: "As I look back at (or have a sense of) my physical self, I expand the lens of my view so that I can see a greater number of objects in the room." Each time you practice this, you increase the panoramic view which will give you a broader perspective of what's going on. Reassociate.

Round 4 = This time, after you arrive at your disassociated location, add auditory elements to that perspective with the following words, "And from my disassociated vantage point, I notice sounds I can hear." Reassociate.

Round 5 = Because the disassociated location is now familiar, now you can increase the speed at which you get there by adding these sentences. "In just a second, I will close my eyes or go into my stare, keeping them closed only as long as necessary for me to go to the disassociated object and look back at my physical body from the disassociated location. (With practice, you are learning how to disassociate during a long blink.) I make certain I'm reassociated into my body at the end of this and every time I do disassociation."

Round 6 = When you feel you have mastered the above, do it with your eyes open. Then do it with movement and finally while talking.

Final comment: The power of being disassociated allows you to do the maneuver on command because you have pre-rehearsed the process and location/object. Make sure you have an object/location in your classroom as well as other locations in your professional and personal life.

Professional Example

One teacher who was transferred two doors down from his previous classroom came to school three days in a row before the normally required reporting day. Having borrowed the key from the secretary, he sat in the corner of the room and determined where he wanted his disassociated spot to be. It was the corner of the window wall where the wall and ceiling met. From there he watched (in his mind) a video of his outstanding teaching moments for twenty minutes. As he left his new room, he realized he kept those aspects from his career that he wanted to have connected with his new classroom.

The second day he anchored his memories of his finest moments of effective discipline and classroom management. The third day, he visualized the toughest students he had ever had and used the technique found in the section, "Review and Rehearsal," p. 146.

When someone has a disassociated professional life because of the amount of stress involved, the necessity of having a personal world and of being associated and having it be positive, becomes imperative. The only way to recover from a disassociated phase of your life is to be associated in a positive way. One of the major differences between being a teacher and being an administrator is the latter's necessity of increasing the amount of disassociation necessary at work.

Personal Example

My wife and I use "couch talks" with our teenagers as one of our situations where we automatically disassociate. This is most helpful because of the emotionality of some of the discussions. The disassociation has greatly decreased our tendency to get "hooked" ("up the ante" or say things you don't mean) into the typical adolescent stimulus response. The results have been that our teenagers are forced to face their situation and figure out what they are going to do.

Going From Disassociated to Associated

On the previous page, it was suggested that it is more appropriate to be disassociated than associated when working with people or conditions which are unpleasant. There are some situations in which it is appropriate to be disassociated even when it is pleasant such as presenting to a group. In such cases, your responsibility is to stay outside yourself and notice how you are doing, responding and adjusting to the group's reactions. In these instances, you can be disassociated to the point that you don't know that your bladder is full or that you are hungry or thirsty until you step off the platform.

When going from a disassociated state (whether because it was stressful or just appropriate to be disassociated) to associated, the speed of transition needs to be respectful of your own style. The emotions that you haven't experienced because you've been disassociated are directly proportionate to what you will experience once you become associated. The emotions could flood into you like water being held back by a levee that is finally open.

Most of us have experienced a moment of surprise stress (accident, emergency, etc.) when we had to act quickly and yet intelligently and rationally. It is only after the accident, (i.e., when the person is at the hospital or being taken care of) that we start to experience how we feel about it. I remember once Gail and I heard our son, Kelly, crying on the front porch. We found him with his forehead gushing blood; he had run into a cement corner. We immediately did the right things; stopped the bleeding, washed the wound, called the hospital and so on. Within a couple of minutes, and sporting a large butterfly bandage, Kelly was ready to go back outside and play. He was four years old and wanted to get back with reality. It was only at that time that Mom and I sat down and somewhat shakily realized how bad it could have been.

The greater the amount of emotional energy we're about to experience as we go from being disassociated to associated, the more we need to let the water be released from the valve slowly. People who work in emergency rooms, law enforcement, firefighters and teachers who discipline are disassociated for a high percentage of the day. Therefore, the transition has to be in a manner that is appropriate for them. This is further explored under "Break State", p. 137, and "Review," p. 145.

An additional note is that we all, from time to time, will find that our personal life will also require us to remain disassociated. Then, a vacation away from both work and home is necessary for recovery. Living with three teenagers, I can assure you that there are times when remaining disassociated at home is more effective.

Thus, it becomes imperative that we sort out our home so that much of it is distinctively different from our professional hours. The following worksheet will assist in that sorting.

WORKSHEET

Going From Disassociated to Associated, con't.

In the space below, describe the style and the method that you use to become associated. How long does it take, where do you do it, what circumstances or factors allow you to increase or decrease the appropriate speed?

1. Describe where "professional" materials are kept at home.

_____

_____

2. Describe how you make the switch from "professional" to "private" (often it is done by going through a "break state"). Include the clothing change and where professional materials and other nonverbal reminders are placed.

_____

_____

_____

3. If and when you are "professional" at home, how do you do it so that the space and time used for "professional" work is appropriately *contained?*

_____

_____

_____

4. Where do you spend your recreational time?

_____

_____

_____

Pay attention to how you decontaminate your bedroom for sleep and rest. I also invite you to consider establishing a "worry" spot and time; restrict yourself to worrying only at that spot and at a set time and faithfully keep to it. (See "Worry Game," p. 139.)

Break State

In the previous two pages, we sorted how we make the transition from professional (disassociated) to personal (associated) life. It was recommended that the transition be done ritualistically (i.e., change professional clothes, read the newspaper, have a cup of coffee, etc.).

Either because of the intensity of what we're disassociated from or the length of time we've been disassociated, there are times when it is more appropriate to have the transition be longer than normal. At these times the break state has to be greater than the one we ritualistically use. It is as if we have two different states; one is disassociated, one associated, and the break state will keep them distinguished and well sorted. We're all aware of the research which shows that when a student sits down and studies for history, remaining in the same body position in the same location to study literature increases the likelihood that during the next day's history test, literary facts may unconsciously begin to creep in.

Since the different mental states are represented, maintained and supported by different physical states, a change between studying history and studying literature will keep the information cleanly sorted. What are some more powerful than normal break state behaviors you have done or could do on those days when it is appropriate to make that transition a little more exact, vivid and sorted than usual?

My own personal pattern seems to be that it is appropriate for me to be disassociated during stressful times and also during quite pleasant times when it is professionally more competent to stay outside myself. An example of this might be when I'm presenting in front of people or working in an intense situation one-on-one. As I make the transition from the disassociated state to the associated state, I often find it is appropriate to very slowly *review* what happened and to *rehearse* future options. This is often assisted by walking slowly, taking my time in terms of breathing, sitting in my car a while before turning on the ignition and leaving the radio off, and driving five miles slower than normal.

You may want to consider what your variables are in terms of the transition break state time period on days of special importance. Describe the variables that will assist you in slowing down the break state transition:

_____

_____

_____

_____

_____

_____

_____

WORKSHEET

Being Disassociated at Home

Sometimes after a professional day in which I've been disassociated, I go through my break state, arrive at home and have full *expectation* to be associated and pleasant and, much to my shock, I may find that I'm quite disappointed. Looking back, in retrospect, what was more appropriate was for me to remain at least partially disassociated as I enter the home/family. Sometimes it seems I leave my professional hat at the doorstep, and with it, my ability to communicate, perceive, and be in rapport and respectful of other humans. One of the signs of this occurring is typified by feelings of "Why me? Don't I deserve . . ." (feeling sorry for myself). If this is an experience you've had, you may want to note it here just to be aware of it so you can program yourself to respond more appropriately in the future by remaining disassociated or knowing how to quickly reenter that disassociated state.

Describe circumstances at home that would warrant your remaining fully or partially disassociated and how you would go about reminding yourself to stay that way.

Circumstances:

_____

_____

_____

Ways to activate the disassociated state (practice disassociating to a given object in each of the different rooms that you typically would be in):

_____

_____

_____

_____

_____

_____

_____

_____

_____

Worry Game
"Shovel while the pile is still small." - *John Klobas*

If and when you are preoccupied with "a worry," the following technique decontaminates your day and energy.

Step 1: List the general area of concern:

_____

_____

Step 2: Guesstimate the number of times you think about it during the day and total amount of time spent:
Number of times: _____ Total amount of time: _____

Step 3: Set aside a definite time and location for your worrying. While you may have to negotiate this on a daily basis, the more consistent you are in keeping your appointment, the more effective this technique. The suggestion is that at the end of each session, you select the time and place for the next day. As ridiculous as this may sound, five to ten minutes is more than enough time for the worry.

Example of time _____ Location _____

Step 4: During this undisturbed time, only think about "downside/negative" scenarios. This is the most important ingredient in the success. Our brain has a tendency to think in ambivalences as characterized by the classic "yes, but . . .".

Step 5: Any time other than the designated worry time, whenever the downside concern comes up, immediately breathe, say, "thank you," to your mind and with great curiosity, say "Now that's a new one; that's going to help me fill up my five to ten minutes; please remind me then." Immediately return to appropriate external reality.

During #4 above, spend the whole time only on downside worries or in total silence. The purpose is to localize worries by associating them with a definite daily time and place. By removing ambivalences, the brain has a very difficult time coming up with more than a couple of minutes of varied worst case scenarios. In effect, the worry that was consuming so much concern oftentimes is thought about during a very boring five to ten minute session. If you decide to do The Worry Game with a safe person, make sure she regulates that you only experience the downside. List the results here.

_____

_____

_____

The above is an adaptation of techniques obtained from Western Behavioral Institute, 1150 Silverade, LaJolla, California, late 1960's.

The Nature of Surprise Stress

The previous pages dealt with gradual stress. There are many models to assist in dealing with this form of tension. At least two issues of *Reader's Digest* a year will have some management system. However, there are times when we are traumatized, when the initial stress stimulus is so vivid and/or unexpected that we are shocked.

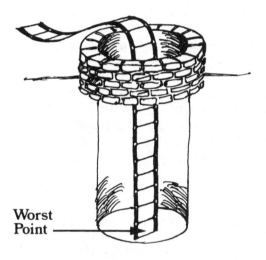

Worst Point

We may suddenly find ourselves at the bottom of the well, and it happens so quickly that we don't remember even falling. We experience being out of breath and lacking resourcefulness.

Techniques for gradual stress management are not applicable for "surprise stress." What are the ingredients for successful stress management in this latter category?

The body-mind relationship is such that when the senses perceive surprise stress, the chemicals released are so strong that the rush is a shock to the body's internal systems. This results in injury and requires a time of recovery. The process of release, injury and recovery is extremely helpful in many life threatening situations. However, in other situations, the initial release is greater than the actual situation warrants, resulting in unnecessary injury.

How do we change our reaction(s)? By distorting time, we slow down our reactions and have more choices. The following activity illustrates how our body gives the mind physiological indicators of stress.

When conducting seminars on NLP and stress management, the following exercise is used to elicit one's first, second and third physiological indicators.*

Step 1: Participants are paired. Each one remembers a very strong, powerful and positive state from the past (technically called "circle of excellence") and they show each other what this state looks like.

Step 2: The pairs now make groups of four. The following roles are assigned: teacher, facilitator and two actors (who role play students/colleagues, principals/parents).

Step 3: The facilitator asks the teacher to turn away from the actors and think of a person(s) who, by a look, voice tone, body posture, or phrase can instantly trigger a lack of resourcefulness in

Footnote: Because of the emotions involved and the sophisticated nature of this exercise, it is recommended that this exercise only be done under the supervision of someone trained in the skills.

himself. This is "surprise stress" (delineated further in the following section).

Step 4: When the teacher has accessed this person(s) that triggers a mentally "stuck" state, he turns to the actors and acts in this triggering manner. Simultaneously, the actors mirror the behavior back.

Step 5: The facilitator watches the teacher. When the teacher is affected by the mimicking actors, the facilitator turns the teacher away from the actors who immediately stop role playing.

Step 6: The teacher takes an additional step away from the actors into that positive state previously established as a circle of excellence. The facilitator respectfully reminds the person to breathe once, and then a second time. Apparently, oxygen comes into the body and is dispensed to all the appropriate vital organs to keep them surviving and to assist in functioning. It is as if the brain gets its maximum amount of oxygen after the other organs; therefore, there's a direct relationship between our breathing and being able to stay resourceful. The cultural adage, "Take a deep breath," is partially correct. If we picture the lungs as a balloon or bag, the first breath taken in doesn't really bring in that much more oxygen. What it does is increase the amount of oxygen expelled afterwards. It is the increase in expelling that creates a vacuum so more oxygen can be taken in on the second breath; hence the NLP expression, "And now take a second breath."

Step 7: The teacher continues to keep his back to the actors, but steps out of the circle (leaving the resourcefulness there) and turns, so as to face the actors.

Step 8: The actors immediately activate behavior which annoys the teacher.

Step 9: As soon as the teacher feels something inside (tension), the teacher turns away from actors (who stop) and reenters the resourceful state. The facilitator reminds the teacher to breathe twice. The facilitator then asks, "What was your initial location of tension/constriction?" Having identified it, the teacher is ready to proceed to #10.

Step 10: The teacher faces the actors again and this time stays long enough to get the initial location of tension plus the second location.

Step 11: Once experiencing the second location, the teacher turns away from actors (as the teacher did in Step 9), steps into the positive, resourceful circle and takes two deep breaths. The facilitator asks if the location of the initial tension was the same as it was thought to be before.

Two insights become apparent. First, what one thinks is his initial location of tension is often somewhere between his tenth and fifteenth location. This shows how well the human mind can isolate and lose touch with the body.

The second insight is the time gap between seeing and/or hearing of external stressors and the sequential order of one location to another. The secret of surprise stress management is your ability to DISTORT reality so that you have more time between when your initial indicator(s) is activated and when you resourcefully respond to the external stressors. This distorted sense of time gives one more choices.

Baseball player Ted Williams always claimed that perceptually he was able to slow down the ball as it approached the plate to the point that he could see the stitching. No wonder he could hit it.

Mary Jo Peppler, who starred for years on the Olympic volleyball team and subsequently coached it, had a favorite drill of standing on a stepladder on one side of the net with a box full of balls and putting one player on the opposite side to react to her spikes. With the ball traveling initially at 90 mph, the player was at a terrible disadvantage. Mary Jo's comment was, "You've got to slow the ball down so that you have more time."

A professional race car driver can go into a turn at a given track at 100 mph and have people passing him because of his lack of speed; likewise, he can go 101 mph quite safely and maintain this position or even move up. At 102 mph, he crashes and burns. To the average driver, there are three choices. However, the professional driver's reality can be distorted to include five gradations between 100 - 101 mph and an additional five between 101 - 102 mph. Because of the professional's ability to distort, the person has more choices.

Many of us have had the experience of being in a near tragic situation when it feels as if time stood still. There is some tentative research which indicates that the body releases certain chemicals to enhance this distortion.

If the baseball, volleyball and race car driver metaphors seem removed from what we do as teachers, think of the last time you had a parent conference during which the appreciative parent said, "I don't know how you do it!" WE are professionals and have learned to distort.

Most of us agree that we are amazingly professional and do incredible things instinctively. However, there are times we do not act as professional as we would wish. These scenarios tend to gnaw at us (often when we are relaxing on weekends and vacations). The gnaw is like an old friend who is asking us for a new choice, another alternative to how we reacted then. Do the following worksheet, "Review." This will help us to listen to our internal friend who says, "Just reminding you of the future possibility of 'x' happening again--have you come up with any alternatives since the last time I broached this subject with you?"

Of course, most of us misinterpret the signal from the old friend and respond with, "Who the heck is bugging me with the same old crap? Don't lay that old guilt trip on me - especially not now."

Skills Used When Reviewing

1) Chronological backtrack: Your memory is like that of the movie film strip with sprocket holes on either side. What looks on the screen like a continuous flow of events is actually the same scene on several individual frames, each frame only slightly different from those on either side of it. The question is which frame initially comes to our mind when the memory of "x" is recalled? Most people recall the frame just before the climax of the disaster.

You want to chronologically back the filmstrip up to a neutral or positive frame. You do this by asking, "What happened before that?" As you back up, your breathing becomes easier and more regular. How much time elapsed or how many changes of location occurred as you backed up?

2) Disassociated Stabilized: See the person (the physical you) in your mind. How far away is he? What object are you at as you look back at him?

3) Grace: You are looking at him outside the well (before the event; while he is still okay). Realize that given the circumstances, he did the best he could. The word "grace" means "unmerited favor."

4) Resource: You know what's about to happen to him but he doesn't. It's like standing on top of a building watching two cars approaching the intersection below. The frame is frozen; reality is at a standstill. As the disassociated observer, look over at him and determine what he needs in order to be okay with what is about to happen. Describe the needed resource.

Now you, the disassociated self, give him the resource (make sure he can see you in this the frozen reality frame outside the well) through a look (visual), voice qualities (auditory) or, if appropriate, by reaching out and touching him (stay at the disassociated object and pretend you are "rubber man/woman," and able to stretch over and touch him). Continue to see him change as you give until, on a scale of 1-10 (10 meaning he is really ready to be perfectly okay with what's about to happen), he is at 9 or better. If the number is other than "9 or better," alter the following three variables:

  a) the resource given. Perhaps add another resource(s) to assist you in giving;

  b) the way you are giving. Vary the VAK;

  c) who is giving. You can always add other people to be at the disassociated object with you.

5) Target state: he is at a "9 or better"; you are disassociated at the object. Let the scenario unfold with each frame appearing <u>only as fast as</u>* you (disassociated at the object) continue to give the resource(s) and he receives, still at 9 or better. You are now watching him actualizing the target/desired state.

In summary, in order to add wisdom to experience we:

1) Chronologically back up out of the well-frame to a neutral or positive frame. Note how much time elapsed or locations have been changed. Now freeze reality, with him knowing that he finally has the person(s) present that he needed.

* Wording developed by Phil and Norma Baretta.

2) Disassociate to an object. Note how far away (distance) it is from him. Use third person pronoun and identify the object.

3) Grace is given; let him off the hook.

4) Resource: Note the needed resource. From the disassociated object, we give VAK and he receives it and changes to 9 or better. This can be varied by adding resources and/or changing how they are given and who gives.

5) Target/desired state. Note the speed of the unfolding scenario is "only as fast" as you can continue to give and he is able to receive and stay at a 9 or better.

The above is as easy as counting the 5 fingers on your hand:

1. Chronological backtrack;
2. Disassociate;
3. Grace;
4. Resource;
5. Target/desired.

Levels of Change

But what are the guidelines for using the above REVIEW process, and how does the severity of the situation alter the steps of the process?

1. If the scenario was very minor, then determine the target state by asking "How would you like to have done it?"

2. If the scenario is minor, but #1 was insufficient to solve, add the question "What would it take in order for you to do it in the way you would like to have done it?"

3. If #1 and #2 are insufficient then it probably wasn't a minor but a regular "garden variety type" of scenario and the above REVIEW outline will be quite adequate.

4. If #3 is insufficient then suspect that the scenario is connected to a CHRONIC pattern. In this case, do the 5 finger steps of the REVIEW but use the earliest example of the pattern. "When did the original scenario occur? Perhaps this is reminding you of an incident when you were younger." The other variable is that the larger the surprise, then it is better that the disassociated location/object be a different location/object from the scenario involved. Ask, "If you could be anywhere you wanted to be, select a place that is so comfortable (i.e., a vacation spot) that you would be able to stay there while watching him?"

5. If #4 is insufficient, then suspect that the chronic scenario is such that it is not enough to change the "younger him" and have the external stressor(s) happen. Go back to the original scene and change all the other people that were present and then change the younger him. By the other people being changed, the external stressor(s) is altered.

In summary, we have two hands. One set of fingers represents the 5 steps of REVIEW and the other hand symbolizes the five Levels of Change.

Is the ability to REVIEW experiences the guarantee that Wisdom will be arriving in tomorrow's mail?

There is a second part of Wisdom: REHEARSING for the future.

Review

One sentence description of the "well":

_____

Which "frame" of the well appears to represent the well (i.e., how far from the bottom, etc.)?

_____

_____

1. You have chronologically backed it up to a different time/place (out of the well); describe the length of time or number of places switched to:

_____

2. You have disassociated at an object. Describe the object and how far away you are from him:

_____

3. You look over at him and realize that given the circumstances, he did the best he could. Grace given.

4. Freeze the frame that is outside the well and, as a disassociated observer, look over at your "physical self" and determine what he needs in order to be okay with what is about to happen. Describe the needed resource.

_____

Give him the resource by looking, sounding and touching appropriately. On a scale of 1 - 10 (10 meaning the person is ready to be okay with what is about to happen), make sure he is 9 or better. What number is he at on the scale?

_____

5. Let the scenario unfold, each frame appearing only as fast as you (from the disassociated position) can give the resource and he can receive it at "9 or better." Comment here on the process.

_____

_____

Comment on how the topic/issue/subject is now viewed differently.

_____

_____

_____

Rehearsal

1. You have completed the "Review" worksheet and are thinking about when you might be in a similar situation in the future. The stimulus that lets you know you are in a similar situation is called a <u>trigger</u>. It is what you would *see* or *hear*, and, in some cases, externally *feel* which corresponds to a particularly stressful situation.

2. <u>Linking</u>: Practice the following:

   a. Think of a <u>trigger</u> and breathe (deep & relaxed).
   Note: As soon as you think of trigger, begin to breathe.

   b. Think of a <u>trigger</u>, breathe, and think of the resource.

   c. Think of a <u>trigger</u>, breathe, resource and begin to see him doing the target state.

3. Allow the target state to have a variety of scenarios (i.e., humorous, serious, etc.).

4. Comment on the above effect (be thorough).

_____

_____

_____

_____

_____

_____

_____

_____

_____

Disciplining With Comfort

The section that follows is not intended to be a panacea or a complete system, but, rather, to comment on generic patterns which occur in discipline situations.

Teachers are often such committed "givers" that they are possessive to the point that the class appears, to a visitor, to be a reflection of the teacher's own identity. As mentioned in a previous section, the operational definition we'll be using for effective discipline is *when the teacher disciplines according to what the student needs rather than how the teacher feels.* The primary variable in determining whether effective discipline will occur or not is the teacher's stress management.

The purpose of discipline is to disrupt the disruption so that the teaching and learning can continue. In essence, the difference between discipline and counseling is that discipline focuses on the behavior and is trying to extinguish it. Counseling focuses on the intention that is generating inappropriateness, presumes the intention is positive on some level, acknowledges its positiveness, and tries to redirect it to a different, more appropriate behavioral outlet. It takes time.

To some extent, discipline focuses on a management atmosphere that is appropriate for the whole class, whereas in counseling the emphasis is on the individual. When a teacher is trying to decide whether to discipline or counsel a pupil, the most critical factor is whether he has the time.

The more effective a teacher is in preventive classroom management techniques, the more opportunities he has for counseling.

If we visit a classroom, the assigned location/seat for the most disruptive child (who we will call Willy Wiggle) often indicates the management skill level of the instructor. If Willy Wiggle is in front row center, we know two things; one, the teacher is working her tail off trying to keep Willy Wiggle (WW) on task, and two, she is successful, because otherwise, all the visuals who would have to look through Willy to see the teacher's instructions wouldn't be able to concentrate. That is why, more often than not, Willy is found in the back part of the room. Superb teachers can handle a WW I and WW II in the same room. The American classroom can't handle a WW III; it explodes in chaos.

All teaching veterans of a WW II will say that the second Willy is more than just an additional WW I. I once heard two teachers with multi-Willys in their room sharing their lunch and jovially referring to their morning experience as having as much order as a war zone. One teacher turned to the other and said, "Well, how was your bunker this morning?" Archie, the other teacher replied, "If they're so kinesthetic with their hands on everything, how come they're not sick more often and stay home?"

A rule of thumb is that you can discipline with authority but counseling is done with rapport. "As a teacher or parent, if you start by counseling, realize you don't have the time necessary and switch to discipline, the child feels emotionally sabotaged." If you initially proceed with trust and then revert to authority, the child feels forsaken.

Disciplining vs. Counseling

Discipline deals directly with behavior. Its purpose is to "disrupt the disruption" so that the teaching/learning can continue. Sometimes we use an "authoritarian" form of discipline ("Because I said so," "You will be sorry if . . .") and, at other times, we employ our rapport, using a personal, friendly or consoling look, touch or voice.

Counseling deals with the "intention" behind the behavior. The purpose of counseling is to acknowledge the student's intention as positive and redirect the intention toward an alternative behavior that is more acceptable in the classroom.

From either current or past experience, record two instances in which you have disciplined someone. Note what behavior you attempted to stop.

Disciplining 1 _____

_____

Disciplining 2 _____

_____

From either current or past experience, record two instances in which you have counseled someone. How did you mentally separate the student's behavior from the intention? How did you acknowledge the intention? How did you facilitate the person to find a more acceptable behavior to fulfill the intention?

Counseling 1 _____

_____

_____

_____

Counseling 2 _____

_____

_____

_____

Consider under what conditions you tend to use an *authoritarian* form of discipline and when you tend to use *rapport*.

If the purpose of discipline is to "disrupt the disruption" so that the teaching/learning can continue, the quicker we disrupt or intervene the better. We start to intervene at the very first sign of inappropriate student behavior.

Disciplining vs. Counseling, con't.

We also want to stop as soon as the student stops the inappropriate behavior, even if we are in midsentence. In a sense we presume that the student was unaware of his inappropriateness; as soon as he stops the behavior, we stop our intervention and continue the teaching/learning. This creates a form of amnesia. The student's image of the day will be a picture of learning as opposed to one of having been disciplined. We are living the principle, "success breeds success."

This worksheet is designed to help you record your experience practicing the skill of noticing how quickly and permanently we can "disrupt disruptions." For each day record:

a) What the student was doing;

b) Whether your intervention was primarily visual, auditory or kinesthetic;

c) What the student did that signaled you to stop;

d) How much time there was between when the student stopped and when you stopped the intervention. How could you shorten it in the future?

Day 1

a) _____

b) _____

c) _____

d) _____

Day 2

a) _____

b) _____

c) _____

d) _____

Day 3

a) _____

b) _____

c) _____

d) _____

"I am doing my best not to think about it, but by trying so hard not to think about it, I can't stop thinking about it."

> *Yankee short stop Paul Zurella, during an 0-28 start. High School valedictorian and Stanford communication graduate.*

Cleaning Up Double Messages

This book has intentionally focused more on the nonverbal aspect of communication for two reasons; (1) it makes up 82% of communication and (2), more of the pedagogical training for teachers has been successful in outlining the verbal systems of communication. (If you haven't been exposed to Instructional Theory Into Practice, put it on your shopping list of future courses.) It is somewhat of a rare exception in this book that the following segment focuses on verbal communication.

"How many times do I have to tell you not . . . ". Sound familiar? Sometimes it seems we get exactly what we are trying to get rid of. How does it happen?

Part of our mind understands the INTENT of spoken messages, and another part of the mind understands LITERALLY what is said. For example, if someone says, "Don't think of blue," what color do you think of? The INTENTION part is thinking of pink, or green, etc., while the LITERAL part is thinking of "blue." Messages with NEGATION ("stop," "don't," "quit," etc.) cause the mind to double focus instead of single focus.

The solution is to say LITERALLY what we INTEND. Because "double messages" are culturally embedded, the process of doing this takes some time, awareness, desire and patience.

Step 1: For one school week, record four messages with negations you or someone else says. Translate these into the LITERAL meaning.

Intention (what is said)   Literal (restated without negation)

Day 1
i.e., "don't talk" _____ = _____"do talk"_____

_____ = _____

_____ = _____

_____ = _____

Day 2

_____ = _____

_____ = _____

_____ = _____

Cleaning Up Double Messages, con't.

_____

Day 3

_____ = _____

_____ = _____

_____ = _____

_____ = _____

Day 4

_____ = _____

_____ = _____

_____ = _____

_____ = _____

Day 5

_____ = _____

_____ = _____

_____ = _____

_____ = _____

The first step in the process of eliminating our double messages was to take a whole week to become aware of their existence. You may want to reflect back and determine in what situations or under what conditions you tend to use them. (Some teachers report it is when they are in a parental state of mind and saying a lot of "shoulds.") The next step is to spend a week catching yourself starting to use a negation, stopping and saying instead, "What I mean to say is . . . ". Record three examples a day.

When you catch yourself starting to say the double message, use the nonverbal cues to support the verbal level.

1. Step off to the side;

2. Breathe;

3. Shift your voice;

4 Calmly say, "What I meant to say is . . . " (and complete the statement).

(#1-3 serve as a "break state.")

Cleaning Up Double Messages, con't.

Intention: "I started to say . . ."   Literal: "What I mean to say is . . ."
Day 1
i.e., *"Stop running . . . "* (step off, breathe, calm)   *"What I mean to say is walk . . ."*

_____   _____

_____   _____

_____   _____

_____   _____

Day 2

_____   _____

_____   _____

_____   _____

Day 3

_____   _____

_____   _____

_____   _____

_____   _____

Day 4

_____   _____

_____   _____

_____   _____

_____   _____

Day 5

_____   _____

_____   _____

_____   _____

_____   _____

Sentences Containing Negative and Positive Statements

Having finished two weeks of "Cleaning Up Double Messages," the obvious question is are there times when we both need and want to use negatives? Primary teachers, out of necessity, have to refer to what not to do.

For the purposes of this worksheet, a "negative" means a description of behavior the class or an individual is doing that is other than desirable and a "positive" is behavior that is desirable. The following is an array of possible sentences with commentary underneath.

1. Negative statement only. Example: THERE IS ENTIRELY TOO MUCH TALKING GOING ON.

Commentary: When we say the negative, our energy level is lower than when we say positives. To say a negative statement only drains the teacher and the students of energy and makes them remember the day as being other than pleasant. AVOID.

2. Positive followed by a negative. Example: I WANT YOU TO BE LISTENING. THERE IS ENTIRELY TOO MUCH TALKING GOING ON.

Commentary: The class will remember the last thing said more strongly than the first thing.

In the military, they have a saying, "Follow the last command first." In remembering, our last impression is often more vivid than a previous impression. If you are going to use a negative, end on a positive.

3. Negative followed by a positive. Example: THERE'S ENTIRELY TOO MUCH TALKING GOING ON. CLASS, I WANT YOU TO LISTEN.

Commentary: Mention the negative before you mention the positive when the class is unaware of the inappropriateness of the behavior. A description of it, especially if done with a neutral, nonverbal voice pattern, is very powerful and appropriate in leading them into the desired behavior.

4. Just a positive. Example: I NEED TO HAVE IT QUIETER.

Commentary: Teachers who have a relationship with a class in which they've developed a lot of responsiveness tend to favor this because it is a very positive statement.

5. Positive to more of a positive. Example: WE'RE PLAYING THE NOTES IN THE BRASS SECTION VERY WELL AND NOW LET'S DO IT EVEN BETTER BY SITTING UP STRAIGHTER AND WITH A LITTLE MORE BLOWING OUT.

Commentary: This pace (what they are doing) / lead (what you want them to do) type of statement is appropriate when you're trying to praise the class on how well they are doing and encourage them to strive for a greater goal or mastery.

Sentences Containing Negative and Positive Statements, con't.

6. Positive - negative - positive. Example: I NEED IT QUIET IN THE ROOM. THERE'S TOO MUCH TALKING GOING ON. EYES UP HERE, LISTENING.

Commentary: The advantage of doing the positive - negative - positive as opposed to the negative - positive is that it allows you to start off on a description of what you want and it also allows your energy level, initially, to be a little more positive.

The reason why the above concepts are so important is that the brain has a part of it that is literal and only understands exactly what is said. If you tell someone, "Don't worry," they have to think of "worrying" to understand what you told them not to think about. Therefore, our description of inappropriate behavior has to be done only when necessary.

The above are guidelines of when and where to use each type of sentence and their respective consequences. For this week, record examples from at least three of the above categories and describe what the situation was when you used them with a comment on whether it would have been more appropriate to have used a different form of the positive - negative pace/lead structure.

1. Category _____

Comment:

_____

_____

2. Category _____

Comment:

_____

_____

3. Category _____

Comment:

_____

_____

4. Category _____

Comment:

_____

Group Discipline

In order to separate your discipline from your learning, you need two spots; one to teach in and one to discipline in. Kinesthetic teachers who utilize the whole classroom or have taken **T**eacher **E**xpectations **S**tudent **A**chievement (TESA) training need to find one spot they are willing to avoid except when disciplining. Visual teachers are already systematically using the front of the room to teach.

The Spot: Overview

In our Education 101 courses, we learned that consistency is the key to being perceived as fair by students. Teachers who are consistent and therefore, fair, have a systematic way of separating the teaching/learning tone from the disciplinary tone. The following segment recommends that you create a spot. If having to physically move to do group discipline doesn't match your style, be eclectic enough to incorporate those aspects which fit in with your style.

Having a spot for group discipline signals to the class, as the teacher enters that spot, that discipline is about to occur. If the teacher assumes a unique facial expression, voice tone, and body posture when in the discipline spot, everyone knows that discipline is occurring. Having the spot in the room allows teacher and students to localize discipline to that spot (much like "The Worry Game," p. 139). When disciplining has ended, the instructor and class can thus return to the teaching/learning. This increases the possibility of amnesty (amnesty and amnesia have the same root word meaning "to pardon or not remember"). The participants of the class remember at the end of the day what was taught rather than what was disciplined.

How far should the discipline spot be from the teaching spot? That depends on your style, how kinesthetic the class is, and the content. A rule of thumb is that the more kinesthetic the students are (i.e., low achievers and lower grades), the greater the distance (exaggeration) between the two should be. If you have a bulletin board or location in the room where school rules are posted, make sure "that" material is at the "spot." One second grade teacher had a class of highly kinesthetic kids, and her perennial methods of discipline were not as effective as they traditionally had been. The advice given to her was, "Because kinesthetics don't hear or see well, you have to *amplify through exaggeration* so that they know that they are being disciplined. Because their concentration span is short, and they are easily distracted, what you do has to be quick and dramatic." Her commitment to being effective was such that within a week, she reported the following scenario:

A metal garbage can, spray painted black, was set in one corner of the room. Behind the can, unseen to the students, was a small pile of rocks a little bigger than a grapefruit, also spray painted black. If the collective behavior was becoming inappropriate, (remember this is group discipline), she walked over to the can, picked up a rock, held it above her head and dropped it into the trash can making a resounding "BOOM!" This signalled nonverbally that one minute of recess had been lost. At the other end of the front of the room was a colorful bulletin board on which a star was placed on a mobile hanging in front of it, indicating when they were doing well that they had either regained a minute or were getting closer to a desired reward (popcorn, extra recess, etc.).

The teacher's energy level was much higher at the end of each day, and the students had immediate feedback of a highly kinesthetic nature on how they were doing as a class.

Another teacher reported that the benefits of the amnesty/amnesia were wonderful. When she went to her spot, she realized that this was not why she selected this profession, but it was very necessary to do. She had taught herself to disassociate before arriving at the spot and was doing what the class needed her to do. The method that assisted her the most was pretending she had the leading role in the play, "The Ogre Who Lived Under the Bridge." This gave her a clear expectation of what her role was while at the spot.

Another teacher who was very skilled in assertive discipline realized that listing students' names on the board contaminated the teaching-learning spot with the discipline spot. She put a board off to the side of the chalkboard. This separated the two spots. Because she was from the Northeast region, where ice hockey was a favorite activity among her students, she wrote "penalty box" at the top of the poster board.

Mrs. Cross-Rhodes had the local high school woodshop build her a simulated stop light out of scrap lumber (she provided the electrical parts which cost about $18). The three switches at the bottom allowed her to have just a red or a green or a yellow light on. The stoplight was located away from the teaching area and showed a green light at the beginning of each day. If she walked towards that spot, the students knew she would be switching it to one of the other colors and were well aware of the consequences and they responded appropriately.

The last example is representative of all the ones given above. In order to be perceived as consistent and fair, we must consider the nonverbal aspect of the discipline system. The next time you hear yourself start a harangue with, "How many times have I . . .", consider how you can represent what you say *nonverbally* - after all, it is 82% of your communication.

The Spot: Transition

Now that you have two spots, one for teaching one for discipline, there has to be a transition from one to the other. At intersections, our traffic patterns would be chaotic and unpredictable if we only had a green light and a red light. The yellow light is needed in traffic; so too it is needed in the classroom. Classrooms where teachers do not have a yellow light are like volcanoes which erupt without warning from the seismographs. On some level, the students are on edge.

Mrs. Cross-Rhodes never goes from green light to red light. From green light, she switches to yellow light and gives the class the opportunity to correct themselves or know they've been warned. Some teachers use a laminated poster board which is used for listing names of students who behave inappropriately. If it is always present, there is a constant reminder of negative and failure.

One teacher has a giant pen spray painted an odd fluorescent color that is kept hidden in the discipline corner. If the class is acting inappropriately, she walks to the spot, exposes the pen, returns to the teaching spot, and continues in her regular calm and friendly manner. She has emotionally used the fluorescent pen as a yellow light to let everyone know that they are in jeopardy.

One high school teacher used a barometer to indicate what mood she perceived herself to be in. At the far end of the scale was the category "Don't ask." It was on very rare occasions that the pointer pointed to that category, but the students knew they were taking chances if they pushed or tested her that day.

A fifth grade teacher had a puppet, Hildebroom, who was the class ombudsman. If the teacher was going to the spot and the class didn't notice, the teacher switched to her Hildebroom voice and announced, "Look out, look out! She's coming!" Likewise, if she was writing on the board and the students were copying, and she realized she wasn't quite up to snuff that day, Hildebroom announced, "She seems a little crabby today, but we know she's trying her best."

Your relationship with the students and the grade level greatly influence your use of the spot and the transition/yellow light to it. At a retirement dinner, I heard a very wise educator describe the difference between teaching fourth grade and below and sixth grade through ninth grade. To the former category, a teacher could say, "Class, I have a slight headache today. I'm wondering if we could just quietly work in our seats." If the teacher has a lot of rapport, the empathy is such that there will be twenty-two little headaches within half an hour. For the latter group, saying, "Class, I have a slight headache" is likely to result in one student in the back of the room whispering to another, "She only thinks she has a headache. It'll be a doozer before we're finished." It's obvious that the use of a vulnerable style of yellow light has to be tempered by many variables.

The point remains, however, that we must have a yellow light/transition when going from teaching to discipline. As transparent as our moods may seem to ourselves, the students still need visual cue(s).

The Spot: Once There

The spot, in and of itself, does not guarantee that the class will know that discipline is about to occur or is occurring. *Location* is but one of four variables that signal nonverbally that discipline is occurring; *facial expressions, voice patterns, body posture (and props)* are other factors which compose the 82%. Therefore, the greater the difference between how you look, sound, and move when in the spot compared with the teaching area, the greater the effectiveness. In the worksheet, "Group Discipline Spot," it is recommended you practice those distinctions.

The Spot: Initially

After practicing the spot with a colleague after school, you're ready to initiate it. This is done best after a natural break (i.e., vacation, three day weekends, etc.) and when the class is in a left brain mood. Whether you want the class to be conscious of the purpose and location is a stylistic decision. It is preferable that during your initial use of the spot, a metaphor/vignette is used (refer to the two examples under "Anchoring with Metaphor," Love One Another and Shut Your Trap).

The Spot: Reaccessing

The section on "Anchoring" includes an explanation of how the reaccessing of a mental state is delineated. If you have effectively established the spot, repeated uses of it allow you to reaccess the class compliance by performing the identical facial, voice and body postures.

One of the most important advantages of having a spot (as opposed to doing group discipline anywhere in the room) is that the spot is an anchor for you to be disassociated and watch the students. When you get the compliance, you will

know when to stop; however, if you do the discipline in a variety of places in the room, it is harder for you to be disassociated and consequently not notice when you have elicited the desired behavior and should stop. If you say more than three or four sentences, you may have triggered an auditory cassette tape in yourself, and you may become associated instead of watching the results you are achieving.

For practice, try doing your disciplinary spiel. When you get the shift you want, stop in the middle of a syllable and leave the rest unspoken. This is one of the finest ways to verify for yourself that the nonverbal aspects are more powerful than the verbal.

On the primary level, we have experimented with putting masking tape on the spot, and much to our delight, after two uses of it, the students monitored the teacher's use of it. There were reports from second to fourth grades, that if the teacher had any kind of a scowl on her face and was not at the spot, the external auditory kids would interrupt the instructor by saying, "Teacher, teacher, you have to be over there to raise your voice."

The Spot: Indelible Memory

The next two items are the two most important variables in the use of the spot. One of the purposes of the spot is to make a lasting impression so that the spot is used less often. When you are finished using the spot, freeze your body posture and your facial expressions. Most teachers find it helpful to lock their jaw and scan the room with a look the students will remember. The axiom is it's okay to make an indelible impression, but it is emotionally unfair to "hunt field mice with an elephant gun." The question of how long to hold the stare/frozen body is based on the length of their concentration span. With third graders, counting "1001" is about the right amount of time. With high school students, you can almost go up to "1001, 1002, 1003."

A comedian once told me that the secret of timing is to start the next line when the second wave of people stop laughing. The next time you're in a group setting in which you are not responsible for the behavior and conduct, notice that there are waves of movement which end a silence or indicate a shift from one mental state to another. This is as true for groups in the hundreds as it is for a classroom. At the beginning of the second wave, the person conducting can still hold the group, but if the second wave is completed and the third wave has started, the presenter loses the "leading edge." Do this sophisticated observation of waves intuitively throughout the day in settings that do not involve discipline.

Mr. B. Marker was establishing a daily routine of silent reading for everyone, including himself. He sat at his desk on the first day pretending to read but was actually peripherally watching his class. As the second wave of restlessness started at minute four, he quietly announced to the class that they could take a social break of one minute. The visual students' tolerance level was greater than four minutes and they were disturbed by the announcement. His purpose was to get in synch with the non-visuals. On day 2, 3,

and 4, he again took his cues from the class; at the start of the second wave, he would announce the social break. Sometime during the second week, the class was conditioned to thinking that the teacher was determining their concentration. He had paced well enough to now lead them. He delayed making the announcement longer each day. Within three weeks, their concentration span was more than ten minutes.

The Spot: Transition Back to the Teaching Area

We know that the body and mind are interrelated and affect each other greatly. Breathing is one of the strongest physiological elements which influences the mind. This is the second most important variable in the use of the spot. After scanning the room, make sure you simultaneously relax the eyes, the body, the jaw and breathe as you break that statue/ posture. Practice breaking the frozen state and breathing after school with a colleague. If you are coaching a colleague, be fastidious in terms of the timing. As the colleague moves away from the spot (remembering "The Ogre Who Lives Under the Bridge"), have her take a second breath before reentering her teaching area. Why? When the teacher holds her breath as she scans the room, the class also holds their breath. By timing it right (start with the second wave), as the teacher takes a breath and simultaneously relaxes her body and starts to move off of the discipline spot, the class will breathe too. This has a powerful effect; everyone is in unison and the amnesty part is more collectively received.

The younger the child, the more he is like those super concentrated balls you can bounce off walls. Kids rebound very quickly and very well from clean, well-sorted, systematic discipline. Adults are more like bowling balls. If we explode, either at an individual pupil or the class, and are associated at the time, it is as if we have the bowling ball shackled to our ankle. We didn't enter our profession to be disciplinarians so we want to disassociate and be an actor when we have to do discipline. Once in a while when visiting a classroom, the following scenario occurs and reinforces the necessity to be disassociated when disciplining.

Violet Mudd is not the happiest of people, but she's trying her best. She's working with student A and three other students have raised their hands, waiting their turn for assistance. Willy Wiggle has just outdone himself in inappropriate behavior. As the teacher barks a retort in Willy's direction, the three kids who are awaiting assistance put their hands down because they instinctively know that Miss Mudd just locked herself on to a bowling ball and no one wants to be around her contaminated state.

The Spot: Styles

The spot can be used in a variety of ways, because what the class needs changes with each situation. To presume that anger and harangues are the only forms in which discipline occurs is a very narrow perspective of the use of the spot. Disappointment, embarrassment, etc. are certainly aspects of the possible emotions which can be displayed. For example, one teacher who had a highly motivated class used the spot by going to it and sheepishly and shyly looking at the class and saying, "My wife was asking me how we're doing on our new unit." There was a long pregnant pause and then the phrase, "I told her we had a lot of potential."

"No one presses our buttons - we expose our panel." Sean Rogers

My Group Discipline Spot

1. Description of the spot.

2. Description of how far it is from my regular teaching area.

3. When I cross the outside perimeter of my teaching area towards my discipline spot, how do the students know that we are in yellow light?

4. When I'm at the spot, a description of how my face, body posture and voice are different from my teaching nonverbals is:

5. When I originally established this spot, it was advised that I do it through a metaphor or vignette. My metaphor/vignette is:

6. Having once established the power of the spot, the purpose of using it afterwards is to reaccess nonverbally the students' strong memory of the initial experience. A rule of thumb is that if I use more than three or four lines to reaccess their memory, I'm diluting the strength of the nonverbal cues. My description of how I reaccessed that spot is (certain look/body posture, 1 - 4 sentences, etc.):

7. To create an indelible mark in their memory, at the end of my time in the spot, I will freeze my face, body posture, and slowly scan the room.

8. As I finish that scan, I will simultaneously breathe, break the frozen body/state and move back towards the teaching arena (this important maneuver should be practiced with a colleague in an empty room. It is the key to the amnesia/pardon).

9. As I move to the teaching area, I've taken at least two breaths and returned to my teaching face, voice and body posture. (Describe the results on a separate piece of paper.)

"Other than Group Discipline"

The concept of being disassociated and breathing applies to one-on-one discipline as much as to group discipline. In the scenario with Violet Mudd, it is not the barking at Willy that bothers the rest of the class. By Halloween, every classroom knows their Willys. Teachers who use a voice pattern that unconsciously cues the class that what is being said only pertains to Willy will still maintain group comfort and those students will keep their hands raised (the teacher is saying, in effect, "The rest of you are fine; I, the teacher, am fine; I love Willy and Willy just needed me to do this."). Two characteristics these teachers have are that they are disassociated when they're doing the discipline and they breathe and break their physiology at the end of it.

A teacher is at the kidney shaped reading table at the back of the room. The students with her are doing fine. One or more students in the rest of the class need to be put back on task. The teacher freezes the group with her by touching a student on either side of her in a calm way, saying in a very relaxed way, "You're doing fine; just a minute." She corrects the student(s) at large, takes a deep breath, breaks her physiology, looks back at the students near her with her face relaxed, releases her touch on either side of those students, and they resume reading.

Vacuum Points

If you watch an individual student acting inappropriately (remember the kinesthetic is very capable of self entertainment), he will go through a variety of movements with little glitches or pauses every 5 - 30 seconds. During those glitches, there's a vacuum in his thinking. If you intervene at the vacuum point, he is very susceptible to being led (those who are certified in NLP know this maneuver as "pattern interruption"). The intervention can be through looks (visual), noise (auditory) or touch (kinesthetic). The auditory and kinesthetic are the more common modes used to interrupt inappropriate behavior. Since the purpose of discipline is to disrupt the disruption so that learning can continue, vacuum points are the premium opportunity.

Because this technique is based so much on perception, formal training is highly recommended. The following is a second substitute:

Round 1: Have a colleague sit in a student's chair and act like Willy Wiggle or his female counterpart, Wandering Wanda. Every time you see Willy or Wanda have any kind of a pause/glitch, raise your left hand indicating you've seen the vacuum point. Do this for 1 1/2 minutes. Stop and debrief if the colleague playing the student can feel the vacuum points inside.

Round 2: If you start to intervene when you see the vacuum, it will have already gone by by the time you intervene. So this round, practice anticipating when the vacuum point will occur. Now do Round 1 again and allow your left hand to raise when the vacuum point occurs as it did the first time. As you gain a sense of Willy and Wanda's pattern, raise your right hand just before the left hand goes up. Your right hand is the anticipation, the left hand is the vacuum point.

Round 3: In this round, intentionally intervene at the vacuum point (remember you have to start as you anticipate it when your right hand was raised) with something overt such as a quick touch to the shoulder or saying the person's name in a raised voice, etc. or be covert (sneeze, drop a book, etc.). Do this over a two minute period. You know you're effective when your colleague, role playing the student, has a hard time getting back into the inappropriate behavior; hence, the name, "pattern interruption."

Round 4: Do the same interventions as before but at times other than the vacuum points. Debrief with your colleague and share which round, 3 or 4, had more of an impact in interrupting the pattern.

There are three corollaries about the body - mind relationship which help emphasize the importance of intervening at the vacuum point.

A) Every mental set is represented and maintained by a certain physiology. The next time you're angry, go stand on your head and see if you can maintain your vehemence.

B) The longer one is in a certain physiology, the deeper the mental set becomes. That's why habitual muscle memory movements reactivate mental states associated with the physiology.

C) The sooner one intervenes with another's physiology, the easier it is to interrupt the mental state.

The next time you see a student acting inappropriately, take 30 seconds to watch the pattern or rhythm and then intervene as soon as possible at the vacuum point. By the way, this can be done when you're greeting the students at the start of the class.

Summary

Personally, I was absent an average of four to five days a year, but only "sick" one or two. I respectfully considered my contract to read "ten *wellness* days a year."

There is an annual award given to "someone of influence." An organization picks someone prominent and then asks them who influenced them the most; the person named receives the award. Several years ago, Jesse Jackson was chosen for this award and named a teacher. Teachers often receive this award, and that makes us proud.

And we have to take care of ourselves. Madeline Hunter said that elementary teachers make 5,000 decisions a day.* They are small but many in number. We cannot give what we don't have. Be WISE. Love Yourself.

---

* Stated during an inservice at Canby School Districts, February, 1989, Canby, Oregon.

Chapter 8

Nonverbal Communications

*". . . 82% of teacher messages are nonverbal."**

Anchors

Research published by the National Education Association indicates:

"The process of education is determined by the process of communication.

"Communication, the major ingredient of education, is composed of two dimensions - verbal and nonverbal (defined as communication without words).

"Humans use nonverbal communication for the following reasons:

1. Words have limitations.

2. Nonverbal signals are powerful.

3. Nonverbal messages are likely to be more genuine.

4. Nonverbal signals can express feelings too disturbing to state.

5. A separate communication channel is necessary to help send complex messages.

"Gestures, body movements and the like are tools we have devel-oped because words were not as effective.

"If there is incongruity between the verbal and the nonverbal, the non-verbal will win hands down.

"It has been contended that 82% of teacher messages are nonverbal.

"Recent evidence from clinical and neurosurgical research indicates that the left hemisphere of the brain is involved primarily in verbal and other analytical functions, while the right hemisphere is responsible for spatial and nonverbal processes."*

Nonverbal Communication: Anchoring

When a teacher consistently uses certain nonverbals with a concept or idea, then the nonverbals and the concept are associated.

One of the major goals of "NLP in Education" is to show instructors how to become more systematic in their behavior. When a teacher's behavior is systematic, the students know, based on the teacher's behavior, what mental

* All quotes on this page are excerpts taken from "Nonverbal Communication" by Patrick Miller (one in the series, *What Research Says to the Teacher,* Washington D.C.: National Education Assocation, 1981), pgs. 4-7. Reprinted with permission.

state to access. In other words, the instructor can reaccess a mental state he has previously created in the students instead of having to create it time and again. This saves the time and energy often involved in doing what Madeline Hunter calls "creating the ANTICIPATORY STATE." For example, if the teacher does the same activity in the same location with the same voice and body posture, the students automatically reaccess the appropriate mental state.

When the association between the teacher's nonverbals and the concept/idea are well established, the association is said to be "anchored."

The study and utilization of anchors is the quickest and most powerful way of understanding nonverbal communication.

Natural Anchors

In one sense, NLP hasn't invented anything new as much as it has discovered patterns of effective communication and of identifying ways of transferring those patterns from people who have them to those who want them. Our world is full of natural anchors; they come in the form of Visual, Auditory and Kinesthetic and any combination of these. Examples abound, from hearing a fire engine to seeing a flashing red light in our rear- view mirror to thinking of an upcoming dental appointment. It isn't a question of whether examples exist or not; they do in every teacher's classroom. The question is whether they are used with purpose and consistency. Any teaching behavior that receives consistent responses from the class is an anchor.

Recognizing Natural Anchors

Natural anchors are those already inside people. The question is which ones we want to avoid (negative anchors) and which ones we want to utilize (positive anchors). Some of those situations in which the natural anchors are present are as follows:

Conferences

One of the purposes of having conferences with the parents of students with whom you want to improve your relationship is to learn what nonverbal anchors are used by parents and which are and are not effective. For example, Mr. James Middle School is having a conference with Sally's parents. James has asked Sally to be present in order to watch how the parents and Sally interact. When the parents and Sally get into some "garbage," James notices that Sally closes her Mom off when her mother becomes anxious and talks faster. On the contrary, Sally does listen better to her Dad when he is anxious but is talking slowly. James memorizes how Dad speaks (his pace, pauses and volume). In the future, when Sally begins to close James off, James will switch to Dad's style of talking and avoid Mom's style.

Previous Teacher's Anchors

During his first year as a self-contained middle school teacher, Mr. Jones becomes aware that four students do not respond when he goes into his emotional harangue location for discipline (see "Decontaminating the Classroom," p. 182). In thinking about it, he realizes these four students all had the same teacher the previous year. During his prep period for the next week, he makes a point of passing by that teacher's classroom. He discovers the teacher averages two emotional outbursts per period. In order to survive, the students have learned to be numb to loud, emotional outbursts from male teachers. When Mr. Jones switches to a much quieter emotional harangue, the whole class responds appropriately.

Mrs. Pri Mary transfers to a new building. The whole school has been inserviced over a two-year period on a particular approach to instructional teaching. Although all teachers use the same verbal commands such as "May I have your attention, please," some teachers are more effective than others because they are more consistent with their accompanying nonverbals. Mary knows one-half of her class had a teacher who was inconsistent in her nonverbals. She watches this teacher asking for the class' attention while she is moving around the room. She realizes that 18% of this teacher's message was communicating, "May I have your attention?" The other 82% of her message was communicating, "Keep moving." Mary presumes that if she physically stands still and says anything other than, "May I have your attention?" (i.c., "Class, eyes up here"), she will get the response from the students that she desires.

Utilizing Previous Anchors

Linking Anchors

I began my teaching career at a school that was a pilot study for implementing Carl Roger's non-directive therapy approach as it applied to education. Through this experience, I developed a lot of interactive techniques for class-room participation. When I moved to a new school district, I found the students inattentive when I did any classroom discussion but very attentive when copying teacher's notes from the board. If they began to wander while I was doing a discussion, I would go to the board and write something they interpreted "having to copy." Once I had their attention again, I would stop and go back to the class dialogue. In effect, I transferred them from their conditioned state to my desired state.

What are some natural anchors in your school environment which will allow you to do likewise?

Sorting Anchors

Vern is a high school counselor who covered for the principal and the vice principal in their absence. Therefore, the students he sometimes had to discipine while acting as V.P. were the same ones with whom he counseled. It became obvious to Vern that after undergoing a disciplining encounter with him, the students were reluctant to share with him as a counselor. Realizing the different outcomes between his position as a counselor and that as a V.P., he used this approach. Whenever he was called upon to act as V.P., he saw the student in the V.P.'s office rather than his own. To distinguish the difference between himself as the counselor and the V.P. on the unconscious level, he took on the mannerisms of the V.P. (voice, proverbial finger, and put on a clip-on tie, etc.).

When are there situations at your school where you take on functions that are not your primary responsibilities? How can you sort, as Vern did, the anchors associated with your primary task from those "fill-in" responsibilities?

Transferring Anchors

Scheduled to be at a conference, I had arranged to have a substitute for a week. I selected the person with mannerisms similar to mine. During the two months before the conference, when he was substituting at our school, we would meet for a few minutes to rehearse my mannerisms and locations for different activities (see worksheet on "Decontaminating the Classroom," p. 182). During his week as substitute, he mimicked well enough to receive the ultimate compliment. The students said, "Oh, you're acting just like Mr. G."

Whenever I cover a teacher's class, especially if the teacher is effective and I'm not well known, I act like the teacher for the first twenty minutes or so. By successfully mimicking another teacher in front of the students who have a good relationship with him, that teacher's credibility and rapport are transferred to me.

When students take specialist courses at my school, such as P.E., Music or Shop, I often walk with the class to the specialist's room for the first several days of the semester. During the following week, I spontaneously "pop in and out" of that class. This transfers my relationship with my class to the specialist. This is especially true if I act like the specialist during the ten minutes before the students leave my room.

Recognizing Anchors

With which other educators do you share your students? _____

Which situations would be appropriate to "link anchors," which to "sort anchors" and which to "transfer anchors"?

_____

_____

What have you gathered from parent conferences and phone calls about the student's "home anchors"?

_____

_____

What are some anchors that are unique to your school (logo, etc.) and how can they be better utilized?

_____

_____

As you reflect on the above, keep in mind the three ingredients that determine the strength of an anchor:
1. Uniqueness;
2. Anchoring at the highest peak of the experience;
3. Exactness of reproduction/duplication.

Right Brain Days

When Routine Anchors are Broken

We're all creatures of habit. There are times in the school year when we are very predictable because normal routines and behaviors are being observed. There are other times during the year when the routine and the anchors associated with them are broken, and the normal avenues of classroom management are diluted (i.e., week before Christmas, week before Spring Break, end of the year, drastic changes in the weather, picture day, homecoming, etc.).

The following section will explain when these two periods occur, how they are connected with the hemispheres of the brain and how to utilize them.

When normal routines are broken, students will shift to using their right brain more. There are specific teaching methods which can transform these "right brain days" into golden opportunities for integrated learning. The teacher can increase or decrease certain teaching styles, as illustrated in the chart below.

The primary level can continue to use the same anchors for classroom management without too much tarnishing, while at the secondary level, teachers often suspend their use of anchors during this time period in order to preserve the effectiveness of the anchor. They pace and lead the students, taking their cues from the mood of the class.

Primary

Mary has taught second grade for fifteen years. She has maintained all the enthusiasm of a rookie or a buck private. Her colleagues have affectionately nicknamed her Private Mary and shortened it to PriMary.

At the beginning of the year, Mary took time to establish a routine for leaving and returning from recess. The students have been trained to be silent once they enter the door from the playground. It's Halloween, and she knows the students are really excited about trick-or-treating that night. Mary knows she has some choices. She can increase her authority by standing at the door, verbally and nonverbally reminding the students to be silent (her finger over her mouth

On Right Brain Days	
Decrease	Increase
reliance on teacher	group dynamics (interactiveness)
teacher lecture	manipulatives
new material	review
reliance on authority	reliance on rapport
critical thinking	creative thought

forming a silent, "shhh"), or she can have students exit out of a door further away, thus preserving the anchor of the regular door.

Junior High/Middle School

Mr. Jr. High History teacher (J.R.) always takes roll from a certain location in the room and begins his lesson from his lectern. Because of his enthusiasm and instructional ability, his students are very attentive. Around the week before Christmas, he realizes the students aren't responding in their usual way. If he continues, he runs the risk of contaminating those anchors. He switches to a new location, expects to cover less content, emphasizes material from the last two chapters he has covered, and creates a review unit.

To make the review unit far more interesting, he plans an academic Bingo game for Wednesday of the last week. Using their books, the students brainstorm at least thirty-five concepts which have been covered over the last two chapters. The teacher lists the concepts on the board. Blank Bingo sheets are distributed. The students fill in their Bingo sheet by selecting 25 of the 35 concepts listed on the board. The teacher asks either a matching, fill-in or a definition of one of the items on the board for column B. If the student has that item, the student puts a small "x" in the corner of the square. If J.R. wants to do a short review, he'll play Bingo. If he wants more in-depth reinforcement, he'll play Blackout (all squares are "x"ed).

High School

Miss H.S. Lit (High School Literature teacher) has a regular routine: Monday is for doing vo-cabulary and an overview of this week's story, Tuesday is silent reading in class, Wednesday is a written review, Thursday, an oral discussion on plot, character and setting and on Friday, a major test. Yesterday was Wednesday and school was closed due to bad weather, and there was a two-hour delay in starting this morning. She anticipates the students to be "different" because of this change in routine. She intentionally starts the lesson in the usual way and is getting the lack of response she expects. Within three minutes, she purposely drops the book in exasperation, steps away from the board area and says, "Class, I hope you don't mind, I'd rather do something different today" (pace). Noticing the students shift to a surprised mental state, she suggests an alternative to their normal procedure; "In place of taking the test on Friday, those students who want an 'A' for this week have the option of role playing the different characters in the story; those who want a 'B' will . . .".

Commentary

In the above examples, the educators were aware of the change in the students' mental state from left brain to right brain. PriMary's choice is of particular interest because if she chooses the normal door to leave/re-enter, she will decrease the appropriate mental state. If her lesson calls for utilization of right brain activities, it would be more effective to use the further door.

On a day with regular routines (left brain days), Miss Lit may not have had any volunteers for her creative alternative plan but very likely will on this particular day. Notice how the activity is "right brain."

It is very common to hear instructors in the lunch room bemoaning the fact that they can't get a new, creative idea from their students. At other times of the year, these same instructors are heard saying, "They're not listening. I've told them, but they're just not listening." In the first case, the students are in their left brain and the teacher wants them in their right brain. In the latter case, the reverse is true; the teacher wants them in their left brain and the students are in their right brain. The days when routine is broken offer wonderful opportunities for creative expression and experiences; take advantage of them. The following form will assist you in identifying and utilizing these times.

Relocating Activities

1. Which days/time of the year are routines naturally broken?

2. Which activities do you currently use which require a lot of right brain ability and to which the students are not as receptive as you would like? How would you move these activities into one of the above time slots?

3. Look at the "Increase/Decrease" chart on p. 169 and select those items which pertain to your subject and grade level. List them here.

4. Briefly outline your plan:

Teaching Left to Right vs. Right to Left

In our traditional methodology courses in college, there is a tendency for educators to be trained in teaching left to right with the left symbolized by teaching part, part, part and the right symbolized by whole. Phonics is an example of left to right where you have the student break the word into smaller chunks called syllables: as you learn those, you end up learning the whole word. That approach is quite appropriate for the average and advanced readers. For the remedial or slow readers the opposite is true. They need the whole before the part. For example, in a literature class for the average and high learners, the teacher can read (part) for 2 - 5 minutes and intersperse an oral commentary on a concept and summarize (whole) one-third of the time. With the low readers, the opposite is true; you spend two-thirds of your time acting out and explaining the overall picture (whole) and one-third of your time actually doing the reading (the parts). When showing a filmstrip or a movie, the lower students need to see the film at the beginning of a unit because it gives them an overall idea of what the unit is about, whereas the advanced students have a choice as to when to see it. The advantage of showing the movie afterward is that the latter group gets to use their own visualization and create their own picture of what they believe they have been reading about.

For this coming week, list an example of teaching a piece of content, either from left to right or right to left and explain how you would have done it the opposite way. Mention what type of audience would be appropriate for each method and what the reaction might be from each if you try this approach with them.

_____

_____

_____

_____

_____

_____

_____

_____

Setting Up for "The Week Before"

We know that the week before any break such as Christmas, Spring Break, summer and, to a lesser extent, Thanksgiving, the students switch to the right side of their brains and have certain right brain capacities in a greater abundance than normal and have other left brain capacities less than normal. How we set up and utilize these capacities is the focus of this paper.

Let's use the two week time period before Spring Break as typical of the above. During that week, the students will have high energy levels, be very creative and spontaneous, and their brains integrate very well because they see more associations. These are the positive attributes. The negative characteristics are distractibility, lack of internal focus control, inability to take in auditory information (lecture) or new information well, and a decrease of respectful responsiveness to authority. Let's say that during the two weeks before Spring Break you were planning to cover three major concepts and reinforce each of those. Our traditional pattern is to teach the 1st concept (T.1st c), reinforce (R.1st c), go to the second concept and teach (T.2nd c), then reinforce (R.2nd c) and likewise teach and reinforce the third concept (T. 3rd c and R. 3rd c).

M	T	W	Th	F	M	T	W	Th	F	M	F
T.1stc.	R.1stc.	T2ndc.		R.2ndc.		T3rdc.		R3rdc.		Spg. Brk.	

The suggestion is to try, as much as possible, to <u>teach</u> the three concepts the two weeks before and then <u>reinforce</u> all three during the week before. In essence, the last week is a "review project."

M	T	W	Th	F	M	T	W	Th	F	M	F
T.1st,	2nd,	3rdc.			R.1st,		2nd,	3rdc.		Spg. Brk.	

Because of the nature of the brain at this time, it's best if we can give more than one interdisciplinary grade for the project. The more we can give interdisciplinary grades for the "week before project," the better. For instance, giving an English grade for a science report is interdisciplinary. Assigning an artistic drawing or graphic symbol on the cover of a history report allows a grade both for art and social studies. Integrative, reinforcement, simulations, roleplay and working in groups (3rd grade through college) are all activities that go extremely well with "the week before." This "cooperative learning" is always beneficial but godsent on right brain weeks.*

Cautions: First, all information concepts have to be visually available (can be found in text/handouts, etc.). Otherwise you spend your time orally reminding them of what you <u>told</u> them the week before. Second, it is important to establish whatever group processes they will be utilizing the week before during the second week before. Form the groups, set down the rules and do a dry run because they are more co-operative with authority and follow directions better two weeks before. Thus you have the rules in place for the week before. Third, make sure if you are using group process, that there is a grade given for "use of time" and that grade is given on a daily basis. Make sure it is posted and given to the students either visually or orally.

* An excellent $5 kit is "Student Team Learning," Center for Social Organization for Schools, 3505 N. Charles, Baltimore, MD 21218, and also David Johnson, Roger Holubec, and Edythe Johnson's *Cooperation in the Classroom* (Edina, Minn.: Interaction Book Co., 1988).

Setting Up for "The Week Before," con't.

1. List the three to four major concepts that you would normally teach during that two week span.

	Teaching	Reinforcing
1st c.	_____	_____
2nd c.	_____	_____
3rd c.	_____	_____

2. Rearrange where you would teach them and where you would reinforce them, using the calendar below. An example for the primary level is "Easter Bunnies." Usually during the last week, the teacher has the class follow some pretty complicated folding and cutting directions (T. 1st c.) and then coloring (R. 1st c). Using the above suggestions, the class does the folding and cutting (T. 1st c.) two weeks before Spring Break while they are still able to listen and follow directions (left brain). Then the bunnies are set aside because they can color the "week before" (R.1st c.) (more right brain).

M	T	W	Th	F	M	T	W	Th	F

3. Describe how you plan to use interdisciplinary activities and utilize multigrades. Make sure you have a checklist of steps involved and due dates with a place for your signature to confirm progress. Remember the students are not hearing/listening well (auditory) and therefore teachers have to be particularly visual and precise.

_____

_____

_____

4. Indicate how you are going to establish groups and how you would give daily feedback for "use of time," etc.

_____

_____

_____

_____

Seasonal Energy Management

As mentioned earlier, teachers are seasonal workers who don't migrate. We have peaks and valleys in terms of energy. One of the purposes of having been in a profession for a certain length of time is that, hopefully, it gives us an overview of knowing what is going to come before it comes. Conversely, when trying new things, we have to give ourselves grace because there are things that we find only after experiencing them.

Make a chart of your season. For example, chart September through Christmas, January through Spring Break and from Spring Break to June. Chart when you think your high and low levels are. Most teachers experience right brain days as requiring more energy than the usual left brain days. The left brain days are more routine in nature and therefore many decisions can be made automatically. Comparatively, the right brain days are different; the class is more "off the wall." And while there are many educational advantages (see "Setting Up for the Week Before"), the teacher's mental state has to be superb. Backtrack before the right brain days occur so that you can mark your planning book and prepare for it.

Keep in mind that medical research indicates that there are some things that will maintain our energy level and things that will increase it. To maintain our energy level, eat appropriate foods and get enough sleep, etc. The only thing that will actually increase our energy level is to exercise. On right brain days, the students' behaviors and activities are vastly different from normal, left brain days. As a result, the teacher often experiences stress and exhaustion from the energy used/confusion of having to cope with such different behaviors. Dreaming assists in the integration of the behavior differences and helps the teacher to recover from a day of coping. One middle school level teacher used the following axiom, "When tired on left brain days, force yourself to exercise; when tired on right brain days, it is okay to nap."

The program has to be initiated at least two weeks before "the week before."

1. Identify right brain days:

_____

_____

2. Plan beginning two weeks before:

A. Food

_____

B. Sleep

_____

C. Activities from "Giving Yourself Love"

_____

D. Exercise

_____

Right Brain Days: Management

On right brain days, students are different than on the traditional left brain days. On those days, how can we be effective and respectful of both ourselves and the students?

We work hard during the year to set up our normal procedures and routines for management. When the right brain days or weeks come, we need to suspend the left brain techniques and switch to something else to preserve the left brain traditions we've established. When the left brain days return, those techniques are intact, and the students automatically go back to those traditions.

First Rule: Preserve routines by setting them aside

Second Rule: Change to different nonverbals

If we don't preserve them, we will tend to force them and contaminate them with a lot of emotional and disciplinary overtones. They won't be as effective then or when the left brain days return.

In order to have students understand unconsciously what is occurring, make sure you change as many of the nonverbals as possible. For instance, if you normally wear a tie, you may want to go without it; if you normally wear a dress, you may want to wear slacks. Since the front board area is normally where most teachers teach, associate this in your mind with the left brain way of managing and therefore on right brain days, use a butcher paper flipchart and teach with them on a side wall. Operate from a side of the room. In fact, you may want to strongly consider having all of the desks turned in that direction. The rule of thumb is that the greater the nonverbal distinctions between left brain and right brain days, the more you preserve the left brain management.

1. Describe your location and normal procedures for your left brain management.

_____

_____

_____

2. Describe how you would change the nonverbals for the right brain day management.

_____

_____

_____

Rule of thumb: while the left brain responds to authority and routine, the right brain responds to rapport and newness . . . do a lot of "pacing and leading."

Surprise Days

So far we have identified consecutive right brain days. We also can predict which single days are right brain days: Homecoming, picture day, Halloween, the first snowfall, etc. A right brain day may "sneak up" spontaneously, however. What's a teacher to do?

A. First, we have to ascertain if it is actually a right brain day (or even a right brain afternoon). One teacher's method of verification is as follows. As soon as the class members have seemed different for at least an hour, the teacher goes out into the hall to listen to the voices coming from the different rooms. If the voices are different (i.e., louder volume, frustrated teachers' voices, etc.), she knows it isn't just her class but actually a right brain day. Many believe that drastic changes in the barometer can tilt people's moods toward the right side of the brain.

B. Secondly, we have to consider how to change the format (use the "Decreasing-Increasing Chart," p. 169). Usually we must have a good grasp of the content in order to change the process. ("Scales of Learning," p. 106.)

C. Third, use the rule of thumb, "Preserve routines by setting them aside and change nonverbals." By doing the ABC's of Surprise Days, we show our insight and flexibility.

A. Describe at least two ways you can verify if a day may have switched the class members to their right brain.

_____

_____

B. Think of a typical lesson and describe how you normally teach it:

_____

_____

_____

How would you change it? (Use the Increase-Decrease chart on p. 169.)

_____

_____

_____

C. Management: This is the item that we want to have well rehearsed so we can immediately change it to "Preserve . . . Change." (See Right Brain Days: Management, p. 176.) Outline your plan.

_____

_____

_____

Anchoring With Metaphors

When an anchor is established under the guise of a metaphor, the lodging of the mental state is on both sides of the brain.   Three examples of this concept follow.

Disciplining Metaphor: "Love One Another"

Having taught high school for eleven years, I was shocked during my first two years of teaching self-contained eighth grade by what turned out to be the "normal" amount of adolescent insensitivity toward one another. While I knew that much of their behavior was outside their range of awareness, I pondered how I could make my classroom a more humane setting. I remembered from my own experience as a teenager that what I needed and wanted most was a safe atmosphere.

One Friday afternoon in September after the students had left, I knew the honeymoon would end sometime during the first two weeks of October. Our permanent relationship for the year would begin to emerge. In surveying my classroom, I picked a location farthest from my normal teaching spot (see "Decontaminating the Classroom," p. 182). It happened to be near a window that had a table with house plants on it. For the next few weeks, I avoided going anywhere near that area.

I waited for the day when the students' insensitivity was particularly strong. I walked over, put a chair in front of the table and steadied the chair while looking up at the light fixture on the ceiling. Since this was unusual behavior, half of the students were confused and, thus, attentive to what I was doing. I proceeded to step up on the chair and then on top of the table and stood under the ceiling light. A hush had come over the classroom as all eyes were riveted on this unusual sight. In a quiet voice, almost a whisper, I began, "Historically, people would gather around the street light after dinner to listen to and talk with people. There are two types of people who often drew large gatherings: politicians and preachers. In order for everyone to see these speakers, someone in the crowd would run into a nearby house and find a box strong enough for the speaker to stand on. (Hence, the term "soapbox.") The preacher would tell the people what they needed to do in life and how they should act towards each other. He would raise his voice, shake his finger at the people while his face would get red as he emphasized, 'People need to love each other, to be kind . . .'". I then mentioned all the behaviors I expected of them (because of how vulnerably receptive they were at that time, all messages had to be single and positive - see "Cleaning up Double Messages," p. 150).

The class was in temporary shock, stunned by the unusual behavior. As I finished, I looked around the room with my body frozen as I silently counted, "1001, 1002, 1003." Stepping from the table to the chair, I simultaneously took a deep breath. I gradually stepped from the chair to the floor with another deep breath (see "Break and Breathe," p. 137). I then returned to the chalkboard area. In a lower-than-normal voice, I proceeded to continue with the lesson. During the next several minutes, I maintained the lower voice as students followed the content and frequently gazed back at the table where the bizarre preacher had been.

Commentary

It's important to consider this was done with eighth graders. It might be quite inappropriate with any age group below the sixth and above the ninth grades. Remember, "It's not appropriate to hunt mice with an elephant gun." This lesson was appropriate for the class because I had learned through experience that their behavior was not a reflection of my teaching style. This point is essential for effective discipline. When I discipline because I have a need to (I'm embarrassed by their behavior, disappointed, or frustrated), then I am doing it out of my own needs. I'm inside myself and am less able to notice the shifts in their behavior. It's imperative that I am disassociated and removed from my feelings at the time of the discipline; otherwise, the elephant gun appears.

One of the purposes and advantages of having a location for group discipline is that it helps separate the mental state of disciplining the students from other classroom activities. As I move from the discipline location back to the instructional area, breathing twice allows me to switch states.

The students, looking back at the table where the preacher had been and then at me at the board, were processing which person they wanted as their teacher. The frozen position (while I silently counted) anchored the image of the mad preacher in their mind. The lowering of my voice as I returned to instructing helped clarify the contrast of myself as the teacher and the haranguer on the table. My hallucination was that the students looked back and forth and knew which person they wanted to have in their room as their instructor.

The anchor was so strong that three weeks later, when they began regressing to their typical adolescent behavior, I got their attention and walked over to the table, carrying the chair. Placing the chair in front of the table, I steadied it, looked at the ceiling light, froze my body and counted to myself. Immediately, the room hushed as they reaccessed the previous experience fully. Remembering to breathe, I left the chair and slowly returned to the instructional spot. Using a softer-than-normal voice, I continued to teach the lesson. The axiom used here was, "Once an anchor is effectively established, reaccessing a part of it recalls the full impact of the previous experience."

In order to maintain the ecology of other classrooms, it's best to forewarn neighboring teachers of the preacher's noise level. One of my teaching neighbors not only figured out what I was doing but was able to utilize the experience. With my permission, he used the NLP technique, QUOTES. For up to three weeks after my harangue, anytime he wanted his class to be kinder or quieter, he would go to the wall separating our classrooms and say, "Boy, you sure are lucky you don't have Mr. G. as a teacher." They would reaccess the experience they had heard through the walls and shift to more appropriate behavior.

"Shut Your Trap"

I once had an unusually loud history class. I established an anchor with this class which proved to be quite effective. Like the previous example, the anchor was set up through the vehicle of a metaphor.

I took two small pieces of 2" x 4" x 6" wood and hinged them together with duct tape. The trim over the classroom door had a lip wide enough to support the 2" x 4". On a day when the noise level was evident to all of us, I placed a chair under the door frame. Standing on the chair, I placed the hinged 2" x 4" on the lip, one piece sitting on top of the other. Since I wasn't acting "normal," I had everyone's attention. I walked to the back of the class, turned and faced the 2" x 4"'s. I launched into an explanation that, historically, before there was glass or screens on the windows, there was a constant problem with flies (I looked at the noisiest students). I took out a jar of honey, stuck in a knife and said, "In order to control these pests (again, I looked at ringleaders), something sweet such as honey was placed as bait in a trap" (I placed some honey on the bottom 2" x 4"). I moved to the back of the class, turned, faced the door and said, "As people went about their normal activities," (I held up a text book to demonstrate class room activities), eventually one of the pests would be caught and would create a most irritating buzzing sound as it tried to free itself." (I'd then mimic the pitch of the ringleader's voice while making a buzzing noise.) "At some point, someone in the household would shout, 'I can't get my work done

with the buzzing going on! Someone shut their trap!'" Running to the front of the room, I jumped on a chair and smashed the top half of the 2" x 4" on the bottom. I froze my body with my back to the class and, with eyes on the trap, I silently counted, "1001, 1002, 1003." I then did "Break and Breathe," p. 137.

Commentary

This procedure was effective for the next two months. In general, the younger the grade level, the longer anchors will last. The older the grade level, the more they have to be suspended at certain times and replaced (see section on "Natural Anchors," p. 166). One of the purposes of the metaphor is to create a parallel between parts of the story (i.e., pests) and the students in the classroom that are represented in the story. It's more powerful if the length of time the teacher looks or points at the student is long enough for the student to unconsciously understand the identification but short enough to avoid their conscious recognition of it.

"Once You Get Its Attention"

Experience affords us an overview of where students are likely to need special assistance. One of the most difficult units I've ever taught is the term paper to eighth graders. In order to simulate a possible high school situation, there were certain conditions established at the beginning of the unit. My lectures required six weeks of arduous listening. The frustration level tended to peak during the fourth or fifth week. I rehearsed the following story and saved it to use at the first sign that their listening was beginning to wane.

"A city slicker wanted to be a weekend gentleman farmer. He purchased a half acre and arranged to rent a mule from the neighboring farmer. Arriving Saturday morning, he harnessed the mule to the plow and tried a variety of ways to get the mule to move. After repeated but futile urgings, he gave up and asked the farmer's assistance. The farmer stopped by the barn to pick up a 2" x 4" (I grabbed a yardstick). The farmer stood in front of the mule with the 2" x 4" hidden. He instructed the city slicker to say 'Giddy-up!' When nothing happened, the farmer hit the mule between the eyes (as I said this, I smashed the yardstick on a student's desk). The mule proceeded to plow nonstop. As dusk came, the man went next door to thank the farmer and to seek an explanation regarding his effectiveness.

The farmer obliged by explaining in his laconic way, 'Even an ass will do well once you get its attention.'"

Commentary

Each year I build into the story the particular aspects which that particular class has so that the identification is made. That night, after doing the story, I taped the yardstick together. For the next four days, I used the yardstick to point out which concepts on the board and overhead screen they needed to pay particular attention to. Vin Scully, the great sports commentator, always does extensive homework on the players and their background. He's well-respected for his ability to use only those statistics and anecdotes which are appropriate. After I've taught a subject or course at least twice, I know the content enough so that I can focus on the process ("Scales of Learning"). By identifying those areas in which the students need special assistance, you can assign more powerful metaphors and anchors to those areas.

Anchoring With Metaphors

1. Which parts of your course or your year do you want to strengthen/enhance?

_____

2. What resource do the students need to help them during those times?

_____

3. What metaphor could be used to deliver that resource?

_____

4. What could be used in the future to anchor the metaphor?

_____

Decontaminating the Classroom

A teacher is involved in a wide variety of activities in a single day. When the instructor only does one particular activity (such as disciplining) in one particular area, the student associates that activity with that one area. Consciously or unconsciously, the teacher is establishing anchors. When the teacher uses areas of the classroom systematically, the class tends to respond quicker and more appropriately because they know what to *expect*. A traditional method of discipline has been to take a student out into the hall and discipline him there. This is a common example of systematically marking off the classroom. One result is that the student stays more relaxed because he is always safe from discipline as long as he is in the classroom.

If the teacher disciplines while using the chalkboard for instruction, the instruction and discipline are both diluted and contaminated. KEEP THEM WELL SORTED.

In the previous worksheet, "My Group Discipline Spot," we anchored our discipline. What are some other activities that we do on a regular basis? By identifying them and allotting specific nonverbals, we increase the clarity of our message. Some activities to consider anchoring are these: logistics (roll, announcements, etc.), counseling/be-friending a student, right brain days, and inspirational/motivational stories.

Select at least three distinct activities and mark off your room in terms of location, face, voice (speed, tone, volume), and body/posture (amount of gesturing, rigidity, standing/sitting, etc.). Use a different location, face, voice, and body posture for each activity.

Activity 1:
Location _____
Face _____
Voice _____
Body Posture _____

Activity 2:
Location _____
Face _____
Voice _____
Body Posture _____

Activity 3:
Location _____
Face _____
Voice _____
Body Posture _____

Watch for the class' response as you move toward a particular area and start to shift into that particular face/voice/body posture. Record your findings.

Academic Anchoring

There are two kinds of anchoring in the classroom. The first anchor is used for repeated and procedural activities. The second is used for **C**oncepts that are **I**mportant and **D**ifficult.

Repeating Academic Anchors

At a local college, a computer education instructor wanted to increase his nonverbal communication with the students. He opened the lesson by positioning himself at the students' far left (K), wearing a graduation hat (V), and talking in a rapid, high voice (A). From that location, he presented the *theoretical* concept for the lesson.

After a 7 - 12 minute monologue, he stepped to the center (K), removed the graduation hat, rolled up his sleeves and put on a construction worker's hard hat (V). His voice became more guttural and slow-paced (A) as he said in a John Wayne drawl, "All right, guys, this is what *we* have to do today to *get it done.*" Having completed that segment of the presentation, he removed his hard hat and rolled down his sleeves. He then stepped behind (K) a $9000 computer which illuminated a 6' x 6' projection of a monitor screen on the wall behind him. Placing his chin in his hands (K), he blinked his eyes in a coy, secretarial way (V). Using an effeminate, rhythmic lilt, he asked, "What would you *like me to do?* "(A). He then followed the students' commands to the letter by

representing their input on the 6' x 6' screen until the students were satisfied they had accomplished their objective.

At that point, his mannerisms shifted as he stepped a yard away from the machine (K). Visually surveying the class, he asked, "Are you satisfied?(A) Are you ready *to test* to see if your program is complete?" If there were changes, he stepped back into the secretarial mode. If not, he put on a motorcycle crash helmet and in a comic relief position, pressed the button to see if they had successfully programmed the instructions. If so, "cheers" appeared on the screen. If not, the screen showed an explosion, indicating that they needed to revamp.

In summary, the instructor used four basic stages:

1. Overall objective (graduation hat);

2. Blueprinting (hard hat);

3. Actual implementation (secretarial);

4. Testing (crash helmet).

Within several days of doing this routine, the students knew how to track the process: they knew the secretary was incapable of answering any questions; the graduate and the hard hat man were receptive only to certain specific categories of questions and assistance. The students quickly learned to point to the area of the room they wanted the instructor to be in order to field their questions.

Concepts that are Important and Difficult (C.I.D.)

Ask yourself:

1. Is the concept appropriate for their Developmental Experience Level (are they capable of understanding)? Am I teaching from the "known" to the "unknown"? What would happen if I taught by explaining from larger concepts ("chunking up")? What would happen if I taught by explaining smaller parts ("chunking down")?

2. How am I teaching the concept now?
   How much visually:
   How much auditorally:
   How much kinesthetically:

Increase the discrimination of the senses being used:
* Visually: size, color, shape, distance, etc.
* Auditorally: volume, pausing, pitch, etc.
* Kinesthetically: texture, temperature, movement, weight, etc.

3. Increase the unused or least used sense. Using the sets of questions immediately above, describe how you would do so.

If the concepts still need assistance, go on to the following section, "**A**nchoring **C**oncepts **I**mportant and **D**ifficult."

C.I.D.
Teaching from Known to Unknown

There are several steps to analyze why certain **C**oncepts are **I**mportant to the teacher and **D**ifficult for the class. One of the first considerations is whether we are teaching from the known to the unknown. This worksheet focuses on that particular ingredient. Because most of education is a process that involves left brain, sequential, logical, small chunk, teaching from part to whole, we often miss the creativity and the simplicity of the right brain. The right brain is an associative hemisphere. When we teach from the known to the unknown, we are accessing the right side of the brain. The instructor can ask himself, "What associations do these students already have in their minds with the concept I'm about to teach?" This is an especially important consideration when working with **C**oncepts that are **I**mportant and **D**ifficult.

Example: "Quarter . . . "
In addition to being associative, the right brain tends to be holistic and grasp the overall concept without going through individual steps. An example was illustrated by a teacher who was teaching time to third and fourth graders. She was trying to get across the idea of "a quarter to" and "a quarter after". She was using the standard approach of chunking down (left brain) and explaining that a quarter is one-fourth of the whole 60 minutes and went into a rather lengthy, several day process of fractions which was somewhat out of the sequence of her main objective.

C.I.D.: Teaching from Known to Unknown, con't.

Using her right brain, she thought about what they might associate with the concept involved. The next day, she went in and masking taped real quarters on the nine and the three of each of the students' clocks. She also put enlarged pictures of quarters on the classroom clock on the 9 and the 3. Without understanding the fraction aspect of "a quarter to" and "a quarter after," all the kids knew that when the big hand was on the nine and three, it's either "a quarter to" or "a quarter after."

Example: "Raise . . ."
Another example is the primary teacher who was teaching "Raise your hand." By using the format below, the teacher discovered the wealth of association the kids had with all the "raisin" commercials on television and just held up a "raisin" prop when she wanted the appropriate response.

Use the worksheet below to explore how you might use the above mentioned concepts for your particular subject area.

1. List a **C**oncept that is **I**mportant and **D**ifficult and is within the students' **D**evelopmental **E**xperience **L**evel.

_____

2. Ask people to assist you (especially those who do not teach the same grade level; family members and noneducators are most welcome). Tell them about the concept and how you're teaching it and ask them to write down the main words you used. List them here.

_____ _____ _____ _____

_____ _____ _____ _____

_____ _____ _____ _____

3. Now have the group "right brainstorm" some other associations or definitions of those same words that might be already within the fund of your students' knowledge.

4. Having taught the concept with the right brain in mind, list the results here and note which students have an easier time with the right brain approach. Are they the same students or different students who have difficulty with the traditional left brain approach?

_____

_____

_____

_____

WORKSHEET

C.I.D.: Changing the Chunking

1. List a **C**oncept that is **I**mportant and **D**ifficult. Make sure the concept passes the following previously presented levels of C.I.D. consideration:

___ within students' **D**evelopmental **E**xperience **L**evel

___ consideration of teaching from **K**nown to **U**nknown

2. The standard teachers' reaction to a C.I.D. is to "chunk down" to smaller bits. This left brain approach is often ideal for "advanced students" and usually quite suitable for the average student. Describe how you would chunk it down.

3. Implement a "chunk down" approach and list results here. Especially pay attention to which students particularly benefit from this approach. Also notice which students seem unassisted by the approach.

4. The other end of the "chunking continuum" is to chunk up. This right brain approach is often much more suited to "remedial level" students. (See "Teaching Left to Right vs. Right to Left," p. 172.) How would you chunk up?

5. Implement a "chunk up" approach and list results here. Especially pay attention to which students particularly benefit from this approach. Also notice which students seem unassisted by the approach.

One advantage of the above analysis and implementation is you get to discover the pattern of which types of students benefit from which approach. Two immediate insights unfold. First, you know which method to use with future classes based on the needs of the average students in those classes. Secondly, whichever approach you use when TEACHING, you can predict which students you will need to RETEACH and how to do so.

C.I.D.: Increasing the Least Used Senses

1. List a **C**oncept that is **I**mportant and **D**ifficult. Make sure the concept passes the following previously presented levels of C.I.D. consideration:

___ within students' **D**evelopmental **E**xperience **L**evel

___ consideration of teaching from **K**nown to **U**nknown

___ consideration of **C**hanging the **C**hunking

2. List how you are currently teaching the concept:

Visuals used_____

_____

Auditories used_____

_____

Kinesthetics used_____

_____

3. Increase the visuals used by considering sizes, colors, shapes, and distances. Increase the auditories used by considering volumes, pauses, pitches, sounds, and voices. Increase the kinesthetics used by considering textures, temperatures, movements, and weights. Describe how you would increase the least used sense.

_____

_____

_____

_____

4. Note the results, especially which students particularly benefit from this approach and which students seem unassisted by it.

_____

_____

_____

_____

_____

Increasing a Sense

Sometimes it is necessary to "add a sense" to build an academic anchor.

A primary classroom teacher was reviewing "telling time" with the class. Between 35 minutes and 55 minutes after the hour (i.e., 8:50); the students typically read 9:50. It was obvious that the students were only using their visual senses. The little hand was actually closer to the 9 than to the 8, so their calculation of 9:50 rather than 8:50 was understandable. The teacher was frustrated and brought the problem to the NLP class. After discussing the idea of increasing the senses for **C**oncepts that are **I**mportant and **D**ifficult, the teacher returned to the classroom and did the following:

Twelve students made a large circle in the room, holding numbers which represented the hours on the clock. The teacher and two students stood inside the circle, one with a yardstick, the other holding a broom handle (one-third longer than the yardstick) to simulate the hands of the clock. On the end of the yardstick, a cowbell was attached. The student with the yardstick representing the hour hand was instructed to move towards the next number and only arrive when the broom handle was at the 12. When the broom handle was aligned with the 12 and the yardstick directly in front of the next number, a student would ring the bell the number of times that corresponded with the number that the yardstick was pointing to. The whole class counted aloud each ring.

When the broom handle was moving between the number 7 and number 11, the teacher repeatedly asked the class, "How many bells have we heard?" In unison, they chimed the appropriate number. Therefore if the broomstick was stopped at the "10", the class knew it was 8:50. The teacher then monitored several students' comprehension by starting the broom handle on a given hour, ringing the bell with an individual student counting aloud, and rotating the broomstick somewhere between the 7 and 11 and asking what time it was.

Anchoring Concepts that are Important and Difficult (A.C.I.D.)

1. Grade level_____ Subject _____

2. Describe your behavior (i.e., do you move around a lot or stay in one place?) Delineate your normal teaching style in terms of Visual, Auditory and Kinesthetic:

_____

_____

_____

3. Select one C.I.D. (Why waste energy on concepts that are either easy to teach or not very important?)

_____

_____

_____

4. Systematically behave differently from your regular behavior as you teach the concept. Suggestion: If the concept is taught in a metaphor/vignette form with a distinctive physical symbol (i.e., prop), the behavior and symbol will be associated with the concepts in the students' minds. To keep the association clear, only use the same behavior and symbol during review.

Plan:

_____

_____

_____

5. Describe results.

_____

_____

The ingredients for anchoring are:

· Anchor done at the peak of the experience;
· Uniqueness of anchor;
· Exactness of reproducing anchor.

Note to reader: A.C.I.D's allow us to look forward to our C.I.D. They're fun. I am putting together a collection of C.I.D's. and A.C.I.D's. If you are interested in sharing yours, fill out the form in the Appendix and send to the address listed in the Appendix. Include your name, school and school address, so that we can include recognition of originator.

Anchoring Concepts that are Important and Difficult

If you have analyzed a **C**oncept that is **I**mportant and **D**ifficult and have tried all the levels of C.I.D. consideration, then you are ready to consider anchoring it. The Sept. 29, 1986 issue of *Newsweek* devoted the cover article to memory. Apparently, the brain creates special long term connections for "firsts." For example, note how fast you recall who you first kissed compared to the third person you ever kissed; or the first class you taught compared to your second; your first car compared to your fourth.

If you want to anchor a C.I.D. (in other words, make it an A.C.I.D.), act differently so that you create a "first" in your students' minds. There are natural A.C.I.D.s - ones in which the anchor (face, voice, body, location and props) are naturally representative or symbolic of concepts, and artificial A.C.I.D.s - ones in which the anchor is connected to the concept only because you make the connection.

A.C.I.D. Example: Dictionary Skills

Miss Dicta S. was instructing the class on how to find a word in the dictionary. Since the concept was difficult, Dicta met with a colleague and did levels of C.I.D. consideration. Dicta's partner thought of "Indians" when the phrase "guide words" was heard. Dicta dressed in appropriate garb and told the story of Lewis and Clark being guided by an Indian named Sacajawea. She had several students come up to an enlarged pretend dictionary, so all students could follow and see if they could be explorers *guided* by words at the top of the page to discover the location of the word they wished to find. To transfer the skill from the front of the room demonstration into the student's body, each student received two feathers from the teacher's Indian head band. As the student opened the dictionary, the student placed the teacher's feather next to the words at the top of the page.

A.C.I.D. Example: Parts of Speech

Mr. Pett was about to teach "Preposition." He brought his daughter's dollhouse to class and put it on a table with a 6" plastic wall around the outside of the table. Mr. Pett introduced "<u>Pre</u>," a very active little white mouse. As the class gathered around the table, "<u>Pre</u>" was placed on the table. As "<u>Pre</u>" scurried around seeking little bits of cheese that had been placed everywhere, the class shouted out all the <u>positions</u> he went to: "inside," "on," "under," "around," etc.

A.C.I.D. Example: Classroom Rules

Mr. Poo taught adolescents and found through experience that teaching why we have <u>rules</u> is an emotional C.I.D. for students of this age group. He therefore created an A.C.I.D. unit. He bought a paperback with crazy old laws (such as "It is against the law to have male and female undergarments on the same clothesline"). He tore the pages apart and gave each student a page which contained at least six funny antiquated laws. Each student selected one law and imagined how the law could possibly have come about. This creative writing assignment resulted in their realization that most of the time, laws pertain to situations that don't happen frequently. Therefore, they learned to "just relax and do what is sensible and we all will be fine." With a calm tone, the rules are introduced.

A.C.I.D. Example: Vowels

While using levels of C.I.D. considerations, a colleague listening to Pri Mary say the vowels real fast ("a, e, i, o, u") thought of the nursery rhyme, "Old McDonald Had a Farm." By borrowing an employee uniform from a local McDonald's restaurant, she was able to teach the sounds quickly, humorously and with great retention. ("And on this farm he had a vowel; a, e, i, o, u.")

A.C.I.D. Example: Zeroes and Decimal Points

Miss Flair taught sixth to eighth grade math for some time and noticed that a certain percentage of students on all these grade levels were unable to distinguish when zeroes next to decimal points were important and when they were optional. For example, the zeroes in "80." and ".08" are essential and yet the following zeroes are optional ("00.8", ".8" and ".80" all have the same value and therefore the zeroes are optional).

She was tired of having students incessantly ask if the above latter set of numbers were all equivalent. This concept, in essence, was an emotional C.I.D. for the teacher (remember, the tongue is the first part of a teacher's body that wears out during the season). Therefore, she arranged the following A.C.I.D. She placed the wastebasket (with an enlarged decimal point on the can) on top of her front table so all could see. She laid a stick on top. Hanging from the stick were separate pieces of papers with the following numbers:

A Mrs. Bonsai was introduced (the movie "Karate Kid" was popular at the time). Miss Flair switched to an Asian accent and explained that it was Mrs. Bonsai's job to trim the unnecessary branches but keep all beautiful ones. Extending her hands between the decimal point and the last paper to the students' left, she asked, "What is the last number other than zero between the decimal point and this end?" In unison the students said, "Four." Then in a very precise, sacred tone, she whispered, "All zeroes between decimal point and last whole number are very important" (as she gently and reverently touched the appropriate "0"). Then, standing in front of the farthest number, she shifted her face and body, and said in a loud, angry voice, "But the zeroes outside are ugly." To the students' surprise, she pulled out gigantic scissors from a hidden location, and proceeded to cut the "optional zero" to shreds while sounding like she was swearing in Japanese.

After the initial shock the students roared with laughter.

When Mrs. Bonsai asked the same series of questions about the number to the right of the decimal sign, they all awaited the violent rage of destroying the "optional zero."

Several days later, one student approached Miss Flair with the question whether ".80" was the same as ".8". The teacher quickly said three syllables sounding like Asian swear words, and the student laughed and left with complete reaccess of the A.C.I.D.

A.C.I.D.: Transferring from Teacher to Student

Doing dramatic teaching without the students getting to practice is like going to a wonderful resort and not taking pictures or buying souvenirs so that you only remember the experiences temporarily. Mementoes reproduce the fine memories and emotions you had while you were there.

Dramatic teaching which comes with A.C.I.D. has to be transferred into the student's body in order to have muscle memory. This is especially true if they are kinesthetic or very young. The following is an example of a teacher doing this.

A string was hung across the blackboard from left to right. The teacher cut out strips of poster board paper and wrote some statements the students had made during previous days, such as:

> Sally said can I borrow your pencil?

The teacher asked a student to come forward and hang the strip on the string by clothespins; the clothespins were supposed to only hold exactly what was said.

> Sally said | can I borrow your pencil? |

The students did the demonstration and, of course, the clothespins represented quotation marks. The color, texture, and size of the clothespins were all important nonverbals in terms of transferring the demonstrated ability into the students' brains. In this case, the teacher used yellow clothespins and bought duplicate sets for her students who replicated the activity with strips at their desk. After that, they went on to the regular worksheet.

Use the form below to systematize the transfer of the A.C.I.D. from you (the teacher) into the students' bodies.

1. Describe what you did which was unique, especially the nonverbals involved.

_____

_____

2. Describe how you're going to duplicate as much as possible those nonverbals in the students' bodies.

_____

_____

3. Record the results you achieved from this exercise.

_____

_____

"I am not a creator. I don't invent my thoughts. I merely separate out some local patterns from the confusing whole."
-- Buckminster Fuller

Other Patterns

Whenever an improvement in communication occurs, it is because the person initially had the perception to notice the improvement. The person is then able to implement improved techniques, based on their perception.

Most of us are conditioned to seek recipe formulas that work with immediate results. This last section contains several of these "recipe formulas" (five transition worksheets). I had thought of beginning this book with these formulas; however, since nonverbal communication is 82% of communication, we need to develop perception as well as technique . . . hence, the last two exercise sheets are a cut above the first five. As you read the following pages, you will undoubtedly discover patterns, in addition to those you have read here, that you and other educators are already doing. The space provided below is to encourage you to record them and share them with others. Enjoy all.

_____

_____

_____

_____

_____

_____

_____

_____

_____

_____

_____

_____

Transition: Freeze Body

The verbal statement, "Class, may I have your attention?" is 18% of the communication, according to research. The other 82% is the teacher's nonverbals at the time the message is given. In a highly kinesthetic teacher's classroom, the teacher tends to be moving while saying, "Class, may I have your attention?" If the students have previously had well trained ITIP* teachers, the students freeze momentarily out of habit and then go right back to whatever they were doing, because 82% of the teacher's communication was saying, "Keep moving." It is the teacher who uses whatever wording they want and accompanies that with a frozen body and a look/stare at the class that allows the students to know that the teacher expects this will happen; this kind of communication increases the likelihood that it will.

1. List your favorite saying which indicates that you want the students' attention.

_____

_____

2. For two days, use the above saying while moving your body; list the reactions here.

_____

_____

_____

3. For days three and four, use the same verbal wording but freeze your body while saying it. List the class' response.

_____

_____

_____

4.   Research shows that when verbal and nonverbal signals are in conflict, the nonverbals win hands down. List any comments or insights which support or disprove this here.

_____

_____

_____

_____

* In the author's opinion, *Instructional Theory into Practice* (e.g., Madeline Hunter, Carol Cummings, etc.) is the best inservice training for left-brain teachers to become competent in their profession.

Transition: Pace Ahead and Lead Through a Whisper

Teachers who are systematic in using certain phrases (such as "May I have your attention," "Eyes up here," or "Okay gang") to get class attention are using verbal anchors well. What if the students won't respond to the above wording? What about the class that is loud (such as on right brain days)? How do you make the transition if they won't respond to the above wording?

The volume of a room collectively can be understood and calibrated.   By using her voice just above the volume of the class and doing so quickly, the teacher will shock or interrupt the class. They will be more outside themselves and more likely to hear.

Teacher's Voice *
Today's Class *

_____
Normal Volume

At this point, you have a very short time span to lead them to something else. Having paced ahead of the class' volume, you have reached a very powerful point. You have two effective lead choices:

1. Drop your voice to a whisper:

paced *
class *

_____
Normal Volume

* whisper

2. Step your voice down to a whisper:

paced *
class *

_____
Normal Voice

* whisper

If you have enough auditory voice control, you can do a stepdown. The stepdown, in some cases, is your only salvation, but it takes more discipline and control to remind yourself to bring it all the way down to the normal range and then below. Therefore, the drop to a whisper will, for most teachers, be far more successful. In either case, either by a direct drop to a whisper or a stepdown, make sure you elongate your sentences, slow your voice down and give it a softer timbre. You will put the class in a more listening mode.

WORKSHEET

Transition: Pace Ahead and Lead Through a Whisper, con't.

1. Describe the day and approximate time when the class noise level was such that asking for their attention would not have been very effective.

_____

_____

2. Use the sharp pace ahead and drop to a whisper. List the results here.

_____

_____

_____

_____

3. Pick another time when asking for their attention would not be very effective; record the day and the time.

_____

_____

4. Use the sharp pace ahead and then lead down, step by step, to a normal voice range and then below it.

5. Describe which technique tends to fit your style better and the results you've achieved with either of them.

_____

_____

_____

_____

_____

_____

_____

_____

Transition: "Raise Your Hand" vs. "ROAR"

Research indicates that 82% of all teacher messages are nonverbal. One of the most vivid examples of this is the teacher's communication on whether the student should raise his hand to answer or should **R**espond with**O**ut **A**rm **R**aised (ROAR). The majority of a teacher's lesson allows for the ROAR, but when the teacher wants to be in control or wants more waiting time, etc., she will switch to "raise your hand." In making that transition, the teacher has several choices.

1. Say the *content*, then verbally say the *process*.

The teacher who says the academic question and then says the process ("raise your hand") afterwards comes across to the students as being punitive or disciplinary in her nonverbal connotations.

2. Verbally say the *process*, then the *content*.

We all know it's better to say the process before the content (i.e., "Students raise your hand if you know the answer to . . .").

3. Nonverbally do *process*, then verbally *content*.

Primary teachers are famous for modeling what they say. This particular technique can be used on all grade levels. The teacher models raising her hand as she says the content question. The exception to this rule is the auditory student who is not following with his eyes and does not see the teacher modeling the hand raised. In this case the teacher has to make some kind of a sound while raising the hand, such as slapping the left hand on the right raised forearm to make a signal which indicates "raise your hand."

Inertia

Class behavior follows the rule of inertia - an object in motion tends to remain in motion; an object that is still tends to remain still. Whatever pattern is in process, it will most likely continue. Therefore, the most important time to model what you want is when you want to change the pattern. For instance, if the class has been doing ROAR and you want to switch to "raise your hand," this is the time (transition) when the teacher needs to model the most. Likewise, if you've been using primarily "raise your hand" and you want to switch to ROAR, you have to indicate it.

Principle

When switching from ROAR to "raise your hand," a change will be elicited if the teacher models it as the content question is being asked.

Transition: "Raise Your Hand" vs."ROAR," con't.

A general axiom is that in a highly visual classroom, the norm is "raise your hand"; in a highly kinesthetic or auditory teacher's classroom, the norm is ROAR. For the next two days, notice whether you have a pattern of doing more ROAR or "raise your hand." Using the following chart, have someone tally your use of each pattern.

	"Raise your hand"	ROAR
Day 1		
Day 2		
Day 3		

2. Now for the next three days, give yourself a check when you are making a transition from ROAR to "raise your hand" and vice versa.

	ROAR → "Raise your hand"	"Raise your hand" → ROAR
Day 1		
Day 2		
Day 3		

3. Notice how many times you have to use a nonverbal signal of either "raise your hand" or ROAR before the students stabilize (inertia settles in) and you can stop modeling. Make your comments here.

_____

_____

_____

_____

Transition: Overlap

Throughout any forty-five minute period, there will be times when the teacher is doing direct instruction and has the class' attention and other times when the students are working on their own. When the teacher changes the format from students working on their own to direct instruction, she needs to gain their attention again. The number of transitions between activities equals the number of times the teacher must get the students' attention. This concept is illustrated by the chart below.

Activity A | Transition | Activity B | etc.

The traditional way of moving through these steps is to finish Activity A and allow some shuffling in the room (e.g., while the class puts the books away). The teacher must then effect a transition and announce the second activity. For example, the teacher has the class answer five questions at the end of the chapter, put their books away, take out another book, and begin Activity B.

The overlap technique saves time by organizing Activity B before Activity A is finished. As the class gets to question number four, the teacher announces, "Before we answer number five, take out your . . .". She announces Activity B, visually gives the directions on the board when all materials are set up, and then proceeds to read #5. The class is automatically into Activity B with less downtime.

```
A  c  t  i  v  i  t  y│A
        A  c  t  i│v  i  t  y     B│
```

Of course, it is important to consider the class and whether the pause/break between Activity A and Activity B is helpful. For example, the greater the percentage of kinesthetics in the classroom, the more that movement is necessary in order to comply with sitting still during Activity B.

WORKSHEET

Transition: Overlap, con't.

1. During the next three days, at least once a day, try the overlap transition technique and briefly describe what was involved.

A._____

_____

B._____

_____

C._____

_____

2. Summarize the overall insights and responses that were elicited from using this type of activity.

_____

_____

_____

_____

_____

Transition: Incomplete Sentences

Often teachers' courses encourage the instructor to have everyone's attention before beginning, yet we know that when we use our voice to pace the lesson* and our nonverbals for management, the students get into the lesson sooner and remember the class as content-oriented. So when should we get their attention before beginning?

If the content is of high enough interest, we can start the lesson and the students will respond; however, if we suspect their interest will not be high enough, we can use "incomplete sentences." Students who are not watching the teacher but hear an abrupt stop in the middle of the opening phrase of a sentence will tend to freeze and look up. This maneuver allows a quick transition to attentiveness. Some examples of these phrases are, "As we see . . ." "Looking at . . ." and "Notice how the . . .". As the inattentive students engage us, repeat the sentence in its entirety and continue.

1. List two of your introductory sentences.

_____

_____

2. For the next three days, use incomplete sentences. Make sure you freeze your body while doing this.

3. List the results.

_____

_____

_____

_____

_____

_____

* See "Pace of Lesson," p. 203.

Transition: Positive Comments

Primary teachers are famous for using positive comments during transitions to indicate to the class which students are exhibiting appropriate behaviors. These students whose names are called are models for the rest of them. Because of their youthfulness and desire to please the teacher, the students respond rather quickly to the model. For example; the teacher might say, "Clear your desk and take out your pencil and pen." Very shortly after that, the teacher may comment, "I like the way Johnny is doing this. Oh! Row four, all of you are ready."

This process works well through the fourth grade. Styles must be adjusted starting with fifth grade, and that adjustment is often based on the relationship of the teacher to the student. A teacher who has strong rapport is able to make vulnerable, positive transition comments such as, "I really appreciate how quickly you're able to get your things ready for our lesson." One of the major differences, of course, is that the fifth grade and above teacher tries to praise collectively instead of praising individuals or small groups.

1. List your grade level:

_____

2. Give four examples of how you currently use positive comments during transition time.

_____

_____

_____

_____

3. What are some other areas where you could increase, further refine or use the concept of positive comments during transition time? List them here.

_____

_____

_____

4. At the end of a week of an increase in positive comments, what insights and responses did you notice in the classroom?

_____

_____

Pace of Lesson

The suggestion was made that it is best to use the nonverbal level of communication for classroom management. This accomplishes several things. If the teacher verbally manages adolescents who are very auditory, the educator runs the risk of their retorting and the situation escalating to an undesirable confrontation. The part of a teacher's body which wears out the fastest during the school year is the tongue. When a teacher uses her tongue for discipline or management, her energy level decreases for the day. When we use nonverbal communication, we can maintain higher energy.

1. During the next week, have a student in each class put a check on the appropriate line for each disciplinary/management, negative comment made.

	Mon	Tues	Wed	Thurs	Fri
1st hour	_____	_____	_____	_____	_____
2nd hour	_____	_____	_____	_____	_____
3rd hour	_____	_____	_____	_____	_____
4th hour	_____	_____	_____	_____	_____
5th hour	_____	_____	_____	_____	_____
6th hour	_____	_____	_____	_____	_____
7th hour	_____	_____	_____	_____	_____

2. Taking into account your normal energy level during the work week, notice if there is an increase or decrease which correlates with the number of checks for that particular day. Make your comments here.

_____

_____

_____

_____

_____

_____

Pace of Lesson, con't.

The correlation between negative disciplinary comments and your energy level is the same for the students hearing those comments and their energy level. Therefore, we want to use the voice for the pace of the lesson and nonverbal signals for management. In order to do the nonverbals, it is usually imperative that the student notice us visually. The exception to this is when a teacher touches a student. Give yourself permission to use a student's name, clear your throat, or use some auditory output system, and then switch to nonverbals such as a hand gesture to indicate what you want (i.e., wave of the hand to indicate, "Turn around . . . get on task").

3. Think of three oral management communications you've done frequently in the past. List them here and, to the right of each, list an equivalent nonverbal you could use for each of these.

A. _____

B. _____

C. _____

4. Try these nonverbals for a week. Remember to give yourself permission to initially use verbal cues to get the students' visual attention. Then you can switch to the nonverbal(s).

5. List your overall reaction to the above process.

_____

_____

_____

_____

Increasing Congruity

In our culture, the more congruent the sender of a message is (the teacher), the more likely the receiver (students) will comply. In North American culture, congruency is perceived when the teacher's weight is equally distributed on both feet and the hands are at the side or in a comfortable gesturing position (other than projected far away from the body such as the pointing finger). With this in mind, the next time you want to increase the likelihood of getting the response you desire, pay attention to your nonverbals, especially to balancing your weight equally on both feet and keeping your body erect.

Placing the weight on both feet can also be interpreted as being confrontive; therefore, what is the difference between being congruent and being confrontive?

In confrontation, the sender will tend to have a part of the torso in a forward slant - the head pointing out or the voice raised or stressed. Feel free to practice being congruent in front of colleagues, other people, or in front of a mirror. One way to do this is to think of a time when you were very congruent and were positive that something was going to happen or you were going to act in a certain way. As you remember, look in a mirror or have people watch you and give you feedback on what particular aspects of your face, voice, or body indicated, with ease, that your full expectation will be met.

Congruency is a way of nonverbally communicating that you fully expect "x" will happen.

1. For two to three days, intentionally take an aspect or a time period of each day and act incongruently. Have one leg out or more weight on one foot than the other, put a hand on your hip, or slant your head. Notice the response you get from the class. Make sure that while you do this, you notice the correlation between the incongruency of your voice and that of your body.

Record your observations below.

Day 1 notes _____

_____

_____

Day 2 notes _____

_____

_____

Day 3 notes _____

_____

_____

WORKSHEET

Increasing Congruity, con't.

2. On days 4 and 5, use a confrontive body and voice. You might also use a pointing finger and push your head out or forward. Record the responses.

Day 4 notes _____
_____
_____

Day 5 notes _____
_____
_____

3. On days 6 & 7, increase the congruency of your voice and your body and notice the responses you get. Record them here.

Day 6 notes _____
_____
_____

Day 7 notes _____
_____
_____

It might be interesting for you to notice whether the congruency of your body tends to lead your voice or whether your voice tends to lead your body. The above is a further refinement of the axiom for secondary teachers, "If you don't touch furniture, your energy level is higher and the class is more attentive."

Summary

As educators, we cannot avoid anchoring. We all do it, consciously or unconsciously. The success of our anchoring techniques depends on how effectively we use them, and effective anchoring involves coordination of the right and left hemispheres.

The left brain is able to select the C.I.D. and analyze using levels of C.I.D. considerations, and the right provides the flair of "increasing the sense" and making the C.I.D. into A.C.I.D. There is a tendency for the following to be true:

I. Left brain preferred teachers always do levels of C.I.D. considerations and, if the concept is still important and difficult, they seek the appropriate prop and skit for it. They are *systematic* and are adding a greater range of behaviors (acting differently).

II. Right brain preferred teachers skip C.I.D. considerations and go directly to A.C.I.D. In fact, they are known to discover props (by frequenting garage sales) and then seek the appropriate C.I.D. They have their range of behaviors and are adding "being systematic." One right brain teacher teased his class on a day when they were a little unruly that they might cause him to be sick and then they would have a substitute. The next day he arrived in his wife's clothing and stayed in her character all day. The students were silently attentive. While his flexibility is to be commended, he wasted his creativity, because his "first" (dressing as a woman) wasn't used to teach a C.I.D.

Events that are "firsts" and unique create synapsis connection for long term memory. Most of us remember where we were on the day President Kennedy was shot.

Advice 1
The first year at a new school we just want to be inconspicuous.

Advice 2
If we do one A.C.I.D. a month, at the end of a year, we will have ten, and by the fourth year, we are doing them weekly and are becoming a legend.

Advice 3
See the movie "Stand and Deliver."*

---

* It is about Jaime Escalante, a math teacher at Los Angeles inner city minority high school, who had the highest percentage of math merit scholarship finalists per high school capita.

Chapter 9

A Parting Thought

"If the human brain were so simple that we could understand it,
we would be so simple that we couldn't."
- Author unknown

A woman who read this book stated, "This is a collection of comments on the obvious." She paused, remembering my introductory remarks about explanation, vignette and worksheets, and added, "But it was only obvious after I read your comments."

While much of this book is a condensed version of the most advanced understanding (NLP) of how humans do and don't educate others, there are many underlying structures that indirectly address more mammoth issues:

1) If the visual approach to reading and spelling is in vogue, then most students will succeed with that. However, educators will then become concerned about the students who are not succeeding, and research will show that the auditory approach will work for some of those students. Therefore, the pendulum will swing to the auditory approach. Hence, either approach will work for most students, and research will be geared to those who arc failing. In essence, there are no panaceas.

Matching Reading Methods of Modality Strength and Global/ Analytic Styles*

Method	Modality Strength/Weakness			Global Analytic Style	
	Visual	Auditory	Tactual	Global	Analytic
Phonic		+			+
Orton-Gillingham	-	+	+		+
Linguistic		+			+
Glass-Analysis		+			+
Whole-Word	+			+	
Language-Experience	+		+	+	
Fernald Word Tracing	_		+	+	
Individualized	+			+	

KEY: - = Weakness   + = Strength
(©Marie Carbo, 1981)

Success with phonics requires an auditory/analytic reading style.

We need to advance to a sophistication that is beyond the "needs of the statistical average."

---

* Marie Carbo, Rita Dunn and Kenneth Dunn, *Teaching Students to Read Through Their Individual Learning Styles* (Englewood Cliffs, NJ: Prentice Hall, 1986), p. 66.

2) Society is putting pressures on education that are causing a whirlpool in curriculum. On the one hand, those who are employing our "C" and below students are demanding we produce graduates with better basic skills (left brain), and on the other hand, those corporations that are hiring our "B" students are baffled by their lack of originality; they want more creativity (right brain). Rubbing these two hands together results in a confusing vortical headache. We need to use right brain methods for the "C" and below students to teach them left brain skills. After we are assured that the "B+" students have learned the left brain knowledge, we need to have them demonstrate their knowledge through right brain activities. In summary, *pace* through their strengths and *lead* to their areas that need to be developed (see "Scales of Learning," p. 106).

3) A cursory look at larger societal issues such as suicide, AIDS, and welfare indicates that nonvisual people who use auditory and kinesthetic modes are the vast majority of all these populations. The question is: are we learning classroom methods that are transferable to social service agencies? Apparently, the ability to have internal focus and to see is indirectly or directly connected to long term planning, which is the fulcrum for changing these populations. This is why such an emphasis was given in *Righting The Educational Conveyor Belt* to "storage." The field of learning styles has matured to the point that we now recognize that one person's preferred input mode (how they learn) may be quite different from their

output (how they teach). We have to go beyond "input" and "output" to focus on "storage." It is the closeted member of the learning styles family. Let's admit how little we understand but be committed to examining. When the U.S. government made the decision to investigate the potential use of plutonium, there was less than a teaspoon in existence; but because of its capacity, millions of dollars were spent in an ASAP fashion.

4) Anchoring: we know phobia is a one-time learning experience. Can we understand how the brain does long-term storage and utilize the methods for content retention? In the appendix, there is a form to submit your own A.C.I.D. Hopefully, it will be used in a future book of A.C.I.D.s.

5) The NLP concept of studying people who do things well is still revolutionary.

For years the counseling profession analyzed why "sick people" were sick. This presupposition produced volumes of labels and libraries of dissertations, resulting both in the patient and counselor stabilizing the ailment. A friend of mine who is an epileptic was required to report annually to a clinic. For years, she was perennially berated for not keeping track of her seizures. Each time, she felt guilty and would start accurately recording them. As she did, the number of seizures increased (see "Cleaning Up Double Messages," p. 150.). Within two months, her inner ecology would instinctively reject the diary-log format. As a result, the seizures would decrease to the point that a year later, the clinic would have to call and remind her to come in ("amnesia of the negative is indeed blissful").

NLP practitioners need to continue to respectfully study "healthy" students who do well, and elicit their strategies so that their formats can be taught to others. At the same time, we have to be much more respectful of *how* to offer these insights that are gathered from one-on-one settings to the education culture that operates in 20 - 35 student group settings. A kennel owner doesn't benefit much from attending a lecture on "Teaching Canine Appropriateness" from a professional who raises only one dog at a time.

Finally, I offer a closing metaphor. Several years ago, a bridge collapsed during a New England storm. Because fatalities were involved, an investigation was in order. A group of graduate students from MIT used the remains of the actual structure to construct a model which collapsed when tested in a wind tunnel. City officials were quick to point out that federal regulations require that bridges and dams be built 200% above the minimum safety criteria. The students made a new model from the blueprint, and it held up fine in the wind tunnel.

The gap between what was intended and what was actually constructed fascinated the MIT people. They set out to test several more bridges, including a quite famous one on the West Coast. The pattern of the gap between the theoretical and actual held true. The blueprint model was always sound, whereas the actual reality required much greater flexibility.

Summary

When the United States military invaded Granada, there were two branches of the armed services lying on the beachhead, the Army and the Marines. The Navy waited on the ship for directions as to when and where to place artillery. The sailors wanted "to deliver" and the soldiers/Marines wanted assistance. As the forces on the beach began to operate long-distance phones to direct the artillery, the military discovered that each branch had made separate contracts with the telecommunications companies, and the systems were incompatible. One soldier used his credit card number, charged the call to his home phone, and contacted his base in North Carolina which patched him through to the Pentagon. The Pentagon then relayed the messages to the ship.

This is much like the left brain teaching system trying to deliver information to the right brain students. "Good intentions are not enough; we have to be effective."

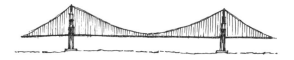

Appendix

Services Offered by Michael Grinder & Associates

National Director of NLP in Education
16303 NE 259th St.
Battle Ground, WA 98604
(206) 687-3238

The following are in precis form. More information is available upon request.

Portland/Vancouver Courses

The following three courses are offered in the greater Portland, Oregon/Vancouver, Washington area during the fall and winter. As part of the course, each enrolled teacher is coached in his/her classroom a minimum of three times.

a) A three credit, 9 week course, "Teaching to the Students' Learning Styles."

b) A three credit, 9 week course, "Visualization: Helping the Students See in Their Minds' Eye."

c) A three credit, 9 week course, "NLP Coaching Model" for administrators and peer coaches.

Outside Portland/Vancouver Courses

The above programs are also offered for districts within a three hour drive from the above area; however, the credits are offered over a 6 week program which includes two coaching visits. Offered during the spring of each year.

Weekend Courses

a) Friday night and Saturday, "Handling the Balance: NLP and Stress Management." 1 credit, 10 hours.

b) Friday night and Saturday, "Disciplining With Comfort." 1 credit, 10 hours (a prerequisite is the above "Handling" course).

c) Friday night through Sunday morning, "Love, Honor and Negotiate" (used with permission from the Barrettas) a couples' communications seminar utilizing NLP strategies.

Schools/Districts

a) Individual schools 1-3 day intensive inservices (includes coaching).

b) Contracts with schools and districts tailored around particular and specific needs.

Shadow Program

Arrangements are made with school districts to have an educator "shadow" (accompany) me for an extended period of time and, in return, become the district's resident expert. Follow up assistance offered to expert.

Summer Institute

For educators during the summer:

"New Trends in Learning Styles" - 9 day NLP institutes in various cities for 5 graduate credits covering:

a) Learning Styles

- Identifying your own and your students' styles
- Teaching multisensory
- Reteaching in a single modality
- Teaching "kids at risk"

b) Rapport; especially with "hard to reach students":

- What is it?
- Why have it?
- Establishing it
- How to test if you have it

c) Visualization - the most important ability a student can have from fifth grade on:

- The strategy effective students use
- External signs of students who are visualizing
- How to "diagnose" a student's spelling strategy

d) Stress Management - stress is closing down from three channels of thinking to one.

- What is your personal pattern of closing down?
- What are your initial signs of closing down?

- Practical methods of staying in a resource state

e) Disciplining With Comfort - we primarily discipline students who are unsuccessful. Those students are often right brain.

- Using visual and kinesthetic techniques to discipline with success
- How to be comfortable while disciplining
- Determine what students need, then act in such a way that the students get what they need
- The difference between counseling and discipline

Advanced Summer Institute

New Trends In Learning Styles - Advanced level (5 graduate level credits). The focus of this course is group dynamics. Michael Grinder meets with this select group one hour earlier than the actual starting time (8:00 - 9:00 a.m.) and debriefs with them from 4:30 - 5:00 p.m.. With this personal attention, participants are tasked in this sophisticated arena. This level is open to:

- Graduates from Michael Grinder's courses; for each previous course, the participant substitutes an advanced level course.
- People who work with groups; administrators and managers. This includes nonteachers. Courses include:

a) Tracking/Platform Skills - Participants will chart Michael Grinder's and others' establishment of nonverbals.

b) Advanced Anchoring - Participants will chart Michael Grinder's and others' systematic utilization of nonverbals.

c) Acknowledging - The study of

handling the clustering of smaller groups within a larger group setting; acknowledging and incorporating the variables of "group dynamics."

d) Metaphors - Identifying when to use them, how to create them, and how to deliver them. They circumvent the resistance of the left brain.

e) Goalsetting - Participants will familiarize themselves with the "Meta" and "Milton" models of communication with emphasis on when to use which form.

Certification in NLP in Education is Open to:

Individuals

Individual educators who have graduated from recognized NLP institutes are eligible for the verification seminar. Participants meet for three weekends during the school year and may choose to be verified in any of the ten content areas presented at the summer institutes. Participants are taught verification techniques (evidence procedure and feedback) and form support systems which assist participants to verify through activity in their own classroom. More information available.

Schools

Qualifications include that 80% of the staff are trained in NLP through course work and in-services. Teachers show competencies in three areas:

a) Identifying styles

b) Anchoring of content for retention

c) Effective use of management techniques.

A Booklist

Education: NLP

Classroom Magic, Lloyd, Linda; an outstanding book for K-8. Each chunk of information is easily digested, outlined for immediate application in your classroom.

Meta-Cation, Jacobson, Sid; for teachers who have an NLP background; a blend of psychology and education

Superteaching, Jensen, Eric; a fine presentation of a teacher's mental attitude (especially look at Ch. 14 on "Discipline").

Education Books

Building Self-Esteem With Koala-Roo Can-Do, Fendel, Laura. "Math Their Way" and "Touch Math" are wonderful inroads into our left brain schooling systems. Like Betty Edwards' work, these programs are more than just about math. They are heralding a shift in perspective. Laura Fendel's and Betty Edwards' work are in that same vein.

Learning and Teaching Style In Theory & Practice, Butler, Kathleen, Ph.D; correlates with many areas, including Bloom's Taxonomy.

Nonverbal Communication, Miller, Patrick; a 33 page, 130 footnote pamphlet put out by the NEA.

NEA has a whole series on "What Research Says to the Teacher."

Peering In On Peers, Cummings, Carol; (and anything else by Cummings). This deals with coaching teachers. 331 8th Ave. S., Edmonds, WA 98020.

Profiling and Utilizing Learning Style, NAASP; summary of educational research and somewhat of an official position.

Put Your Mother On the Ceiling, DeMille, Richard; activities for parents and teachers to help children develop their creative visualization capacity. Done in a manner so that being reality-oriented is also fostered.

Reach More - Faster Teaching Makes A Difference, Cummings, Carol; a distillment of many of ITIP's concepts.

Switch On Your Brain, Cutler-Stuart, Margaret and Parker, Allen; explores educational kinesiology; how to change the mind via physical motion.

Teacher, Ashton Warner, Sylvia; an educational classic. An example of the instructor using the student's view of reality to teach reading and writing.

Teaching for Transfer, Motivation, Reinforcement and Retention, Hunter, Madeline; pioneer of <u>I</u>nstructional <u>T</u>heory <u>I</u>nto <u>P</u>ractice (and anything else by her).

Teaching Students Through Their Individual Learning Styles, Dunn, Rita & Kenneth; the matron of learning styles.

Teaching to Modality Strengths: A Common Sense Approach to Learning; Drs. Swassing and Barbe; a filmstrip cassette by Zaner Bloser.

The Lind Method of Accelerated Learning, Schmid, Charles, Ph.D.; excellent audio cassette set; great eclectic presenter.

The 4MAT System, McCarthy, Bernice; a very complex teaching model.

What Works, U.S. Department of Education; precis form, excellent content.

In Their Own Way, Armstrong, Thomas; uses Gardner's *Frames of Mind* as a backdrop to examine how our schools are inflexible towards "different learners." Outstanding concepts, readability and references.

The I Hate Mathematics Book and *Math for Smarty Pants*, Burns, Marilyn.

Educational Books: Hemispherology

Drawing On the Right Side of the Brain; Edwards, Betty.

Unicorns Are Real, Meister Vitale, Barbara; a right brain approach to learning for teachers and parents.

Use Both Sides of Your Brain, Buzan, Tony; a leader in the field.

Writing the Natural Way, Rico, Gabriele. Uses mind maps.

Education: Visualization

Picture This, Rose, Laura; series of multi-sensory exercises for students to recall and picture past experiences.

Visualizing and Verbalizing, Bell, Nanci; connects what you see in your mind and how to describe it and, of course, when you see words, pictures are created in your mind. A must-read for teachers.

Imaging, Seyba, Mary; visual right exercises to increase focus control of your mind. Ideal as warm up for creative thinking (i.e., writing).

200 Ways of Using Imagery in the Classroom, Bagley and Hess; succinct introduction and guidelines to imagery with easy to implement imagery in all curriculum areas.

Mind's Eye, Escondido School District; structuring and implementing a district wide program that utilizes visualization in a reading program.

"An Educator's Guide to the Best Recent Books On the Human Brain," 1988. Compiled by Dr. Robert Sylvester, University of Oregon.

Recent dramatic advances in the neurosciences are moving us toward a clearer understanding of the three pounds of matter that defines our profession, and a number of excellent books are making these new developments accessible to general readers. These books will provide educators who are principally concerned with mental processes (i.e., teaching, learning styles, motivation) with an important functional understanding of the brain mechanisms that operate such processes. Brain and mind operate conceptually as an integrated unit, much as computer hardware and software cannot function without each other. It is important that educators understand both brain and mind.

Respected neuroscientists and science writers wrote the twenty-four informative and sometimes controversial books in the basic reading list below. The books are arranged topically and somewhat sequentially within topics. All

books have been published since 1983. Most include excellent illustrations, and can be read by intelligent educators who have a very limited background in biology, chemistry and cognitive psychology. Many are available in paperback. You might begin with Michael Gazzaniga's *Mind Matters: How the Mind and Brain Interact to Create Our Conscious Lives* (1988, Houghton Mifflin), a fascinating non-technical introduction to basic brain/mind questions that affect educators. Continue with The Diagram Group's easily read, well-illustrated *The Brain: A User's Manual* (1987, Putnam). Robert Ornstein and R. Thompson's *The Amazing Brain* (1984, Houghton Mifflin) is a bit more technical, but David Macaulay's delightful and informative illustrations clarify and enhance the text. Marion Diamond, A. Scheibel, and L. Elson's imaginative *The Human Brain Coloring Book* (1985, Harper and Row) uses the tactile experience of coloring to help you grasp brain relationships that are generally abstractions to non-neuroscientists. Richard Fisher's *Brain Games: 134 Original Scientific Games That Reveal How Your Mind Works* (1983, Schocken) provides another delightful way of exploring the complexities of your brain.

Two fine books emerged from the excellent PBS-TV series on the brain. Richard Restak's *The Brain* (1984, Bantam) is a print discussion/expansion of the individual programs, and Floyd Bloom, A. Lazerson, and L. Hofstadter's comprehensive *Brain, Mind, and Behavior* (1985, Freeman) is the accompanying textbook for the TV series. Peter Nathan's *The Nervous System* (1983, Oxford University Press) and Jean Pierre Changeux's *Neuronal Man: The Biology of Mind* (1985, Pantheon) are a bit more technical than the foregoing books, but well worth the effort. Sarah Friedman, K. Klivington, and R. Peterson's *The Brain, Cognition and Education* (1986, Academic Press) places existing neuroscience research into a very useful educational perspective.

Several books provide fascinating background descriptions of specific educationally significant developments in the neurosciences during the last twenty-five years, and they will provide you with a view of the cooperative/competitive human side of neuroscience research. Michael Gazzaniga's *The Social Brain: Discovering the Networks of the Mind* (1985, Basic) describes the extensive split-brain research that captivated the attention of educators, initiated the learning styles movement, and led to the currently dominant modular theory of brain organization that Howard Gardner developed further for educators in *Frames of Mind: The Theory of Multiple Intelligences* (1983, Basic). Susan Allport's *Explorers of the Black Box: The Search for the Cellular Basis of Memory* (1986, Norton) tells the story of the extensive work on sea slugs that led to the discovery of what happens within individual neurons when learning occurs. At the macrolevel, Israel Rosenfield's *The Invention of Memory: A New View of the Brain* (1988, Basic) examines memory theory and research from the perspective of the development and organization of memory within large neural networks. Jon Franklin's *Molecules of the Mind: The Brave New World of Molecular Psychology* (1987, Atheneum) describes the endorphin discoveries and subsequent related work that led to our current understanding of the molecular basis of neural activity. Richard Bergland's *The Fabric of Mind:*

A Radical New Understanding of the Brain and How It Works (1985, Viking) expands this research into the development of the new wet-brain theory that argues that the brain is one of the endocrine glands. Jeremy Campbell's lively *Winston Churchill's Afternoon Nap: a Wide-Awake Inquiry into the Human Nature of Time* (1986, Simon and Schuster) describes recent research in various body/brain rhythms and cycles that can affect educational performance (as well as many other aspects of human life). Nancy Andreasen's *The Broken Brain: The Biological Revolution in Psychiatry* (1984, Harper and Row) provides a nontechnical introduction to new perspectives of mental illness and its treatment. Robert Julien's *A Primer of Drug Action* (1985, Freeman) and Solomon Snyder's *Drugs and the Brain* (1986, Scientific American Library) provide related useful background information on drugs and the brain.

Finally, three fascinating books that will make intellectual demands on you, but that will also materially expand your professional vision: Humberto Maturana and F. Varela's *The Tree of Knowledge: The Biological Roots of Human Understanding* (1987, New Science Library) suggests an inspiring unified scientific conception of mind/matter/life. Patricia Smith Churchland's *Neurophilosophy: Toward a Unified Science of Mind/Brain* (1986, MIT Press) is a fine introduction to philosophy for those interested in neuroscience, and a fine introduction to neuroscience for those interested in philosophy. Marvin Minsky's *The Society of Mind* (1986, Simon and Schuster) combines what we know about brains and computers into a truly mind-boggling book that he organized much like he believes our brain is organized. Start reading somewhere in this list. Continue reading as your time and interest dictate and discover your profession's exciting future!

NLP Basics

Frogs Into Princes, Bandler, Richard and Grinder, John; introduction to NLP.

Reframing, Bandler & Grinder; advanced reframing techniques.

NLP Vol. I, Dilts, Grinder, Bandler, Cameron-Bandler & DeLozier.

Practical Magic, Lankton; NLP integrated into therapies.

Roots of Neuro Linguistic Programming, Dilts; reference guide to NLP.

Tranceformations, Bandler & Grinder.

The Imprint Method, Cameron-Bandler, Gordon, Lebeau; a guide to reproducing competence.

Using Your Brain For A Change, Bandler, Richard; using submodalities to make changes.

Organizations

Charles Schmid
The Lind Institute
Box 14487
San Francisco, CA 94114

Eric Jensen
Supercamp
Box 2011
Del Mar, CA 92014

Grinder DeLozier & Associates
200 7th Ave., Suite 100
Santa Cruz, CA 95062

(Check with them for NLP Centers in your area.)

Lara Ewing
5603 W. Virginia Ave.
Lakewood, CO 80226

Late Bloomers Educational Consulting Services
Thomas Armstrong
P.O. Box 5435
Santa Rosa, CA 95402

Laura Grinder Resource Center
1803 Mission St., Ste. 406
Santa Cruz, CA 95060

Mim Rona
120 Queens Parade East
Newport, NSW 2106
Australia

Nils Sellaeg
Interaction
P.O. Box 1266
Vika, 0111
Oslo 1, Norway

New Learning Pathways
S 6000 E. Evans
Bldg. 2 #250
Denver, CO 80222

Pam McAbee & Cliff Nesbit
275 So. 19th St., #700
Philadelphia, PA 19103

Southern California
Center for NLP
Phil and Norma Barretta
929 Barhugh
San Pedro, CA 90731

Steve and Connirae Andreas
1221 Left Hand Canyon Dr.
Boulder, CO 80302

Thomas Grinder
4939 Del Mar Ave.
San Diego, CA 92107

Check your area for Learning Styles Associations.

Anchoring Concepts that are Important & Difficult

This is one of the most enjoyable areas of educational communication. If you have a C.I.D. that you successfully turned into an A.C.I.D., please use the form below and mail in the process. With enough of them, we'll publish a book with your contribution acknowledged.

1. Description of C.I.D.:

_____

_____

2. Grade level and subject area:

_____

_____

3. Description of what was causing the C.I.D.:

_____

_____

_____

4. Your plan for anchoring:

_____

_____

_____

5. Reaccess of anchor (optional):

_____

_____

6. Results and comments:

_____

_____

7. Your name, district, address, city, state:

_____

_____

_____

Mail to:
Michael Grinder & Associates
16303 NE 259th Street
Battle Ground, Washington 98604

Glossary

Since this book is used as a text in courses, some of the glossary entries have longer definitions/commentaries than usual. This allows the book to be used as a reference.

A.C.I.D.
A nchoring
C oncepts that are
I mportant to the teacher and
D ifficult for the class to understand
(See Anchors.)

Anchors
Association of teacher behaviors with concepts. Four kinds: natural (i.e., stoplight); artificial; repeating and A.C.I.D. Three variables that determine strength of anchors: uniqueness; done at peak; exactness of reproduction.

Associated
When one is inside his/her body and experiences. Excellent mental state for pleasant experiences. The only way to replenish self (see "Giving Yourself Love").

Break & Breathe
The maneuver at the end of disciplining. Allows teacher and student to have amnesty (amnesia). If done well, it unifies class. Following "break and breathe," remember to begin softer and slower in voice.

Break state
When one interrupts what is occurring. Ideal when going from a heavily disassociated state to a pleasant associated state.

C.I.D (Concept that is Important and Difficult) levels of consideration
Analyze via: 1) Is concept within their development level? 2) teach from known to unknown 3) chunk up: go global or metaphoric (right brain); chunk down: make into smaller, more specific steps (left brain) 4) increase least used sense.

Conveyor belt teacher
Main stream.

Corridor teacher
Special Education, Chapter 1, resource room, etc.

Cultures
Education is a culture with certain presuppositions. The subcultures are primary, third and fourth grades, early adolescent, high school and Special Education. Each has its own perceptual filters of processing and reacting. The more we understand our subcultural patterns of verbal and especially nonverbal communication and how these patterns stem from the "statistical average" students, the more options we can allow ourselves for those students who are outside the average.

Days
Left brain: most of the school year (except inner city and Special Education).
Right brain: when routines are broken (holidays, snow closures, assemblies, etc.).
Flat left: day(s) following right brain days.

Decontaminating
Sorting the class mental state by systematically associating (anchoring) them with nonverbals (i.e., location, etc.). Examples: sorting discipline from teaching; sorting professional life from home life.

Disassociated
When one is outside his/her body. A good strategy for stressful times.

Discipline
Effective discipline is when you act like they need you to act.
Remember:
1) avoid auditory output channel (because of tendency to press the "cassette of sermonettes"); 2) decontaminate ("the spot"); 3) be disassociated; 4) break and breathe; and 5) keep your voice lower and slower as you return to teaching.

Exit Directions
End of transition from "direct instruction" (TEACH) to students doing independent work. List directives visually.

Hemispherology
Study of functions of each side of brain. Left: logical, sequential, reality oriented, has internal focus. How school operates.
Right: Visual neurological indicators and kinesthetic behavioral indicators. See SPECIALTY.

Houdini
The tendency for instructors to teach/test by showing information, then having information disappear and then reappear rearranged. The disappear phase is labeled "Houdini." Kinesthetic students are confused by Houdini. "Getting rid of Houdini" helps the kinesthetic student.

Indicators
Two kinds which indicate modes of processing: 1) Neurological: physiological cues; 2) Behavioral cues. The more the information is not readily available (they have to mentally search for it), the more the neurological cues are seen. The pause before speaking is most likely a time of searching. "How" questions increase the listener's process of searching.

Kids at risk
Two causes: 1) psychological 2) learning styles which are incompatible with teacher/testing styles.

Lead
After pacing (following) another person, you switch to a more appropriate physiology and they follow.

Learning
Combination of input and storage. Educators do a good job of checking that students have learned by doing review.

Learning styles
On a fundamental level, it is the preferred sense/mode of processing information. On a more sophisticated level, the process is divided into "input," "storage," and "output."

Levels of change
Categories of reviewing:
1) target state;
2) resource;
3) #1-5 of standard review;
4) earliest representation of current chronic pattern;
5) changing everyone else, then "him/her" in earliest scenario.

Linguistic
Information from senses stored in language.

Manipulation
When acting in such a way that you don't have permission from another.

Metaphors
Parallel representation of a concept/message. Conveys a "whole idea." Addresses listener's right brain. It's helpful for circumventing the listener's left brain, logical insistance/resistance.

Modality
We store information in the five senses. For school, we primarily use three; the visual (seeing), auditory (hearing) and kinesthetic (body). Our "preferred mode" is the one used when in stress; "capacities" are the modes one can function in when resourceful (breathing)/relaxed.

Neuro
Five senses used to bring in information.

Nonverbal
All aspects of communication apart from literal words; therefore, face/voice/body/locations,etc. Research published by the NEA indicates it is 82% of all communication.

Pace
When one respectfully mirrors (follows) another's physiology (voice - 100%; face 75%; body 50%; gestures = "wait your turn").

Rapport
When one enters another's world. There are two kinds: 1) Preferred rapport of professional - when the other enters "my world" (tendency of the left brain "plaque mentality") 2) Necessary rapport when working with kids at risk; the teacher enters the student's world. It is done by respectfully mirroring the other's physiology and nonverbals. It is a nonverbal way of acknowledgment. The purpose of entering their world is to lead them to a more appropriate mental state via changing their physiology as they follow your lead.

Respectfully mirroring
Pacing which is done outside their awareness and you have permission.

RETEACH
After TEACHING, working one-on-one; usually with translators, gearing down to their individual mode(s).

Retrieval
Combination of storage and output. We need First Review to check that the information got into the student, then Second Review to ensure that information is stored appropriately for use/demonstration. From the fourth grade on, the demonstration is a test and therefore the information has to be stored visually; hence, the importance of "Visualization."

REHEARSAL
Programming future process of linking trigger-breathing-resource and target state.

REVIEW
Debrief process:
1) chronological backtrack
2) disassociate
3) grace
4) resource
5) target state

Scales of Learning
Relationship between process and content. Process: how something is done. Content: what's being done. Axiom: if you are going "heavy" (unknown) on one, be "light" (familiar) on the other.

223

S.P.E.C.I.A.LT.Y.

Right brain students are a SPECIALTY item on the conveyor belt:

S low processing;
P erson to person;
E ntertainment;
C oncrete objects;
I ntuitive;
A ssociative memory;
L ousy left brain ability;
T ouch;
Y Why?

Storage

Visual characteristics: speed and change of order (see Visualization). Auditory characteristics: sequential and entire chunk. Kinesthetic characteristics: muscle memory.

Stress

A dissonance between what we expect/want/are used to and what is happening. Results in contraction of body (tension). There are two kinds:

1. Gradual = seasonal
2. Surprise stress = traumatic shock (three phases: release of chemical, injury to system from release/utilization of chemical; recovery from injury). The body is a barometer of tension and the mind interprets the meaning. The body is wired with a prehistoric release mechanism (fight or flight). Effective stress management includes rewiring so that the intensity appropriately matches the actual situation. Skills include: Distortion of time and acknowledging to initial signals; use of REVIEW and REHEARSAL.

TEACH

Group setting; multisensory.

Teaching

Left to right: standard way of teaching average student and ideal for 3.5 GPA students. "Part, part, then whole;" "give them the label and then the experience."
Right to left: good for remedial and kinesthetic students; give experience, then the label-term-jargon.

Transferring from teacher to student

What to focus on after A.C.I.D.

Translator

VO = **V**isual **O**nly;
AO = **A**uditory **O**nly;
KO = **K**inesthetic **O**nly ("Knocked Out of system").

Visualization

The visual left brain sees letters, words, sentences, passages and internal focus; an essential skill from the fourth grade on. It gives the student the ability to rearrange items. A corollary ability is long term planning. The visual right brain sees concrete objects, excellent for non word, spatial skills, (such as engineering and geometry). High distractibility (external focus) Visualization is the process of putting already stored information into the visual left mode. Done through speed and change of order. Visual properties such as color, size, and shape often help. See "Scales of Learning" and "Moving A Student From the Visual Right to the Visual Left."
Teacher's behaviors that assist = 1) still body/arms 2) flat high voice 3) talking at a slow pace 4) increase the length of sentences.

Bibliography

Anderson, Jill. *Thinking, Changing, Rearranging: Improving Self-Esteem in Young People.* Portland, OR: Metamorphous Press, 1981.

Armstrong, Thomas. *In Their Own Way.* Los Angeles: J.P. Tarcher, Inc., 1987.

Bateson, Gregory. *Steps to an Ecology of Mind.* New York: Harper & Row, 1972.

Beecher, Henry K. *The Measurement of Subjective Response.* New York: Oxford University Press, 1959.

Bell, Nanci. *Visualizing & Verbalizing.* Paso Robles, CA: Academy of Reading Publications, 1986.

Carbo, Marie; Dunn, Rita; and Dunn, Kenneth. *Teaching Students to Read Through Their Individual Learning Styles.* Englewood Cliffs, NJ: Prentice Hall, 1986.

Cummings, Dr. Carol. *Teaching Makes A Difference.* Edmonds, WA: Teaching, Inc., 1980.

_____. *Managing To Teach.* Edmonds, WA: Teaching Inc., 1983.

Ferguson, Marilyn. *Aquarian Conspiracy.* Los Angeles, CA: J.P. Tarcher, 1980.

Goodlad, John. *A Place Called School.* New York: McGraw-Hill, 1984.

Holmes, Thomas and Rahe. "The Social Readjustment Rating Scale." *Journal of Psychosomatic Research,* 11, 1967.

Johnson, David; Holubec, Roger; and Johnson, Edythe. *Cooperation in the Classroom.* Edina, Minn.: Interaction Book Co., 1988.

Lee, Scout. *The Excellence Principle.* Portland, OR: Metamorphous Press, 1989.

Lewis, Byron and Pucelik, Frank. *Magic Demystified.* Portland, OR: Metamorphous Press, 1982.

Lloyd, Linda. *Classroom Magic.* Portland, OR: Metamorphous Press, 1982.

McCarthy, Dr. Bernice. *4MAT.* Barrington, Ill: Excel, Inc., 1981.

Miller, Patrick. *Nonverbal Communication.* Washington, D.C.: National Education Association, 1981.

Naisbitt, John. *Megatrends.* New York: Warner Books, 1984.

O'Connor, Joseph. *Not Pulling Strings.* Portland, OR: Metamorphous Press, 1989.

Vitale, Barbara Meister. *Unicorns Are Real.* Rolling Hills Estates, CA: Jalmar Press, 1982.

Warner, Sylvia Ashton. *Teacher.* New York: Simon and Schuster, 1963.

Index

Metamorphous Press

Metamorphous Press is a publisher and distributor of books and other media providing resources for personal growth and positive change. **Metamorphous Press** publishes and distributes leading-edge ideas that help people strengthen their unique talents and discover that we are all responsible for our own realities.

Many of our titles have centered around NeuroLinguistic Programming (NLP). NLP is an exciting, practical, and powerful model of human communication systems that has been able to connect observable patterns of behavior and language to the processes that underlie them.

Metamorphous Press provides selections in many subject areas such as communication, health and fitness, education, business and sales, therapy, selections for young persons, and other subjects of general and specific interest. Our products are available in fine bookstores around the world. Among our Distributors for North America are:

Baker & Taylor　　　　　　　　The Distributors
Bookpeople　　　　　　　　　　Inland Book Co.
New Leaf Distributors　　　　　Moving Books, Inc.
Pacific Pipeline　　　　　　　　Quality Books

For those of you overseas, we are distributed by:

Airlift (UK, Western Europe)
Specialist Publications (Australia)

New selections are added regularly and availability and prices change, so call for a current catalog or to be put on our mailing list. If you have difficulty finding our products in your favorite store or if you prefer to order by mail, we will be happy to make our books and other products available to you directly. Your involvement and your interest in what we do is always welcome. Please write or call at:

Metamorphous Press
P.O. Box 10616
Portland, OR 97210-0616
(503) 228-4972
TOLL FREE ORDER LINE
1-800-937-7771
FAX (503) 223-9117

Red Seal Educational Series

Classroom Magic
Amazing Technology for Teachers and Home Schoolers
Linda Lloyd
Daily lesson strategies for teaching success with
students of all learning styles.
ISBN 1-55552-014-6 $14.95

Not Pulling Strings
Joseph O'Connor
Shows how teaching and performing music
can be improved effortlessly.
ISBN 1-55552-000-6 $9.95

Righting The Educational Conveyor Belt, 2nd Ed.
Michael Grinder, National Director of NLP in Education
Fascinating technology for classroom management
and creating the conditions for learning.
ISBN 1-55552-036-7 $17.95

Thinking, Changing, Rearranging
Improving Self-Esteem in Young People
Jill Anderson
Workbook/manual using NLP and Rational Emotive
Therapy principles to develop positive self-esteem in children of all ages.
ISBN 0-943920-30-2 $7.50

Books

Childmade
Cynde Gregory
Handbook for teachers and parents to experience the joy of developing creative writing skills in children $10.95

Classroom Magic: Amazing Technology for Teachers and Home Schoolers
Linda Lloyd
Daily lesson strategies for teaching success with students of all learning styles. $14.95

Everyday Genius: Restoring Children's Natural Joy of Learning—And Yours Too
Peter Kline
Practical, powerful ideas, games and exercises for encouraging the love of learning
in children of all ages. $11.95

How Do You Draw Dinosaurs?
D.C. DuBosque
Build self-esteem through successful creative drawing experiences. $6.95

Master Teaching Techniques
Bernard Cleveland
Teach children how to learn subject matter by developing and modifying learning patterns. $16.95

Mega Teaching and Learning
C. Van Nagel, Robert Siudzinski, MaryAnn & Ed Reese
A revolutionary approach to identifying and eliminating learning blocks. $24.95

Meta-Cation I: Prescriptions For Some Ailing Educational Processes
Sid Jacobson
Helps you explore belief systems about learning and how to avoid getting stuck. $11.95

Meta-Cation Vol. II: New Improved Formulas For Thinking About Thinking
Sid Jacobson
Roadmaps to discovering learning strengths and weaknesses. $11.95

Meta-Cation Vol. III: Powerful Applications For Strong Relief
Sid Jacobson
Self-paced learning program to find solutions to the most common teaching problems (keyed to Vol. II). $11.95

Not Pulling Strings
Joseph O'Connor
Shows how teaching and performing music can be improved effortlessly. $9.95

Righting The Educational Conveyor Belt, 2nd Ed.
Michael Grinder
Fascinating technology for classroom management and creating the conditions for learning. $17.95

Superlearning
Sheila Ostrander & Lynn Schroeder
Examine startling implications of epoch-making discoveries that multiply human abilities in all areas. $14.95

Super Teaching
Eric Jensen
Latest on Accelerated Learning, Bio-Energy, Visualization, NLP, music and much more. $19.50

Thinking, Changing, Rearranging: Improving Self-Esteem in Young People
Jill Anderson
Workbook/manual using NLP and Rational Emotive Therapy principles to develop
positive self-esteem in children of all ages. $7.50

Willie & His Friends
Self-esteem building text and cassettes featuring 12 metaphorical teaching tales
and a meditation by Virginia Satir. Complete set. $35.00

Wimp Buster: The Integrity Brigade
Vida C. Baron, M.D.
Presents an innovative new approach to the problems of drug abuse by students
and an antidote to the "wimp malady." Instructional and inspirational for educators. $9.95

CASSETTE TAPES

ONE TO GROW ON SERIES
Trenna Daniells
Exciting, non-violent stories that teach self-reliance for children ages 4-12. Dramatized with original music and sound effects, the stories encourage children to approach life with positive attitudes, helping to build self-esteem from an early age. Tapes sold separately or in money-saving book-style sets.

Maylene The Mermaid (All Things Change)
Egar & The Land of The Twoids (Courage & Confidence)
Exploring and Developing Your Senses
The Girl Who Looked to Find Where Happiness Lives (Happiness Lives Within You)
Oliver's Adventures on Monkey Island (It's OK To Be Different)
Matthew's New Jungle Friends (Making Friends By Being Yourself)
Aaron & Wish The Dog (Turning Problems Into Opportunities)
The Purple Planet Phatos (You Can Make A Difference)
Travis & The Dragon (Accepting Others As They Are)
Timothy Chicken Learns To Lead (Don't Blame Others)
Lily's Big Lesson (Honesty & Positive Thinking)
Frog's Magic Journey (You're OK The Way You Are)

TURNING POINT FOR TEACHERS
Created by Eric Jensen, the author of *Superteaching,* these tapes offer a world of leading edge technology for educators. They include areas such as:

- Uses of NLP for student success
- Attitude adjustment and motivation
- Accelerated Learning
- Leadership

- Self-esteem
- Positive classroom discipline
- Presentation success skills

LEARNING FORUM AUDIO COURSES
Success Through Alpha Learning
Success Through Writing

VIDEO TAPES

- Increase math confidence and success
- Develop a winning attitude
- Increase memory

- Build test-taking skills for better grades
- How to take "quantum leaps" in reading speed
- Develop better personal skills in the classroom

SOFTWARE (for Apple II & III)

- NLP software for Apple II, ages 12-adult
- Pac-man type programs for typing skills
- Math marksmanship and fundamentals
- Math strategies for memorization

- How to make spelling a sport
- Visualization and memory
- Macintosh software for NLP skills and personal change

These are only a few of the resources we offer. If you cannot find our products at your favorite bookstore, you can order directly from us. To order, receive our free catalog, or be included on our mail list, call or write:

Metamorphous Press
P.O. Box 10616
Portland, OR 97210-0616
(503) 228-4972

TOLL FREE ORDER LINE
1-800-937-7771

FAX (503) 223-9117

All orders shipped prepaid UPS unless otherwise requested. We accept VISA, Mastercard, American Express and Optima. Shipping and handling charges are $3.50 for the first item and $0.75 for each additional item. Foreign orders shipped prepaid in USD $3.50 for the first item and USD $0.75 for each additional. Ship surface unless otherwise specified. Please write or call directly to determine alternate charges. Prices and availability subject to change without notice.